CANADIAN CLUB

Birthright Citizenship and National Belonging

Birth-based citizenship is widely considered to be the most secure claim to political belonging. Despite the general belief that liberal democracies are formed through consent, in fact, most people are members of a political community by virtue of the circumstances of their birth. In *Canadian Club*, Lois Harder tracks the development of Canada's *Citizenship Act* from its first iteration in 1947 to the provisions governing the citizenship of children born abroad to Canadian parents with the assistance of reproductive technologies. Reviewing a range of cases, Harder reveals how membership in the Canadian political community relies on norms surrounding gender, family, and sexuality, as well as presumptions regarding the constitution of "authentic" national identity, racial hierarchy, and the rightness of settler colonialism.

Canadian Club concludes with a consideration of alternative approaches to forming political communities. Ultimately, it asks whether birth-based citizenship is the best we can do and what a more democratic and socially just alternative might look like.

LOIS HARDER is Dean of the Faculty of Social Sciences and a professor of political science at the University of Victoria.

Canadian Club

Birthright Citizenship and National Belonging

LOIS HARDER

UNIVERSITY OF TORONTO PRESS
Toronto Buffalo London

© University of Toronto Press 2022
Toronto Buffalo London
utorontopress.com

ISBN 978-1-4875-4766-0 (cloth)
ISBN 978-1-4875-4860-5 (paper)
ISBN 978-1-4875-5076-9 (EPUB)
ISBN 978-1-4875-4922-0 (PDF)

Library and Archives Canada Cataloguing in Publication

Title: Canadian club : birthright citizenship and national belonging / Lois Harder.
Names: Harder, Lois, 1966– author.
Description: Includes bibliographical references and index.
Identifiers: Canadiana (print) 20220273871 | Canadiana (ebook) 20220274037 |
ISBN 9781487548605 (paper) | ISBN 9781487547660 (cloth) |
ISBN 9781487550769 (EPUB) | ISBN 9781487549220 (PDF)
Subjects: LCSH: Citizenship – Canada. | LCSH: Canada. Citizenship Act.
Classification: LCC JL187.H37 2022 | DDC 323.60971 – dc23

We wish to acknowledge the land on which the University of Toronto Press
operates. This land is the traditional territory of the Wendat, the Anishnaabeg, the
Haudenosaunee, the Métis, and the Mississaugas of the Credit First Nation.

This book has been published with the help of a grant from the Federation for the
Humanities and Social Sciences, through the Awards to Scholarly Publications
Program, using funds provided by the Social Sciences and Humanities Research
Council of Canada.

University of Toronto Press acknowledges the financial support of the Government of
Canada, the Canada Council for the Arts, and the Ontario Arts Council, an agency of
the Government of Ontario, for its publishing activities.

Canada Council   Conseil des Arts
for the Arts   du Canada

ONTARIO ARTS COUNCIL
CONSEIL DES ARTS DE L'ONTARIO
an Ontario government agency
un organisme du gouvernement de l'Ontario

Funded by the   Financé par le
Government   gouvernement
of Canada   du Canada

Canadä

Contents

Acknowledgments

This book has been very, very long in the making. Over more than a decade, I have juggled the demands of significant university administrative positions and the persistent fascination with how the Canadian state has named or refused its citizens. I have been endlessly surprised by the ways in which norms – of gender, sexuality, race, family, and class, and of what it means to be a Canadian – can be stitched together, unpicked, and restitched as we attempt to construct the political community. How might we, as Canadians, or simply as people engaged with others in the task of governance, do better? And more broadly, what does birth-based membership make possible and what does it prevent? These questions have been fodder for conference papers, invited presentations, senior undergraduate and graduate seminars, and myriad conversations with both the suspecting and the unsuspecting. I have benefited from the generosity of many people who offered their encouragement, enthusiasm, and friendship. Support has come in all forms – research assistance, reference compiling, great questions, time, space, funds, wine, dinner, cake, wisdom, love. My gratitude overcomes me.

For most of my professional career, I have worked at or near the Department of Political Science at the University of Alberta. It has been a rich intellectual community with a capacious and thus generative sense of the discipline. My colleagues and my students have been a source of great inspiration. Thanks, in particular, are owed to Jurgita Kornijenko, Maya Seshia, and Margot Challborn for their excellent research support and to Yasmeen Abu-Laban, Rob Aitken, Isabel Altamirano, Roger Epp, Cressida Heyes, Catherine Kellogg, Fiona Nicoll, Steve Patten, and Lyubov Zhyznomirska for their various engagements with this project. Beyond my former department, Eric Adams, Kim Armstrong, Rainer Bauböck, Davina Bhandar, John Clarke, Carla Cuglietta, Costica Dumbrava, Megan Gaucher, Jon Goldberg-Hiller, Nisha Nath, Peter Nyers, George Pavlich, Tyler Waye, and Ian Quigley have listened to, read, and commented on various pieces, or all the pieces, in ways that have sharpened my analysis, and for which they cannot be held accountable.

Much of the writing for this project emerged during time spent as a visiting fellow at the Eccles Centre for American Studies at the British Library and as a visiting scholar at the Centre for Law, Gender, and Sexuality at Kent University. Kate Bedford and Emily Grabham were wonderful hosts and intellectual interlocutors during these visits.

I am also very grateful to the people who shared their first-hand citizenship experiences with me. The generosity of Laurence Caron, Don Chapman, Douglas Chute, and Bill Janzen has made this a better book.

Pieces of the analysis, scattered through the introduction, chapters 3, 5, and 7, and the conclusion have appeared in the following journal articles:

"In Canada of All Places: National Belonging and the Lost Canadians,"
  Citizenship Studies 14, no. 2 (March 2010): 203–20.
Lois Harder and Lyubov Zhyznomirska, "Claims of Belonging: Recent Tales
  of Trouble in Canadian Citizenship," *Ethnicities* 12, no. 3 (June 2012):
  293–316.
"Does Sperm Have a Flag? On Biological Relationship and National Mem-
  bership," *Canadian Journal of Law and Society* 30, no. 1 (2015): 109–125.
"'Maternity Tourism,' Civic Integration, and *Jus Soli* Citizenship in Canada,"
  Revue Européenne des Migrations Internationales (REMI) vol. 36, no. 4
  (2020): 35–54.

I have also presented early iterations of the book in conference papers at the annual meetings of the Canadian Political Science Association, the Western Political Science Association, the International Studies Association, the Law and Society Association, the Law and Society Association of Australia and New Zealand, the Canadian Law and Society Association, the American Political Science Association, and the European Consortium for Political Research, as well as in seminars at the University of Kent, the University of Hawai'i, Trent University, and the University of Alberta. I want to thank the conference and panel organizers for these events. Their work is critical to the scholarly endeavour and an essential contribution to knowledge.

Rebecca Cory, Bailey Sousa, and Daniel Quinlan have played critical roles in getting this book across the finish line. Rebecca's patience, writing strategies, and coaching helped me persist. Bailey blocked the time in my calendar and ran interference. Daniel's enthusiasm for the project and careful shepherding of the review and publication process kept the wheels turning. I am also very grateful to the Aid for Scholarly Publishing Program for their contribution to this work and to Matthew Kudelka for his careful and patient copy editing.

In so many ways, family lies at the heart of this project, as a concept, as biographical motivation, and as lived experience. My father came to Canada as a child fleeing religious persecution, and my mother was born to parents who had only recently arrived in Canada under the same conditions. Ultimately, they navigated Canada's terms of belonging with considerable success, but the stories of the struggles along the way fed an empathy and curiosity in me that has helped fuel this project. I am so very grateful to Eric and Anne for their inspiration, work ethic, and love. My siblings and their families (Lawrence, Dale, Marilyn, Ken, Doris, Ernie, Claire, and Ryan) have politely withstood the rehearsal of many of the book's arguments, undoubtedly baffled by what was taking me so long, but loving and supporting me along the way. And my stepsons Noah and Alec are the future to whom this work points.

Finally, ultimately, my beloved Curtis. This book could not have happened without his patience, grace, and unwavering faith in me. He held my hand, sometimes my head, and always my heart. This book is for him.

CANADIAN CLUB

Birthright Citizenship and National Belonging

1
Introduction

The function of imagination is not to make strange things settled, so much as to make settled things strange; not so much to make wonders facts as to make facts wonders.
– G.K. Chesterton, *The Defendant: Essays*, 32

One morning, in the spring of 2008, my clock radio awakened me with a CBC news story describing the plight of people who thought they were Canadian but whose citizenship had suddenly been cast into doubt. As part of the implementation of the Western Hemisphere Travel Initiative (WHTI), a post–9/11 initiative to enhance border security, Canadians were newly required to provide a passport to enter the United States. In making their passport applications, a remarkable number of people were having the discombobulating experience of being told that their citizenship was in question or that they did not have Canadian citizenship at all. I was immediately curious. "How does it come to be," my political scientist brain wondered, "that the state can suddenly question the inclusion of long-time residents – indeed, people who understood themselves to be lifelong, birthright citizens?"

I was in the early goings of exploring the state's interest in governing personal relationships – the bedrooms of the nation, as it were[1] – when this story came across the airwaves, and it instantly attracted me because it was clear that people's citizenship difficulties were arising from the peculiar circumstances of their births and the configurations and activities of their families. Some people had grown up in border towns where the closest hospital was in the United States and their birth registration detailing their Canadian parentage had not been completed. Others were born in Canada before 1977 but had a father who had taken out citizenship elsewhere, and, as minor children, had lost their own Canadian citizenship in the bargain.[2] And for Second World War brides, but especially their children, the citizenship surprise largely applied to people who were born abroad and landed in Canada after 1 January 1947, the day that

Canada's first *Citizenship Act* came into effect.[3] Timing, and the marital status of the parents at a child's birth, mattered.

While the WHTI was a catalyst for these realizations, the issues giving rise to these citizenship difficulties certainly predated its announcement. A University of Victoria demographer who appeared before the House of Commons Standing Committee on Citizenship and Immigration in 2007 suggested that there were six possible scenarios that could lead to difficulties with people's claims to Canadian citizenship on the basis of birthright. Potentially tens of thousands of people could be affected, although, as Dr Edmonston cautioned, only a portion of those people would be aware of, or concerned with addressing, their precarious citizenship status.[4] Such were the circumstances through which "lost Canadians" became something of a political phenomenon – and a liability.

As far as the news media and their attentive publics were concerned, this exercise of the overweening power of the Canadian state had clearly gone too far. It was one thing to deny or impede the citizenship of people who tried to gain access to the country illegally, but these lost Canadians were kin. After all, they had a birthright claim to belonging in the Canadian state but for the operation of some abstract technicality, outdated, sexist rule, or random time frame. Many of these lost Canadians had lived their lives in Canada, voted, paid taxes, and even held passports. In those cases, both birth and a longtime commitment to the country made the Canadian state's challenge to their citizenship particularly unjust.

More intriguingly, at least for me, some of the highest-profile cases of lost Canadians concerned people whose ties to Canada were considerably more ephemeral. These were people who, for example, were born in Britain, fathered by a Canadian soldier during the Second World War, but other than lineage had no connection to Canada, having never lived in the country (or only briefly).[5] In the precedent-setting Supreme Court decision in *Benner*, a man who had lived much of his adult life in the United States and had managed to acquire a serious criminal record succeeded in rectifying his "lost" status by persuading the court (and rightly so) that Canadian women should be able to pass on their citizenship under the same conditions as Canadian men. The fact that foreign-born children claiming Canadian citizenship through their mothers had to undergo a security check, when the children of Canadian fathers did not, was clearly a sex-based infringement on equality.[6] Benner's status as a Canadian was not a function of commitment to the country, shared values, or good behaviour, but rather of his blood tie to a Canadian parent. His case (minus the details about his manslaughter and theft convictions) subsequently came to define a subset of similarly affected lost Canadians as "Benner babies."[7]

While the various means through which one could become a lost Canadian provided my entrée into this exploration of birthright citizenship law, a number of other situations in which the Canadian state was prepared to challenge people's birthright citizenship claims quickly emerged. The interpretation of "parent" in situations involving children born abroad and conceived with the assistance of reproductive technologies; and debates over whether Canada should maintain its *jus soli* citizenship in light of so-called maternity tourists, provide additional grist for my reflections on birth criteria as the basis for political membership.

The stories that connect birth and citizenship are deeply paradoxical. At one level, we know that formal citizenship – whether in Canada or anywhere else in the world – is based on criteria of birth. Even in this globalizing era of extensive migration, the vast majority of people who can answer the question "how did you become a citizen?" say "birth to a citizen parent" (*jus sanguinis* – right of blood) or "birth in the territory" (*jus soli* – right of soil).[8] Yet this relationship between birth and citizenship – or what Jacqueline Stevens has so compellingly demonstrated as the kinship basis of political membership – is not at all what liberal democracy is supposed to be about.[9] The social contract – which undergirds modern democratic nation-states – declares that membership in the polity is based on consent. As rational individuals we agree to submit to the authority of the sovereign, and on the basis of our consent we become members of the sovereign body – that is, citizens of the state. In truth, however, only a tiny fraction of our fellow citizens have explicitly consented to sovereign authority. And even these citizens, who attained citizenship through the immigration process, are understood to be "naturalized" – an ecological metaphor denoting the integration of a foreign species into a new environment, complete with the capacity of that species to reproduce in its new surroundings.[10] In Canadian citizenship law – and characteristic of settler societies – the consent of immigrant parents ensures the subsequent enactment of birthright citizenship claims for their children.

Relatedly, settler societies are also characterized by a "self-indigenization" of the colonizing population, a process that can be understood in at least two valences. The first involves a "societal unification" through intermarriage and racial mixedness.[11] Samuel de Champlain's articulation of this vision to his Indigenous allies went something like "our young men will marry your daughters, and we shall become one people."[12] Adam Gaudry and Darryl Leroux note that this vision has been overstated and that it confuses what is effectively an assimilative project with hybridity.[13] The second valence mobilizes a combination of sovereign authority and racial innocence, obscuring the violent processes of colonial dispossession and inserting settlers (and especially those of French and British origin) as the original people, or at least the legitimate people, as per the ecological process of "naturalization." Henderson observes that the predominant narrative of Canadian citizenship "confuses citizenship as a right to political or civil membership with citizenship as a right to presence in the territory" while ignoring the treaty right to be present in Canada.[14] As

Audra Simpson explains, the settler state, in its newness, exerts "an aggressive regulatory fixation on demarcating, through time, the boundaries and the content of the 'we' of community … These populations are to be … harmonized into a form of constructed, rights-bearing kin through citizenship."[15] Here the paradox of consent-based, liberal democracy founded on kinship is perpetually haunted by the never quite obscured violence of its founding conditions and the derogation of treaty.

Political theorist Jacqueline Stevens makes a persuasive argument for locating kinship at the centre of discussions of political membership, and it is her work – or rather, my interpretation and application of it – that undergirds my analysis of Canada's birthright citizenship laws.[16] Unlike most citizenship theorists, whose analytical focus concerns the rights, obligations, and entitlements that emerge from citizenship status and are denied to those who lack that status, Stevens asks the prior question of the conditions that give rise to membership in the first place.[17] As Stevens notes, "the idea among sophisticated scholars is that nations are not based on 'blood ties' (whereas families are), and therefore it makes no sense to turn to the family for ontological or historical (as opposed to psychoanalytical) understandings of the nation."[18] Rather, Stevens asks us to notice how criteria of birth are fundamental to citizenship (families make the state) but also how families are *not* natural, biological creations, but defined through the law (states make families). Indeed, it is the specificity of these rules that gives rise to particular states. As Stevens points out, what makes a state is not human reproduction per se, but the detailed rules that govern that reproduction. In the absence of kinship rules there would be humans, but not Canadians, Americans, or any other national identity.[19]

Parentage and Gender

Because all countries use criteria of birth as the basis for national citizenship determination, and because parental status generally implies the right to confer citizenship on one's progeny, whom the law names as a parent is directly associated with whom the law names as a citizen. This is Stevens's point regarding the state's prerogative to define the family. And while the process of designating parents and children seems, at first glance, to be a straightforward matter, biological fact and socio-legal circumstances do not necessarily align. In fact, the rules that govern who may be designated a legal parent vary depending on the national or subnational jurisdiction and change over time. That said, there are some long-standing historical norms for parentage determination that form the reference point for contemporary innovations. With regard to fathers, the historical and contemporary legal presumption is that the husband (or common law male partner) of a woman who gives birth in the context of the marriage (or cohabiting relationship) is the father. Paternity can be disputed, but even with evidence that a husband is not the biological father of a child born in the context of a marriage, courts have often reinforced the husband/father connection, regardless of the biological evidence.[20] This imposition of paternity reinforced the patriarch as head of the household; moreover, it protected children from illegitimacy, that is, from the status of *filius nullius,* or child of no one. Illegitimacy meant that an actually existing, living being could not command the status of a legal person, nor could that non-person claim rights to lineage, to inherit or pass on his own wealth.[21] Mothers – people who give birth – could create bare life, but only husbands/fathers could confer full humanity and full entry into the social realm. Here we have a vivid illustration of gender hierarchy and the work of the law in ensuring its production and perpetuation.

In the absence of marriage, only the mother could be known for certain. Nature – sanctified by law – was seen to do the work of parentage determination in the case of motherhood. This is still largely the case, although adoption, the legal recognition of same-sex relationships, and the advent of reproductive technologies and surrogacy have complicated determinations of motherhood as well. That said, in Canada the birth mother is understood to be a legal mother – at least in the first instance.

These norms of parental determination are central to many of the contested citizenship cases I consider. Prior to Canada's first *Citizenship Act* in 1947, Canadian women who married foreigners automatically acquired the citizenship of their husbands.[22] Dual nationality (like polygamy) was not a possibility, at least in part because of a concern about divided loyalties.[23] Marriage implied a familial loyalty, and that familial loyalty tracked directly through the husband to the state. To marry a foreigner, then, was to adopt a new nationality and eschew membership in one's birthplace. With the passage of the 1947 *Citizenship Act,* marriage to a foreigner no longer cancelled women's Canadian citizenship status, but their born-abroad children were only entitled to the citizenship of their fathers.

Canada also made use of these rules to protect its male soldiers from the responsibilities they – and the Canadian state – owed to foreign sweethearts and as well as to children arising from wartime liaisons. As I elaborate in chapter 2, since marriage turned husbands into fathers, the Canadian military's refusal to grant permissions to marry to its soldiers in advance of the D-Day invasion helped Canada avoid "creating widows and orphans."[24] That is, these refusals helped Canada avoid its obligations to foreign women and their infants.

With the Report of the Royal Commission on the Status of Women in 1971, and the successful activism of the second wave of the women's movement, the issue of women's equality was very much in the forefront when the Canadian government decided to overhaul the *Citizenship Act* in the mid-1970s. With the passage of the 1977 *Citizenship Act,* children born after 15 February 1977 could acquire birthright citizenship from either Canadian parent regardless of their wedlock status. Yet this provision was not retroactive. In its wisdom, the Canadian government enabled people who had been born abroad to Canadian mothers prior to 1977 a two-year window to apply for citizenship – but in these cases, the applicants had to pass a security check. Gender equality applied only to citizenship acquisition for newly born Canadians. Older ones had to prove their worthiness.

Most recently, the *Citizenship Act* has been confronted by the brave new world of parentage determination in an era of reproductive technologies and the legal recognition of same-sex relationships. Initially, both the federal government and the Federal Court of Appeal were adamant that in cases of children born abroad with the assistance of reproductive technologies, a child could acquire Canadian citizenship only if she was genetically related to her Canadian parent.[25] As of July 2020, the government broadened its interpretation of parent to include Canadians who are not biologically related to children born in the context of their relationships – in this specific case, the Canadian, non-biological, same-sex partner of a Dutch woman.[26] This decision restores, in fact, the long-standing dictum that marriage turns husbands into fathers regardless of their biological relationship to their children – but this has now been extended to same-sex relationships.

These parentage machinations provide fascinating insights about gender; they also expose the Canadian state's willingness to challenge the certainty of birthright citizenship when the opportunity arises. Birthright citizenship is often defended on the grounds that it protects citizens from the vagaries of politics and the whims of particular ideological projects. Yet as the many cases I describe below clearly demonstrate, birthright is a less solid guarantee of belonging than its proponents believe it to be. Birth is assailable, and more than that, it undergirds a global system of inequality, what Ayelet Shachar so aptly describes as the birthright lottery.[27] While many vectors of identity – gender, race, class, and so on – impact one's life chances, *where* one is born matters a great deal. Officially, the story is that all citizenships are equal, but given the global maldistribution of wealth, opportunity, and governance by the rule of law, it is clear that some citizenships are a great deal more valuable than others. It is this observation that undergirds my argument, and my provocation, to consider the alternatives to birthright membership. I, too, am deeply worried about the prospects of statelessness and citizenship-stripping, and I fully support a strong and enduring claim to citizenship. My question, though, is whether we could devise more equitable rules for belonging that could enable more people to demand accountable governments and access to resources, a demand that is made more real when it is possible to leave. But exit is not enough. People should also be able to join new political communities and to become members of those communities based on principles of connection, subjection to governance, and consent, while also having the assurance of sustained inclusion.

In telling these stories of the instability of birthright citizenship, and in making a case for an alternative approach to establishing political membership based on connection (including time and residency), subjection to governance, and consent, I acknowledge that such an exercise might also be read as a settlement project, and one that might well be accused of disregarding the long-standing political communities of Indigenous nations. This is not my intention. In the first instance, the intellectual exercise I am undertaking is an attempt to undo the paradox of birth-based membership criteria in liberal democratic polities so as to envision some principles for a more rigorously consent-based political community. Thinking about such a community relationally, ideally its existence would be predicated on respect for the autonomy and self-determination of Indigenous nations within a structure of ethically negotiated and variably overlapping interdependent[28] or independent sovereignties. Moreover, prior to colonization – and in some cases to this day – Indigenous communities had citizenship/membership criteria that did not necessarily rely on birth and certainly not on race, instead emphasizing community recognition, participation, and commitment. Such approaches could offer inspiration for alternative citizenship models and, perhaps, for alternative formulations of the Canadian state's relationship with Indigenous political communities that extend well beyond the limits of liberal democratic theorizing.[29] To date, however, the membership components of the Canadian state-making project have entailed the incorporation, dispossession, and elimination of Indigenous political societies – not exactly an ideal liberal-democratic outcome, though arguably not a surprising result of its material manifestation.

Blood, Nation, and Race

A key attraction surrounding Canadians facing questions about their citizenship was their celebration of the nation. Throughout their stories, the lost Canadians expressed a national belonging that marked a territorial and ancestral inheritance whose existence "in the blood" legitimated their claims for national membership. Witness some representative statements from lost Canadians: "It is my Canadian blood that works overtime when I'm here";[30] "It's me; it's my total identity. It supersedes being wife, mother, daughter, or anything … I, sir, am a Canadian. To the roots of me, to the spirit of me, to the soul of me, I'm Canadian."[31] These impassioned claims to Canada were not articulated simply as a choice; rather it was as though national identity, even a national identity in a country that prides itself on its immigrant founding – a settler society – was part of a person's genetic code. Canada *has* these people, it *constitutes* them; they are powerless to resist the country's hold on their identities. Such testimonials, along with news reports, House of Commons debates, and legal arguments, enfold the lost Canadians' assertions of an organic connection to Canada. Their narratives express an economy of desire in which the lost Canadians long for inclusion in Canada (and are deeply pained by exclusion from it), while

Canadians who are more certain of their citizenship status are affirmed in the worthiness of their national identity. This economy serves to re-enchant the Canadian nation, providing a roster of performances through which Canada is perpetually reimagined and its desirableness is reinforced.[32]

Given Canada's pride in its commitment to multiculturalism, often taken as evidence of the civic character of Canadian nationalism, and its self-representation as a settler society, the appeal to Canadian ancestry might appear puzzling. Jacqueline Stevens can, again, help us here. Stevens takes aim at the distinction between ethnic and civic nationalism by interrogating the assertion that ethnic forms of national identity are based on birth, whereas civic national identities are constituted through consensual processes within the territorial borders of the state. According to this logic, affiliation through blood ties sets up a kind of genetic prescription for the political community through which the code of belonging is locked in. By contrast, the "facts" of bounded territory do not prescribe how people operate within those boundaries. In contrast to Indigenous conceptions of land as a living entity and constitutive of political communities,[33] civic nationalism renders territory as, effectively, a blank slate on which the population can determine its governing principles and rules of affiliation.[34] Yet as Stevens points out, "territory as the criterion for membership only defers the site of birth invocations from the *politically constituted* family to the *politically constituted* territory. The effect of the citizenship criterion of birth in the territory is to sacralize the political borders, not to defetishize birth as a membership criterion."[35]

To be clear, though, Stevens's argument is not that the sacralization of territory is akin to the prescriptive community of blood – that, in the end, all nationalisms are ethnic. Rather, it is the reverse. The bounds of blood (or kinship) and the bounds of territory are products of law, which means that both are subject to alteration and reimagining, if on different grounds. All nationalisms are civic. And if we choose to perceive the nation as a construction of rules and commitments, we might well decide to dispense altogether with the sacralization of blood and territory as the basis for political community.

Ayelet Shachar, in her efforts to promote a concept of *jus nexi*, or citizenship through genuine connection, provides us with a compelling example of how the apparent openness of civic nationalism gives way to a rigid territorial sacralization.[36] With regard to *jus soli* (birth in the territory), Shachar observes that birthright citizenship is both under- and over-inclusive. The concept can be under-inclusive, for example, when it denies citizenship to a child who, through a mere accident of birth, arrived in the national territory as an infant but otherwise spent his entire life in the country. With regard to the over-inclusive functioning of territory, one could note the remarkable case of a child born on an airplane over Canadian airspace and who was, indeed, granted Canadian citizenship. The child's mother was Ugandan, and she boarded the Northwest Airlines plane in Amsterdam, travelling to Boston. The mother went into labour during the flight and delivered the child over the east coast of Canada. And while Canadian officials were initially uncertain about the child's eligibility for citizenship, the government ultimately concluded that "Canadian territory – and, as a result, the full reach of Canadian sovereignty – extends to [its] airspace."[37] This over-inclusive tendency is what is at issue in contemporary debates surrounding "maternity tourism," which I explore in chapter 7. To the extent that this is a phenomenon worthy of political attention, one might note that the anxiety this situation provokes adheres to the behaviour of racialized women who, in seeking a better life for their children, are seen as fraudulent "takers" whose Canadian infants are guilty by association. In any event, Shachar's point here is that holding fast to the fact of one's birth in the territory bears only passing relationship to one's engagement in the political community. And while she does not, in fact, oppose birth-based citizenship determination, her argument is that the rigidity of its operations in certain national contexts – including Canada – fails to adequately reflect more substantive principles of citizenship.

The attachment narratives of the most vocal lost Canadians are also remarkable for the deep but largely unspoken racial structures on which they rest. Implicitly and sometimes explicitly, these claims to Canadian identity are also rooted in race, that is, in whiteness. Strategies such as invoking commitment to Canada via a father's military service, lineage going back to a Father of Confederation, and "Canadian blood" were especially effective for lost Canadians in their efforts to persuade the public and federal politicians of the validity of their claims to Canadian membership. Notably, such strategies were imbued with a Canadian national identity saturated with whiteness and masculinity and firmly tied to a nostalgic rendering of the country's colonial heritage. But these invocations disregard Canada's dispossession of Indigenous peoples, thus participating in the "indigenization" of white settlers (discussed earlier); they also bifurcate Canadian settlement stories, roping off the preferred and welcomed settlers from those whose presence in Canada was complicated by the Atlantic slave trade, Asian exclusion and continuous journey legislation, head taxes, and an immigration system that explicitly preferred northern Europeans.[38] This rhetorical strategy has been particularly effective at reproducing a racial hierarchy in which white people, regardless of when they immigrated to Canada, are understood as part of the nation, whereas a racialized person whose family has lived in Canada for generations finds their connection to the country a source of regular interrogation *qua* "but where are you from, really?" By staking their legitimacy on their ancestry, lost Canadians mobilize a strategy that juxtaposes their assertions of authenticity against those of racialized others, effectively asserting that racialized settlers' attachment to Canadian-ness is less worthy, or at least less long-lasting.

As many critical scholars of Canadian nationalism have pointed out, white supremacy is endemic to Canadian nationalism, and in turn, Canadian nationalism constructs a racialized sense of home.[39] While multiculturalism has been an artefact of Canadian public policy since 1971, its existence has always rested on the juxtaposition of "authentic" Canadians with both Indigenous peoples and "newcomers." This discursive formulation places people of French but especially English ancestry at the centre of "authenticity." As Nandita Sharma explains, the racialization and regulation of diverse Indigenous peoples into "Indians" and the changing hierarchical organization of various racialized populations over time – "Blacks," "Asians," "southern" and "eastern" "Europeans" – have been articulated in opposition to "Canadian-ness."[40] Multiculturalism thus works to reinforce rather than undermine the language of authenticity.

Of course, the "other" to the "authentic" does play a crucial role in national identity construction. Moreover, in the context of the ruse of liberal consent, immigrants are especially important since they are the only citizens in contemporary nation-states who deliberately affirm the authority of the sovereign through their "adoption" of/by a new political society. In Bonnie Honig's illuminating examination of the role of foreigners in sustaining liberal democracies, she observes that when so-called outsiders choose to become members of a polity they provide a vehicle for nationalism by articulating a narrative of the nation's choice-worthiness.[41] Honig invokes Sanford Levinson's observation that immigrant naturalization ceremonies perform a kind of "national liturgy": "With a hope and a prayer and an oath, the gap of consent is filled. Immigrant naturalization ceremonies – frequently publicized on the front pages of the nation's newspapers – testify to the fundamental consentworthiness of the regime by symbolically representing the consent that is effectively unattainable for native-born citizens of a liberal regime."[42] Thus, even while immigrants are confirming the desirability of their chosen nation-state, they are exposing the fact that most citizens do not, in fact, actively consent to the authority of the sovereign.

People asserting a birthright claim to Canadian citizenship inject an intriguing liminality into this discussion as they are neither entirely within nor outside of the nation-state, at least while their statuses are disputed. For the lost Canadians, this situation is especially poignant, as they have been called out of the Canadian fold and obliged to make their consent explicit, an act of validating their attachment to Canada that they feel should not be required of them. In their insistence that they are (misplaced) citizens rather than immigrants, and in their assertions that they should not have to undertake the processes and expenses to which immigrants are subjected, they are effectively arguing that they should be understood as part of the national family. And families, as the story goes, are not constructed by rational consent, but by affection and blood.

In a number of their public representations, lost Canadians – at least of the "ordinary" variety that I explore in chapter 5 – make their case for citizenship with righteous indignation. Of course, there is no shortage of injustice in the workings and interpretations of Canada's *Citizenship Act*, but the dynamic that interests me here is the sense of entitlement with which some lost Canadians made their claims, and the willingness of politicians, the media, and the Canadian public to share their moral outrage. Don Chapman, the self-proclaimed leader of the lost Canadians, is a notable example. His book, recounting his efforts to address the provisions of the *Citizenship Act* that created lost Canadians, relies on the juxtaposition of "real Canadians" whose citizenship had nonetheless been refused and "immigrants" whose national attachment is presumptively both weaker and more readily assured by the Canadian state.[43] The outrage of these authentic-but-lost Canadians contrasts sharply with the affection that is expected of racialized Canadians, be they birthright or naturalized citizens. For naturalizing citizens, and for people whose birthright claims are inflected by racial difference or security concerns – as well as the ways in which race and security are often bound together – a righteous sense of entitlement to citizenship is simply unacceptable. Instead, as Sara Ahmed observes, people in these categories are expected to portray a normative "happiness" and gratitude, regardless of their treatment at the hands of state officials and the broader community.[44] Thus, we can expand on Honig's insight regarding the critical role of foreigners in shoring up the desirability of settler societies. While the performance of gratitude underscores Canada's worthiness as a political community of choice, so too does the indignation of otherwise "authentic" Canadians whose citizenship is denied.

When birth criteria provide the foundation for membership in political communities, blood-based structures of belonging and their racial associations are infused with the logic of citizenship. Global mobility, diasporic communities, and even multiculturalism do, of course, disrupt strict delineations of race and place. And, more fundamentally, family, kinship, and race are all social forms – imaginative concepts whose power comes from the extent to which we invest them with immutability. Birth criteria provide an expeditious means to name community members, but they do more than that. They set up systems of citizen/alien, belonging/exclusion, and authentic/forgery; they can inspire xenophobia and define the limits of our "non-emergency expressions of compassion";[45] and they restrict participation in self-governance and self-determination. Given that birth-based membership has so many faults, it is worth considering some alternatives.

Time

In her remarkable book, *The Political Value of Time,* Elizabeth Cohen argues that durational time has been largely absent from political theories of legitimacy or justice, since, like the family, we associate it with nature and thus take it for granted.[46] Time, unlike property, wealth, or privilege, appears to be a highly egalitarian measure or proxy in politics since "the clock ticks and calendar days pass at the same rate regardless of one's social class, status, birth or other personal characteristics."[47] Yet time also has significant political value. The coming into force of legislation, waiting periods to establish permanent residency and subsequently citizenship, and passport and visa expiration dates all reflect the power of time. Furthermore, and as the lost Canadians demonstrate so poignantly, relative to territorial borders, temporal borders are extremely efficient and cost-effective. As Cohen asserts, "a temporal boundary can impose a surgical precision on political power that geography cannot."[48] This is especially true for fixed, single-moment boundaries, and it describes the dilemmas faced by many of the lost Canadians as they contend with the proximity of their birthdates to the passage of Canada's various citizenship acts.[49] The hard deadline of 1 January 1947, for example, was the last bulwark in the Harper Conservatives' efforts to restrict the extension of Canada's citizenship provisions to the children of Canadian soldiers. To be born on 31 December 1946 in Britain to the unmarried wartime sweetheart of a Canadian soldier meant, definitively, that one was *not* a Canadian, a fact that remained true until 11 June 2015. Countdown boundaries are an improvement over the single moment-boundary, as they can accommodate more complexity and thus distribute power across a wider stretch of time.[50] As noted earlier, the 1977 *Citizenship Act* provided that children of Canadian mothers born abroad prior to 1977 had two years to apply for citizenship, and in fact, that boundary was later extended several times. Nonetheless, "once the time window has elapsed, the door slams shut."[51]

Time's political value goes well beyond defining borders. Time is also extremely helpful in commensurating competing values. When, for example, we argue over the appropriate residency period that a prospective immigrant should complete prior to becoming a citizen, the debate may engage arguments that include a desire not to "cheapen" citizenship by making the time too short; a sense that people need time to become acclimatized to their new community; the significant investment of time necessary to enhance loyalty; and the notion that people who are subjected to the state's governance should be able to participate in their governance as quickly as possible. Reasonable people might argue that a proper rehearsal of these distinct rationales is substantively important to the integrity of democratic deliberation. Or one might feel that the divisions that competing values can wreak are best addressed through a proxy agreement around time, leaving the contested norms with the sleeping dogs. Time, it is fair to say, does a lot of political work in the realm of citizenship.

Telling the Tale

While the news stories of lost Canadians were the initial inspiration for this project, once I began researching the law, policy, and politics that created their predicaments, I found myself engaged in a kind of historical biography of the birthright citizenship provisions of Canada's citizenship acts. The trajectory of my argument is both linear and reflexive, exploring the various birthright provisions as they manifested in people's lived experiences and the Canadian state's successive attempts to address the injustices in those experiences. Generally speaking, the state's initial response to claims of unjust treatment has been defensive and negative.[52] With the assistance of judicial judgments, public support, and political will, however, positive change has also been realized, through special dispensation, legislative reform, or interpretive practice. That narrative arc frames chapters 2 through 5, all of which engage stories in which paying heed to the injustice in people's denied or challenged citizenship claims is a relatively straightforward exercise, albeit made awkward by appeals to "Canadian ethnicity" and national symbolism rather than to a more substantive attachment to Canada. Chapter 6 also engages the legal pitfalls of the citizenship legislation that created lost Canadians, but it focuses on adults whose criminality and threat to state security propelled the lower courts, at least, to moderate the principle of birthright entitlement. The chapter ends with the unique case of Zakaria Amari, the only Canadian to have his citizenship revoked under the Harper government's anti-terror reforms to the *Citizenship Act.* Chapter 7 then turns to the Canadian state's actions to limit the citizenship claims of babies, in the context of children who were born abroad with the assistance of reproductive technologies but are not genetically related to their Canadian parent(s), as well as children born in Canada to foreign parents. Having made the case, then, that birthright citizenship is less secure than we might think, and that it generates an exclusive form of national identity rooted in Canada's colonial past and racialized whiteness, I examine alternative proposals for political membership, both moderate and radical.

Chapters 2 and 3 examine Canada's first *Citizenship Act,* which came into force in 1947 in the wake of Canada's national coming of age during the Second World War. The analysis explores the situation prior to the passage of the legislation, in particular the unique circumstances of Canadian soldiers abroad and the primarily British and Dutch women with whom they interacted. In its postwar enthusiasm for nation-building, the Canadian government advanced a public performance of welcoming soldiers home to Canada with their foreign brides and children, but this warmth was subtended by concerns about protecting Canada from women of unfit character, absolving the Canadian state from responsibility for Canadian-sired children born out of wedlock, and keeping a careful eye on the costs of patriation. The provisions of Canada's first *Citizenship Act* reflected some of these concerns, notably by removing citizenship from naturalized Canadians who subsequently lived outside Canada for more than six years, and, as noted above, by including wedlock provisions that restricted *jus sanguinis* citizenship to children of married Canadian fathers or unmarried Canadian mothers.[53] The passage of Canada's first *Citizenship Act* was the occasion for a fresh and highly symbolic articulation of an independent national identity. In its celebration of a very mid-twentieth-century sense of diversity, what we might call diversity-in-whiteness, the legislation and the context in which it arose are highly informative of the social dynamics of the time.

While chapter 2 considers the period leading up to the passage of Canada's first *Citizenship Act*, chapter 3 engages the consequences of that Act for war brides and their children. Due to the workings of the loss provisions of the 1947 Act as well as the fact that different citizenship rules applied to people who became citizens before and after 1947, a number of war brides and their children found themselves struggling to assert or reclaim their Canadian citizenship. I also explore two cases in which children of Canadian soldiers, who were raised in Europe by adoptive fathers, attempted to trace their Canadian heritage without an intention to claim citizenship. The significance of fathers' wartime service underscores the rhetorical force of these claims, but the Canadian state's concerns to limit its obligations to these emergent citizens is also very much alive in the struggles of these people. Gender, sexual norms, race, and age track through all of these stories, illustrating the complexities of making the "Canadian people" and the settler-colonial Canadian nation, as well as the resonant emotional performances that ultimately compelled the Canadian state to act.

Chapters 4 and 5 look beyond the war brides and their children to consider the consequences of the 1947 *Citizenship Act* for a broader range of would-be Canadians. These consequences would lead to the passage of a new citizenship act that came into effect on 15 February 1977. Although this new act rectified the gender and marital status discrimination of its predecessor, it was not retroactive. Thus, different laws governed one's Canadian citizenship depending on when one was born – before 1 January 1947; between then and 14 February 1977; and after. While "lost Canadians" resulted from each of these Acts independently, the coexistence of different rules, even when earlier legislation had effectively been repealed, added further confusion and complication, both for people trying to sort out their own status and for public officials charged with administering the law(s). With the coming into force of the equality provisions of Canada's *Charter of Rights and Freedoms* in 1985, the unequal treatment this situation created came under increasing scrutiny.

Chapter 4 focuses on the parliamentary debate surrounding the 1977 Act. Equality was a central focus, and more specifically, that birthright and naturalized Canadians should enjoy equal citizenship and that Canadian women should be able to pass along their citizenship to their foreign-born children, regardless of their wedlock status. The question of whether the legislation should be retroactive – whether the children born before 15 February 1977 to Canadian citizen mothers should be entitled to apply for citizenship – was given lengthy consideration. Many parliamentarians were in favour of this extended eligibility, but the public servants in the Ministry of Citizenship and Immigration were considerably more circumspect. Ultimately, the Act would enable people born abroad to Canadian mothers prior to 15 February 1977 a two-year opportunity (subsequently extended) to apply for citizenship, but they would be required to pass a security check and swear an oath of allegiance. This created a situation in which the born-abroad children of married Canadian mothers were seemingly more dangerous than the born-abroad children of married Canadian fathers. The 1977 Act was also notable for enabling dual citizenship and for a provision that allowed second-generation born-abroad Canadians to retain their citizenship if they affirmed their intention by age twenty-eight.

Chapter 5 examines three situations of citizenship loss occasioned by the operation of the 1947 *Citizenship Act* and intensified in their injustice by the non-retroactive corrections of the 1977 Act. The first situation considers the ongoing gender inequities in birthright citizenship entitlement. I consider two cases in which children within the same family had differential access to Canadian citizenship by virtue of being born before or after 15 February 1977. In the first case, decided prior to the coming into force of the *Charter of Rights and Freedoms,* the rule affected a child born abroad to a Canadian father who was cohabiting with the child's mother – and thus the child was born out of wedlock. His younger siblings, born after 1977, were deemed Canadian citizens. In the second case, a married Canadian mother applied for Canadian citizenship for her US-born children who had lost their citizenship when their Canadian father became an American citizen. Because the older child was eighteen at the time of application, he was deemed ineligible, while his younger brother, as a minor, was granted citizenship. In this case, a *Charter* argument provided extra weight to the case. The second situation focuses on people who were born in Canada but lost their citizenship when, as minor children, their "responsible parent" took citizenship in a foreign country. This situation is exemplified in the highest-profile lost Canadian, Don Chapman, whose tireless efforts on behalf of a range of people caught up in the complications of Canada's *Citizenship Acts* would ultimately lead to reforms in 2008 and 2014. Chapman's case is especially compelling for my argument because of the ways in which his deployment of patriotic nationalism constrains broader considerations of the terms of political membership and articulates a hierarchy of belonging. The third situation focuses on wedlock provisions and citizenship affirmation requirements for born-abroad citizens. Some members of the Mennonite community were particularly impacted by these rules, having moved between Canada, Mexico, and other Central and Latin American countries over the trajectory of Canada's various citizenship acts. These people assumed that their Canadian citizenship remained intact, not least because they were regularly issued Canadian citizenship certificates and passports. With heightened scrutiny of the citizenship of born-abroad children, beginning in the 2000s, however, many of these people found their citizenship called into question.

In chapter 6, I pull on the security thread that has lurked in the background of Canada's 1947 and 1977 *Citizenship* Acts. While the high-profile lost Canadians could rely on their national commitment and personal integrity to make a political case for legislative reform, a major impetus for changing the law, arguably, came from judicial decisions involving Canadians with much more nefarious records. These cases illustrate the extent to which the Canadian state is prepared to use the technicalities of birthright provisions to deny citizenship to people it feels are unworthy of political membership. While most of these cases ultimately upheld the birthright claim of the defendant, the various arguments and judicial findings demonstrate that birth-based claims are more precarious than one might presume, besides revealing a reluctance to countenance rights-based arguments when other approaches to legal argumentation might be found. The issues of criminality and security set the table for a consideration of whose bad behaviour we must accept as part of the national community and who can be expelled because of bad behaviour. Given my interest in alternatives to birthright citizenship, the issues of revocation and banishment are of obvious importance, since, as birthright proponents argue, in the absence of a birthright guarantee, what stops the state or a motivated government from expatriating people it doesn't like? The singular case of Zakaria Amara, the only Canadian to have his citizenship stripped under anti-terrorism law – and subsequently reinstated – is illustrative here. But this concern also begs the question. What does it say about a democratic polity if we are loyal to our kin, even when they behave badly, but deeply suspicious of non-kin even when they are law-abiding and earnestly desire to be part of the political community? So, leaning into the limit case of security, the chapter examines the underlying dynamics of inclusion and exclusion in birthright citizenship and the fundamental importance of an inclusive political membership.

In the last empirical chapter of this book, I examine two situations of contested birthright citizenship that have not been a part of the trajectory of lost Canadians – children born abroad with the assistance of reproductive technologies and children born on Canadian soil to foreign parents. Throughout most of the history of Canada's *Citizenship Act,* figuring out who was a parent – and thus who was the child of a Canadian parent – was relatively uncomplicated. Heterosexual marriage and binary understandings of gender did the job. In light of assisted conception and same-sex relationships, however, the definition of parent has become considerably more complicated. And while Canada's domestic legal provisions are increasingly taking these new realities into account, the *Citizenship Act* – or at least its interpretation by citizenship officials and judges – has been impressively resistant. It was not until the summer of 2020 that the federal government was compelled to broaden its definitions of parent and child to include children conceived with the assistance of reproductive technologies, regardless of genetic or gestational relationship. To be a Canadian was in the blood. Children born on Canadian soil to foreign parents have also created a frisson of political interest, particularly in the last decade. In fact, such babies represent, at the most generous estimate, 1.4 per cent of total births in Canada, but they – or rather, their mothers – have been cast as fraudulent queue-jumpers. Indeed, the harm caused by so-called maternity tourists – stereotypically Asian – was deemed sufficiently egregious that the Harper government seriously contemplated limiting *jus soli* citizenship to the children of citizens and permanent residents. The bureaucratic hassle and cost – largely to the provinces – ultimately persuaded the government to leave the *jus soli* provisions unchanged. The Conservative Party would revisit the issue at its 2018 convention, passing a resolution to pursue limitations to *jus soli*. These situations are particularly interesting because they sharpen our focus on the kinship dimensions of citizenship. What is being contested, after all, is not so much the citizenship of the infants but rather the identity and behaviour of the parents. It is the adults who are expected to embody the connection to the nation, as the Canadian soldier fathers so clearly did for so many lost Canadians. And if parents are adjudged to fall short in that regard, the political membership of the children becomes a matter of debate and contention.

The book's final chapter sets out the case for considering bases other than birth as the criteria for political membership. Beginning with a careful analysis of the work of a number of prominent scholars of liberal-democratic citizenship, I outline key features of an alternative model, one that includes consent, connection – primarily through residence – time, and subjection to governance. I have approached this task with a great deal of caution, knowing that xenophobic nationalism motivates many proposals for the abandonment of birthright citizenship, and certainly not wanting to align myself with such a project. The most vociferous proponents of ending birthright citizenship have a much more limited conception of their political project than the one that is advanced by most of the thinkers in this concluding chapter – and also by me. As it turns out, populist opponents of birthright are opposed not to birthright citizenship as a whole, but rather to extending it to the children of people they deem undesirable. This argument starts with the children of illegal immigrants, refugees, and "maternity tourists" and proceeds to a range of racialized groups who are regarded as threats to the dominant culture. Given the vitriol with which proponents advance their arguments in favour of limiting birthright citizenship, this assignation of threat seems, at best, misplaced.

I am well aware that making the case for reimagining the basis for citizenship is, in practical terms, a non-starter. Yet I would argue that this speculative exercise – based as it is on a rich history of the Canadian state's variable rules of membership as seen in the experiences of lost Canadians and a few others – is valuable as a spur to interrogate the terms on which we live together. And even if this broader argumentative gambit around political membership is a bridge too far, I do hope readers will find these remarkable stories both engaging and thought-provoking. They have much to tell us about who we are and, thus, who we could be.

2

Operation Daddy, War Brides, and the Making of Canadians: Canadian Citizenship Law, or the Canadian National Family

In February 2014, Canada's Minister of Citizenship and Immigration, Chris Alexander, rose in the House of Commons to outline the provisions of Bill C-24, a series of amendments to Canada's *Citizenship Act*. Alexander's speech drew from a deep well of nationalist oratory, invoking the citizenship practices of ancient Greece, citing origins in God's covenant with the Israelites, and over-writing Canada's violent colonial history to assert that Canadian citizenship has "involved" the languages, cultures, and love of the land of First Nations and Inuit people.[1] The speech included reference to the explorers Jacques Cartier, Samuel de Champlain, and "Mathieu da Costa, whom we honour during Black History Month every year in Canada."[2] The War of 1812 made an appearance, including its contribution to British North America's population through the addition of fleeing, British-sympathetic Americans.[3] As the story unfolded, the ambitions and struggles of the virtuous, dedicated people who would be Canadians produced rule of law, government free of corruption, a system of responsible government, and, ultimately, a *Citizenship Act* in 1947.[4] The government's 2014 amendments, Alexander proclaimed, could thus be read as an extension of this impressive legacy.

Much of the minister's speech was, in fact, devoted to justifying the legislation's title – *Strengthening Canada's Citizenship Act* – and thus focused on various amendments to make the acquisition of Canadian citizenship more difficult, as well as measures to rescind Canadian citizenship from dual nationals convicted in Canada or abroad of terrorism, treason, or espionage. However, the carrot to the Act's many sticks was a set of provisions to address the precarious citizenship status of foreign-born brides but especially the children of Canada's Second World War veterans. The minister described the extension of Canadian citizenship to people born before 1947 as a means to ensure that "we take the final steps to make sure that the lost Canadians, the children of those who fought in World War II, those who were among the most committed to the defence and service of this country, enjoy all the benefits of Canadians, not just in the first generation but also in succeeding generations, as governed by the provisions of this law."[5] These amendments serve as a bookend to the Lost Canadians saga, as the war brides and their children represent both the first category of lost Canadians created by the operation of Canada's inaugural *Citizenship Act* of 1947 and the last set of lost Canadians whose status has merited the Canadian government's legislative attention.[6]

The obvious question here would be, "What took them so long?," but my interest is different. I want to understand how it is that Canada – a settler society – came to incorporate birthright as the basis for citizenship in the first place and how war, family, and the British Empire were central to the shaping of Canada's first citizenship act. In this chapter, I set out the context for the *Citizenship Act* of 1947, but with particular attention to the race and gender dimensions of its development, as well as to the complex work of meaning-making that surrounded the figures of the war brides and their role in launching Canada's brave new nationhood. In the following pages, I build on this background to examine the texts and media coverage of the citizenship difficulties and legal challenges brought by the spouses and children of Second World War veterans as a direct result of the provisions of the *Citizenship Act*. These stories will help illustrate how birth, lineage, and national attachment are mutually reinforcing in the formulation of demands for political inclusion. The fact that successive governments resisted the citizenship claims of some Canadian veterans' children demonstrates that political calculations shape membership criteria, even when those criteria are defined by the seeming unassailability of birth. Thus, while abandoning birthright may risk the possible exclusion of people from the political community, I argue that birthright itself does not provide a failsafe. As Ayelet Shachar observes, and as I elaborate in chapter 8, birthright citizenship is both overinclusive – granting citizenship to people without substantive attachment to the political community – and underinclusive – withholding membership from people directly affected by a particular state's policies.[7] Veterans, war brides, and their children provide rich illustrations for this discussion.

Getting to Citizenship

Although 1867 marks the year of Canada's formation as a nation-state, as far as the Fathers of Confederation were concerned, the country's status as a British Dominion and thus a continued member of the Commonwealth obviated the need for a unique national membership. Instead, to be a Canadian was to be a British subject, as Sir John A. Macdonald's famous declaration "British I was born, and British I will die" explicitly conveyed. This retention of British subject status in Canada strikingly distinguished Canada's approach to citizenship from that of the Americans in the former British colonies to the south. With the Declaration of Independence, Americans' allegiance to the monarch – which they had acquired upon their birth in the sovereign's territories – was snapped.[8] Instead, as the story goes, Americans became *citizens* by consenting to their political membership in the new republic. As might already be apparent, however, the birth/consent distinction that supposedly distinguishes between subjects and citizens is false.

In many ways, the retention of British subjecthood in the Dominion of Canada was a brutal assertion. Rather than proclaiming a fresh identity for a new political community, the retention of British subjecthood as the status of Canadian political belonging restated the conquest of French Canada and largely erased the nation-to-nation basis of the British Crown's treaties with Indigenous peoples. Post-Confederation British subject status did not, however, manifest itself as a universally accessible *jus soli* principle. Rather, membership in Canada was defined by racial and gender criteria. Those Indigenous men recognized as Status Indians were offered enfranchisement – a kind of naturalization process through which Indian status was traded for assimilation as full members of the Canadian polity.[9] In legal terms, the alternative to enfranchisement was to be a ward of the federal government. Wardship was infantilizing, but such a status ensured some semblance of Indigenous community and identity. In the trade-off between enfranchisement and wardship, then, it was hardly surprising that enfranchisement was largely rejected.[10]

With regard to post-Confederation settlers, the Canadian government expressed a clear preference for white Europeans, and especially fellow British subjects from the UK and former British subjects from the US.[11] Given the Canadian government's designs on western settlement, however, and the limited supply of these desired immigrants, Liberal governments, in particular, were willing to extend political membership to eastern, central, and southern Europeans – though not without considerable debate and popular resistance.[12] In terms of national membership, Europeans who migrated to Canada could become naturalized as British subjects, and their Canadian-born children would receive British subject status by virtue of birth in the territory (*jus soli*). By contrast, the prospects for settlement and political membership for Asian and South Asian migrants were much more fraught. The Canadian government and influential industrialists were highly desirous of their labour, but provincial governments (especially in British Columbia) and labour organizations, as well as a number of social reform organizations, opposed Asian settlement. Thus, as Reg Whitaker explains, despite the federal government's preference for permanent settlement, short-term contracts for racialized migrant workers were permitted on occasion.[13] South Asians from India posed a particular conundrum for Canada's immigration officials because, of course, they *were* British subjects. The Canadian government attempted to finesse this situation by limiting migration from India through the imposition of the "continuous journey" regulation. Migrants had to arrive in Canada as the end point in one continuous trip from their country of birth or citizenship.[14]

Debates about whether or not Asian women as well as men should be permitted to migrate were particularly contentious. Enakshi Dua elaborates a lively debate in which those who opposed the migration of Asian women argued that the presence of these racialized women in Canada would encourage permanent Asian settlement through the establishment of families, or, alternatively, foster prostitution and licentious behaviour. In any case, the opponents asserted, women from China, Japan, and South Asia should not be permitted to come to Canada. For their part, proponents argued that allowing Asian women to enter Canada would help alleviate the risk of miscegenation and reduce crime by ensuring moral order. Thus, went the argument, limited migration of women could be encouraged, but given the supposed fecundity of these women, their numbers should be strictly controlled.[15]

In the early part of the twentieth century, some Japanese, Indian, and (many fewer) Chinese immigrants did manage to settle in Canada. Importantly, though, people from China and Japan were considered aliens, and while not formally prohibited from naturalization, they were often excluded by virtue of the racist application of "good character" qualifications by state officials. Canadian-born children of alien Asian migrants were also deemed aliens.[16]

As a settler-society, then, membership in the Canadian nation-state was a hybrid of naturalization and birthright claims that worked in tandem to build membership in the political community – a membership that was idealized as racially white and gendered male. Until the passage of Canada's *Citizenship Act* in 1946, wives were understood to acquire the citizenship of their husbands upon marriage. Thus, Canadian women who married foreign men lost their Canadian citizenship. Asian women who married Canadian men became Canadians; moreover, applying the same logic, though in the context of Indigenous communities, the *Indian Act* provided that Status Indian women who married non-Status men lost their status, whereas non-Status women who married Status men, became Status Indians. As the dictums of coverture made clear, in marriage two people became one, and that one was the husband.[17]

Until the passage of Canada's first *Citizenship Act* in 1946 (which came into force on 1 January 1947), the British subject status that defined membership in the Canadian polity was articulated through a series of immigration acts, naturalization acts, and the *Canadian Nationals Act* (1921) – the last of these necessitated by Canada's obligations to the League of Nations.[18] As Paul Martin Sr, the architect of Canada's first citizenship act, would ruefully observe, "there are few countries in the world who define their citizenship within the clauses of an immigration act."[19] For Martin, the consent-based trappings of immigration and naturalization did not invoke a model membership process, which he regarded as a process of inclusion, since "the real purpose and intent of [the Immigration Act] is to exclude certain classes of people."[20]

The *Citizenship Act* of 1947

The impetus for a law that would finally articulate Canadian citizenship, distinct (but not divorced) from British subjecthood, arose over the course of the Second World War in response to Secretary of State Martin's encounters with the European graves of Canadian soldiers. These fallen had been designated as "British subjects" rather than "Canadians," and Martin felt that this failure to recognize the soldiers' sacrifice to Canada and to honour Canada's significant contribution to the Allied war effort needed to be addressed through a distinctive national citizenship.[21] There had been at least one previous attempt to establish Canadian citizenship – in 1931, coincident with the Statute of Westminster. As Martin described the rationale behind that initiative, C.H. Cahan, the legislation's promoter, "felt, as I feel that the time had come when Canada, having matured into full nationhood, should give her people the right of being able to designate themselves Canadian citizens."[22] The Canadian state, envisioned as a child of the British motherland, had come of age.

Martin argued passionately for a big tent vision of Canadian identity:

> Our citizenship is made up not only of people born in this country and of people who acquired domicile as British subjects under the Immigration Act, but of many thousands of new Canadians living in all parts of our country who have come from other lands and who have made a notable contribution to the development of Canada. Many of those people came here without being able to speak the two languages of the country and without being accustomed to its traditions. Most of them have rendered notable service to Canada. We should not lose the opportunity of impressing ourselves and reminding them that just as we are glad to welcome them to our shores, now that they are here they should enjoy with us the full measure of partnership in the Canadian community.[23]

The Conservative leader of the Opposition, John Diefenbaker, seemed to share Martin's capacious vision of citizenship, arguing that it was incumbent upon Canada to develop "unity out of diversity" and, in particular, "a citizenship free from racial origin and unhyphenated."[24] For Diefenbaker, the path to this unified Canadian identity would be further enabled by the abolition of census questions that required the reporting of "paternal racial origin." As an example of the inanity of this requirement, Diefenbaker quoted an informational pamphlet for census completion. "As a general rule," the pamphlet stated, "a person's racial origin is to be traced through his father, eg. if a person's father is English and his mother French, the racial origin shall be entered as English, while a person whose father is French and whose mother is English, shall be entered as French."[25] Indeed, there is a rankling in this gendered logic for determining national – or in the language of the time, racial – derivation. But Diefenbaker's insight had limited reach. Citing the Americans as an admirable example of how to register racial origins, Diefenbaker noted, positively, that only naturalized citizens had to register on the basis of racial origin, and the only separation was that of "negro, Indian, Chinese and Japanese races."[26] Diefenbaker's conception of unhyphenated Canadians thus remained restricted to white people. And while he obviously felt that women had a role to play in conveying a national/racial identity, he did not offer any objections to the patriarchal vestiges of citizenship determination that imbued the 1947 Act. True enough, the act did newly entitle women to keep their own citizenship upon marriage to a foreigner, but children of the marriage gained their father's status, and there was no provision for dual citizenship until 1977.

Diefenbaker's desire to establish an unhyphenated national identity for white people was further restricted by a preference for immigration from the British Empire and the retention of British subject status as an extension of the new designation of Canadian citizen. He was particularly displeased that British subjects had to meet the same residency requirements as immigrants from other countries. ""I ask the minister to explain why ... should a British subject coming into Canada and properly entering this country under our immigration law be required to go through the same formalities as persons coming from other parts of the world?"[27] Several parliamentarians echoed this concern regarding the *Citizenship Act*'s lack of expedited residency provisions for British subjects. Progressive Conservative MP T.L. Church, for example, worried that "this measure represents a notice to the mother country that we do not want any more of them over here."[28] Other MPs, particularly from Quebec, felt that the *Citizenship Act* cleaved rather too much to Britain, with Mr Maxime Raymond arguing that "far from being a symbol of nationhood, this bill as it now reads is a symbol of colonialism."[29]

One would expect the designing of a citizenship act from the ground up to occasion some careful thought about birthright citizenship. Those kinds of debates, however, if they did occur in the Canadian context, are not included in the public record. There was some consideration of limiting *jus soli*, since a law that granted citizenship on the basis of birth in the territory had the potential to include racialized populations that had been excluded from membership under previous practice and legislation. In the final version, the British *jus soli* tradition was carried through into the new Canadian law, with citizenship being attainable both through birth in the territory and through *jus sanguinis* – birth to a citizen father (in the case of married parents) or a citizen mother (in the case of a child born out of wedlock). It was the *jus sanguinis* provisions that would prove particularly contentious for the children of Canada's veterans.

The metaphor of the family figured centrally in these discussions of identity and belonging. As we can see from invocations of "the motherland," Canada's "coming of age," and paternal delineations of ethnic and national identity, the connection between family and nation (a term that finds its origins in *nasci* – birth) was never far from the logic underscoring citizenship. Of course, a hallmark of liberal modernity was the effort to envision a form of political society distinct from the family. This was a way of constituting the polity without a hereditary monarchy – without the king. Yet, as many political theorists have observed, the political and the familial are densely entangled. Kennan Ferguson, for example, notes that conceptions of sovereignty in political theory as in political debate rely on the organization of authority within the family as a fundamental metaphor for the operation of authority through the structures of the state. Even as liberal (and other) thinkers articulate a vision of the family as a deeply private, even pre-political arrangement, families nonetheless form a touchstone for the right ordering of political society. As Ferguson explains, "if God no longer forms the basis of political legitimacy, as in the divine right of Kings, then other legitimizations must take his place ... One pattern appears repeatedly, families are the site of natural, prepolitical authority, and the proper state is that which develops from and expands that source of power."[30]

Families, then, offer a model for the operation of power and the naturalization of power differentials. The subordination of wives and children and an explicitly gendered order of authority are central to this model, but all for the greater good of realizing a shared project animated by care and concern.[31] "Once a small-scale ideal commonality can be built (or at least bought into)," Ferguson argues, "the only obstacle to a perfectly functioning larger community is the question of scale."[32]

Ferguson's central observation is that the deployment of the familial metaphor as the basis for political authority presumes (a) that families are harmonious places with a shared vision and (b) that a state, so ordered, similarly produces harmony. This metaphor was certainly alive and well in the realization of Canada's first citizenship act. In Secretary of State Martin's words, "there is no finer club in the world than the club I would characterize as the Canadian family."[33]

Ultimately, Canada's first *Citizenship Act* established a unique Canadian citizenship while retaining British subject status, and required five years of residency for everyone seeking citizenship, regardless of British subject status. That said, British subjects were entitled to less arduous application procedures once the residency requirement had been met, and people who had served in the armed forces were required to establish only one year of residency in the country. As well, in order to ensure that no one lost their status as a result of the coming into force of the *Citizenship Act*, automatic citizenship was granted to people who had been naturalized in Canada, non-Canadian British subjects who had lived in Canada for five years or more, and non-Canadian women who had married citizens (or rather, men who became citizens with the coming into force of the Act) and had landed in Canada.[34] Martin would later attest that he would have preferred to eliminate British subject status entirely, but regarded its inclusion as a political necessity to ensure the bill's passage.[35]

Martin was rather more successful at articulating his capacious and nascent multicultural conception of Canadian membership in the orchestration of the first citizenship ceremony. Indeed, he asserted that one of the *Citizenship Act's* major aims was to provide for "a more effective and impressive ceremony of admission to the Canadian family."[36] Held in the "august chambers of the Supreme Court" on 3 January 1947 (albeit *before* that Court had acquired the stature of Canada's supreme judicial authority), the event planners did their utmost to gather a broad representation of Canadian settlers.[37] The ceremony was, indeed, heavily symbolic, since most of the people who received citizenship certificates in that first ceremony were already citizens by virtue of the Act itself and were not required by law to pledge allegiance or otherwise express their desire for membership in the Canadian polity. Prime Minister Mackenzie King and Secretary of State Martin received the first two citizenship certificates; other recipients included Wasyl Elnyiak, an elderly Ukrainian farmer who had been "discovered ... after a long search through the immigration department's records," and Mrs Stanley Mynarski of Winnipeg, who wore her son's Victoria Cross and received "applause equal to that given to the prime minister."[38] Mrs Mynarski's contribution to Canada, as a mother to a heroic soldier, articulated the reproductive contribution to the nation that was expected of women. The fact that she was identified by the convention of the day, through her husband's name rather than her own – as Mrs Stanley Mynarski – reinforced the absent presence of the *paterfamilias* and her role as a conduit of masculinity from father to son. Additional participants in Canada's first citizenship ceremony included "Giuseppe Agostini, a conductor for the CBC [Canadian Broadcasting Corporation]; Kjeld Beichman, a Danish-born potter from New Brunswick; Maurice Labrosse of Ottawa and his Aberdeenshire bride; Yousef Karsh, the famous photographer; Mrs R.P. Steeves of Vancouver; Gerhard Ens of Rosthern Saskatchewan; and Andrew B. MacRae, a descendant of one of the oldest families in Prince Edward Island."[39] In this collection of newly certified Canadians, then, the nation was being articulated geographically, both within Canada and in terms of settler source countries (Asian countries and African and Caribbean colonies being notably absent, as well as Indigenous communities), as well as in terms of contribution – to the arts, to public service (military duty and elected office), and to the nation-making work of agricultural production and mothering. Men were rendered in their full names, while women were uniformly subsumed to their spouses. In this evocative description then, we find the embodiment of Canadian citizenship in its first formal expression.

The War Brides – Canada's "Most Excellent" Citizens

Scholars of nationalism have demonstrated persuasively that violence and war are central events in the articulation of nations and national identity.[40] Nonetheless, as the war bride story richly illustrates, birth and generational reproduction are also worthy contenders in the expression of national formation. Jacqueline Stevens suggests that the interplay of birth and death is what animates national belonging. "States claim the monopoly on the prerogative to define the family because only legal kinship rules playing on fantasies about birth and death ensure national attachments that might lead large populations to risk their lives and to kill others."[41] The combination of the generationality of families (i.e., as individuals we live through time by virtue of being marked by ancestors and marking progeny) and the kinship basis of state membership (i.e., the state's rules of attachment that constitute both families and political membership) creates nation-state identities worthy of sacrifice and even death.

The families produced as a result of the wartime romances of Canadian soldiers and northern European (but overwhelmingly British) women were among the liveliest and most desirable members to be welcomed to the Canadian national club. The war brides provided both an ancestral connection to the motherland and the promise of a new, racially and culturally desirable generation of young Canadians. Out of the ashes of war, the Canadian nation emerged in the fertile bodies of British maidens. But this cheery, "good news" story with all of its trappings of love, marriage, and baby carriages was also the product of a great deal of interpretive fashioning. Several other renderings of the encounters between Canadian soldiers and foreign women were in circulation during the war years, interpretations that were considerably more tawdry, or more reflective of the material conditions of thousands of young men posted overseas, the effects of bombing, rationing, injury, and death, Canadian sweethearts and families left behind, and the interplay of familiarity and foreignness in the European–Canadian encounter. The press and Parliament exuded a great deal of romanticism when the war brides arrived in Canada, and that romanticism has attained an ever higher lustre over time. Yet this bedazzling obscures both the politics and the human dimension of the war bride story, features that are, nonetheless, very much alive in the bureaucratic and judicial struggles concerning their citizenship and that of their children.[42]

Canada entered the Second World War on 10 September 1939, and on 28 January 1940, church bells rang in the English heathlands, celebrating the wedding of a Canadian soldier and a young woman of Aldershot.[43] By the end of the war, 44,885 more weddings would be celebrated, as well as 2,674 marriages between Canadian soldiers and women of other nationalities.[44] Given that most Canadian soldiers did not participate in a sustained military campaign until the summer of 1944, they had a considerable amount of time to develop relationships.[45] That said, these commitments emerged from a much broader terrain of sexual encounters. Historian John Costello recounts that "Canadian troops stationed in the south of England ... acquired the worst wartime record as violent lovers, and ... extracted the most savage vengeance on those girls who jilted them."[46] By contrast, renowned writer and wartime journalist Mavis Gallant observed that Canadian soldiers were often characterized as naive, chaste boys from the colony. In her recounting of this particular anecdotal form, "English girls, avid for marriage were said to leap on any passing Canadian and drag him into blacked-out doorways for goings-on too shameful to describe – the soldier meanwhile clinging to a lamppost and protesting, 'No, no, I'm engaged to a nice girl in Regina!'"[47] Between these extremes, however, the familiar gendered tropes of "boys will be boys" and the shaming of women engaged in non- or extra-marital sexual encounters were frequently and vividly expressed. The extraordinary social circumstances of the war extended men's sexual licence in the face of the prospect of death in battle while heightening anxiety in light of women's employment in male workplaces, their everyday existence in communities evacuated of male, familial authority, and their chronic desperation under circumstances of rationing and repeated aerial bombardment.

This gendered sexual economy also found expression in Canada's military regulations regarding permissions to marry, provisions for illegitimate children, and the transporting and citizenship of Canadian soldiers' foreign fiancées, wives, and children. Despite the significant number of marriages that did manage to occur, Canadian soldiers encountered stiff restrictions when they sought permission to marry from their commanding officers, and even when that permission was granted, the logistics of conducting a wedding in the context of frequent troop movements often thwarted their best intentions. The regulations governing permissions to marry grew more stringent as the war progressed. Initially there were no regulations for naval and air force personnel, whereas soldiers in the army had to have their commanding officers' permission only if the new bride was to receive a dependant's allowance.[48] Eight months after the first Aldershot wedding, however, the rules were tightened: men under nineteen and their fiancées under twenty-one now required parental permission, as well as attestation by the commanding officer that the soldier understood his financial responsibilities and was debt-free and that the bride was of sound moral character.[49] One year later, in December 1941, in light of reports of bigamous marriages, further restrictions were imposed. A prospective groom was now required to declare his current marital status, his likely ability to sustain his family after discharge, and his consent to a forced savings of $200 at the rate of a $10 per month deduction from his pay to finance his dependants' passage to Canada.[50] The prospective bride required a responsible citizen to vouch for her good character, and the couple was required to wait an additional two months before the wedding could be celebrated.[51]

Commanding officers, as well as the chaplains to whom they divested much of this marriage-sanctioning responsibility, freely imposed their own moral judgments about the suitability of the marriages they were asked to authorize, and they readily enforced prohibitions against religious, ethnic, and racial mixing. Protestant/Catholic unions were actively discouraged, and the commanding officers of French-speaking units were known to refuse permission for marriages to British women. C.P. Stacey and Barbara Wilson note that by "January 1943 … there had yet to be a marriage of a member of Le Régiment de la Chaudière in Britain – and the regiment had been there since August 1941."[52] Once Canadian troops were engaged in battle on the continent, marriages were governed by Canadian Army North West Europe Routine Order No. 788, which instructed commanding officers to dissuade marriages in foreign lands, especially when "'differences of race, religion, and customs' left them 'open to obvious risks to future happiness.'"[53] This order evidently had only limited effect, or perhaps the commanding officers saw more similarity than difference in the prospective marriages they were asked to endorse. Yet the logic underlying the order reveals the Canadian military's concern, undoubtedly shared by their political overseers, with enforcing a particular ethnic (read moral) character on these emergent families. As families go, after all, so goes the nation.

The combination of a disordered social context, concentrations of young people, and strictures on marriage unsurprisingly led to thousands of births out of wedlock. Reliable statistics are not available, but one estimate puts the figure at 23,000. In this vein, the Canadian military's remarkably modest figures reported that the British civil courts had notified Canadian military headquarters of 414 maintenance orders by August 1945, that Canadian soldiers voluntarily acknowledged 283 children, and that another 144 awards were made to these children by the Dependant's Allowance Board.[54] For its part, the UK General Register Office recorded 1945 as having the highest illegitimacy rate on record, at 9.35 per cent of live births.[55] In any event, the severity of the problem was sufficient to capture the attention of Canada's High Commissioner to the United Kingdom, senior military officials, and the Minister of Defence.[56] When the *Toronto Evening Telegram* offered the remaining monies in its British war victims' fund to support "'the immediate relief … of the children, legitimate or otherwise,' of Canadians who had served in Britain," Canadian officials readily accepted, assigning the task of administering the aid to Department of Veterans Affairs.[57] With that arrangement made, however, Canada systematically absolved itself of any future responsibilities for the illegitimate children of Canadian soldiers. Historian Jeffrey Keshen notes that by the autumn of 1946, the Canadian military was refusing requests to locate discharged men with respect to paternity claims. In the military's assessment, by that time all legitimate cases would have been filed and the veterans were "once more private citizens … entitled to protection."[58] This refusal of responsibility continued to play out in Canadian citizenship law until the 2014 amendments to the *Citizenship Act*.

The Canadian government was largely able to evade the thorny challenges posed by the unacknowledged illegitimate children of its soldiers; however, the citizenship status of war brides and their children (whether born before or after the mothers' marriages to soldier fathers) required more careful attention. Prior to 1 January 1947, this status was governed through a series of Privy Council Orders, the most significant being P.C. 858, since the vast majority of war brides entered Canada under its authority. Signed in February 1945, P.C. 858 granted dependents (wives, widows, and children under eighteen) who applied, entry to Canada, landed status upon admission, and the same national status designation as the husband/father. Specifically, paragraph 3 of the order stated: "Every dependent who is permitted to enter Canada ... shall for the purpose of Canadian immigration law be deemed to be a Canadian citizen if the member of the forces upon whom he is dependent is a Canadian citizen and shall be deemed to have Canadian domicile if the said member has Canadian domicile."[59]

The language of "Canadian citizen" in this order is worth noting, particularly since the Canadian government insisted that "Canadian citizenship" did not exist as a status before 1 January 1947. According to this rationale, the status designation "Canadian citizen" only officially existed in, and for the purposes of, Canadian immigration law, where it was defined as "a person born in Canada who has not become an alien." The courts have not uniformly agreed with this limited interpretation of Canadian citizenship prior to 1947, but the case of record – *Taylor v. Canada* (2007) – does uphold this view, and it was this interpretation that initially led the Harper government to insist that it was impossible to extend that status back through time.[60] P.C. 858 also included provisions requiring a medical examination prior to the journey to Canada and deferring admission for dependents diagnosed with a contagious or infectious disease or an illness that might compromise public health or the safety of the dependent on the voyage.

The majority of war brides and children made the journey to Canada in a series of sailings organized over the course of 1946. The first sailing of "Operation Daddy," as the press dubbed the war bride patriation, was made on 5 February 1946 and included one thousand war brides. By the time the operation was completed, 43,454 women and 20,997 children had been transported to Canada, enduring the seasickness of the Atlantic crossing and, for many of them, long train rides to their final destinations in unfamiliar and more or less welcoming communities.[61] The Canadian government's efforts to ensure the safe passage and settlement of its soldiers' new families were truly impressive. Despite reservations among some government and military officials that carte blanche admission for soldiers' dependents would inevitably grant Canadian citizenship to otherwise unworthy characters, and despite resistance from Canadians who disapproved of foreign women capturing "the cream of Canada's young men," the overwhelming concern of officials was how quickly both the troops and their families could arrive on Canadian soil and begin the exciting work of building the postwar Canadian nation.[62] In Operation Daddy, the Canadian government's desire to recognize the contributions of Canadian

soldiers to the war effort aligned with a desire to re-establish a properly gendered social order, fortify the Canadian gene pool with British stock, and ensure
that British cultural traditions and emotional ties would flow through subsequent generations.[63]

It is also worth noting the "bridal" formulation as the characterization of these
wives of Canadian servicemen. Brides, of course, are so much more romantic,
youthful, and full of promise than "wives." Moreover, as Sydney Matrix astutely
notes, the designation war bride located these women in a particular moment
in Canadian military and nation-building history and "underscores their commitment to the nation via their sacred vows of loyalty to its servicemen."[64] The
foreigner – this time in the guise of rosy-cheeked, blushing white brides – did
the magical work of re-enchanting the nation.[65] As feminist theorists of nationalism have pointed out, projects of national articulation rely heavily on women's
cultural and reproductive labour to ensure the intergenerational transmission
of preferred political identities and to mark the boundaries of belonging.[66] And
while the war brides were newcomers, their exalted national heritage and ties to
the motherland reinforced Canada's preferred origin story even as the country
embarked on an increasingly independent future.

Even in the best of circumstances, the process of settlement and integration
is challenging. And while a 1947 national survey by the Department of Veterans
Affairs found that the marriages between Canadian servicemen and the women
they met abroad were "as successful as even the most optimistic could expect,"
unsurprisingly, some relationships could not withstand the displacement, the
effects of what we now recognize as post-traumatic stress, or the more quo-
tidian disappointments of intimate life.[67] The Canadian government had not
made financial provisions for British women (or their families) to return to
the United Kingdom, and the cost of doing so meant that boarding the boat
in Liverpool committed the vast majority of these women and children to a
lifetime in Canada. Furthermore, and homesickness aside, the news from the
UK and Europe was unlikely to induce visions of a happy alternative. Devas-
tated cities and continued rationing had to be weighed against undoubtedly
variable, though not bomb-ravaged, conditions in Canada.[68] That said, there
were instances of return – elaborated vividly in the case of *Taylor v. Canada*,
discussed in the next chapter. The government wanted the war brides to remain
in Canada, but if they returned from whence they came, the *Citizenship Act*
ensured that the divorce was complete, removing Canadian citizenship for
those who did manage the round trip.

This rehearsal of the war brides' migration highlights several factors that
would gain significance as their citizenship struggles, and those of their children, began to unfold. The statuses of marriage and legitimacy in determining
citizenship, the relationship between the provisions of P.C. 858 and those of the
Citizenship Act of 1947, the consequences of staying or going, and the emotional

purchase of war service, family, ethnic origins, and national attachment resonated from the Aldershot church steeple to Ottawa's Peace Tower. People with British origins and a direct connection to a central moment in Canada's national formation were exalted subjects, and in that context, the encounter between war brides and children with the technical rules that articulate citizenship and its loss was easily rendered as a grave injustice, an inexplicable act of self-denial.[69] The fact that it was a white British identity that commanded such a strong claim to authenticity in Canada, even in the early decades of the twenty-first century, demonstrates that it takes more than a formally non-racialized immigration policy and official multiculturalism to undermine the effectiveness of birthright and lineage in maintaining the white racialized identity of a settler state. Yet it is also true that Canadian governments, and the British-history-loving Harper government in particular, steadfastly resisted the citizenship claims of Canadian veterans' children for many years.

The following chapter examines the provisions of the *Citizenship Act* that produced lost Canadians out of war brides and their children and examines several contemporary instances in which war brides, but especially war children, confronted Canadian citizenship law. While the issues raised in these examples were resolved by the 2014 amendments, Canadian governments' long reluctance to address their citizenship difficulties points to the interplay of romanticism and complexity in the figures of the war brides and their children, and of certainty and opacity in birthright citizenship.

3

Feminine Virtues and Lost Canadians

The previous chapter's contextualization of Canada's 1947 *Citizenship Act* and the circumstances surrounding the war brides' entry to Canada set the stage for an analysis of the family, nation, gender, and race as they figured in the efforts of war brides, but especially their children, to negotiate the loss provisions of the Act. Through this analysis we will see how the tensions between the natural and the formal/legal are at work in articulating a white, reproductive, and highly patriarchal structure for membership in the Canadian polity. Political science, as Jacqueline Stevens observes, generally regards affiliations of family, race, and gender as preconstituted, arriving fully formed in the public sphere rather than being actively produced in and through law and policy as well as through various cultural expressions.[1] In applying Stevens's approach of examining the rules of membership and their manifestations of family, gender, race, and nation, we can identify the productive work – both subtle and obvious – that creates political identities and reinforces masculine, British origin as pre-eminent in the hierarchy of Canadian belonging. A favoured lineage of attachments is seemingly so compelling as to blind us to alternative forms of asserting political belonging, including residence and contribution to the public good.

As we've seen, Canada's first *Citizenship Act* reflected a compromise between retaining the vestiges of British colonial status in British subjecthood, including modestly preferential access for British migrants, and a more independent conception of the Canadian nation. Debates surrounding the *Citizenship Act*, and the citizenship status of war brides in particular, also reflected some ambivalence over whether family members of Canadians should enjoy expedited access to national membership. Canada's legislators did ultimately determine that foreign-born wives and children with British subject status and lawful admission to Canada as permanent residents would become Canadian citizens at the commencement of the Act.[2] This provision effectively rolled the status designations of Privy Council Order 858 – which granted the wives and children of Canadian servicemen the same citizenship status as that of their husbands – into the new *Citizenship Act*. That said, however, Canadian citizens born outside of Canada were also subject to loss provisions. A person born abroad was required to declare his retention of Canadian citizenship before his twenty-second (later, his twenty-fourth) birthday.[3] Canadian citizens who were not "natural born" (i.e., born in Canada or born to a citizen father if the parents were married, or to a citizen mother if born out of wedlock) ceased to hold citizenship if they resided outside of Canada for at least six consecutive years, with some provisos for people working abroad (or spouses and minor children of people working abroad) in public service for Canada or as an employee of a Canadian-owned firm or international agency.[4] Thus, while people born in Canada could leave the country for virtually their entire lives without losing citizenship, a person who had been naturalized and thus pledged allegiance to Canada would be understood to have withdrawn that allegiance after an absence of six years. Birth according to the rules trumped a consciously declared statement of commitment when it came to the retention of citizenship. That said, even natural-born children could lose their citizenship if their "responsible parent" – their fathers if the parents were married, otherwise their mothers – took out citizenship in another country.[5]

The citizenship status of the war brides was derived through marriage and governed by immigration law and the loss provisions of the *Citizenship Act* noted earlier. Thus, those war brides who ultimately decided to leave Canada for good also lost their Canadian citizenship after the threshold number of consecutive years abroad. There does not seem to be any record of these returnees contesting the loss of their citizenship. More revealing, though, are the news reports and parliamentary testimony concerning the citizenship status of war brides who remained in Canada. Their difficulties have largely arisen in situations where they have been asked to provide a citizenship certificate in order to acquire a passport or other citizenship-based entitlement. Acquiring a citizenship certificate requires landing documents, marriage certificates, and other related documentation that may be challenging to produce several decades after their original acquisition. Moreover, citizenship and immigration officials may not necessarily be well-informed about the rules that apply to the war brides' citizenship, leading to misinterpretations of the regulations and a great deal of stress and frustration. When applying for a passport, for example, Gwen Zradicka was erroneously informed that she had lost her Canadian citizenship because she had divorced her Canadian soldier husband.[6] Priscilla Corrie, who had a social insurance number, received a government pension, and was previously issued a Canadian passport (expired in 1999), had her passport application denied in 2008 when she was unable to produce a birth certificate or her landing records.[7] Born to British parents in Ceylon in 1923, her birth certificate was lost at sea when her father perished in a shipwreck. She arrived in Canada to join her soldier husband in 1943, but her landing documents had been lost as well. Unable to produce the documents that passport officials insisted were necessary for her passport renewal, she was prevented from attending her grandsons' weddings in Australia, visiting a new great-grandchild, and embarking on an Alaskan cruise with her son and daughter-in-law. The publicity surrounding Mrs Corrie's case prompted the government to reconsider, and one business day after her passport struggles were reported in the *Vancouver Sun*, she was told that her driver's licence, health insurance card, two photos, and $75 would be all she required to receive a citizenship card. With those things, her passport application could proceed immediately.[8]

The reporting on Mrs Corrie's case is indicative of the claim to Canadian belonging exercised by the symbol of the British war bride. As an elderly woman who can trace her connection to Canada through her marriage to a Canadian soldier, Corrie's lost papers are represented as completely comprehensible. Of course, lost documents are a regular feature of citizenship, immigration, and especially refugee determinations, but in less sympathetic cases, the fact of lost papers is just as easily interpreted as a function of carelessness, subterfuge, or fraud. Of course, without the intervention of a concerned journalist (even the efforts of a sympathetic MP had failed to elicit government attention), Corrie might have remained trapped in the suspicions, or at least foot-dragging, of Citizenship and Immigration Canada (CIC) officials.[9] But as the journalist clearly recognized, grandmotherly Mrs Corrie was sure to win her case against CIC's rule-boundedness once her plight was publicized. Indeed, the injustice of Corrie's treatment gained additional force through the journalist's juxtaposition of Corrie's situation with a description of the Surrey passport office in which "all of these other immigrants who couldn't even speak English … were getting their passports," and the irony of immigration officials' willingness to rely on the attestations of family members to identify a group of Tamils who had recently arrived in Vancouver on a rusted freighter in dubious circumstances.[10] As the *Vancouver Sun*'s journalist quoted Mrs Corrie: "I have lots of family who will vouch for me and say that I'm Canadian. But that's not good enough."[11] Ultimately, though, the political liability posed by Mrs Corrie spurred the government to action. Her exalted status as an elderly war bride who was simply seeking to engage in appropriate grandmothering activities provided sufficient enhancement of her claims to citizenship to ensure her place at the front of the queue at the Kelowna passport office.

Mrs Corrie's citizenship challenges represent the extreme end of the circumstances faced by war brides in the post-1947 period. For those war brides who have faced similar difficulties, the issues of citizenship determination have turned on a lack of clarity about the rules governing the unique circumstances of their entry to Canada and challenges in producing the necessary documentation. Media attention, the work of elected representatives, and advocates for war brides and lost Canadians have been instrumental in assisting these women in clarifying their status and gaining the necessary documentation.

The citizenship situation for their children, by contrast, has been more ambiguous, since it straddles the line between immigration and birthright citizenship and the magical moment of 1 January 1947. Moreover, the fact that the contested cases involve children born out of wedlock or marriages that came apart has added further emotional charge to their arguments for Canadian belonging, while underscoring the tenuousness of a national identity and political membership that hinges on blood.

The leading illustration of these precarious circumstances, and of the language of belonging that accompanies preferred claims to national membership, is the case of Joe Taylor.[12] Taylor's struggle to assert Canadian citizenship began in 2003 when he applied for citizenship and was denied. Taylor was born in Britain in 1944, before his British mother and Canadian soldier father were permitted to marry.[13] As a result, Taylor derived his citizenship at birth, from his mother. And although his parents did marry four months later, the marriage did not erase the status of out-of-wedlock birth. After his father returned to the west coast of Canada after the war, he sent for his new bride and baby. Taylor and his mother were granted status under P.C. 858 when they landed in Canada. The marriage did not last, with the judicial record suggesting that the former soldier, perhaps suffering from what we would now call post-traumatic stress disorder, was a violent spouse.[14] In 1946, after only a few months of Canadian residency, Joe and his mother returned to Britain, where Taylor grew up and lived his adult life.[15] He had virtually no contact with his Canadian father, who died in 1999, but considers himself a Canadian nonetheless.

Taylor was denied Canadian citizenship on the grounds that he was born out of wedlock and thus derived his citizenship from his mother, that he had continuously resided outside of Canada for more than six years, and that he had not reaffirmed his citizenship by age twenty-four.[16] On this basis, Taylor launched a *Charter* claim, arguing that the wedlock and notification provisions of the 1947 *Citizenship Act* violated the equality (s. 15) and due process (s. 7) provisions of the *Charter of Rights and Freedoms*. Of course, the *Charter* came into force only in 1982 and the equality provisions were further delayed until 1985, well after Canada's citizenship laws had determined Mr Taylor's status. Moreover, the Supreme Court of Canada has established that the *Charter* should not apply either retroactively or retrospectively. But in particular cases, the court has found it necessary to balance a *Charter* claim made in the interest of seeking redress for an old event, in which case the Charter should not apply, against the contemporary effects of a law that was passed before 1985, in which case the Court has found that *Charter* rights should apply.[17] In *Benner v. Canada* (1997) and *Augier v. Canada* (2004), the Supreme Court decided that pre-*Charter* statutes had contemporary effects and hence were subject to the *Charter*'s application. Each of these cases (discussed in greater depth in chapter 6) involved the denial of citizenship status to a child based on the sex and/ or marital status of the "responsible parent." When Taylor's case was heard at the Federal Court, Justice Martineau similarly held that the *Charter's* equality provisions could be applied to the 1947 *Citizenship Act*. Thus, denying Taylor the capacity to derive citizenship from his father was a violation of the gender and marital status equality protections of the *Charter*. Furthermore, Justice Martineau ruled that the requirement to affirm citizenship by age twenty-four was a violation of the *Charter's* due process provisions since the Government of Canada had not provided adequate notice of the condition to those who might be affected by it.[18]

The federal government, however, was not satisfied with this outcome and appealed the decision. In 2007, the Federal Court of Appeal reversed the lower court's ruling, finding that Taylor's citizenship was an "old event" and observing that "it would be odd to use the Charter ... to challenge a 1947 statute which was repealed by a 1977 statute that Parliament did not wish to have retroactive effects."[19] The Federal Court of Appeal also held that Taylor was subject to the loss provisions of the *Citizenship Act* of 1947 and that due process had been fulfilled through the publication of the legislation itself.[20] The court cases brought considerable media attention to Taylor, and again, the resulting public pressure succeeded in persuading the Minister of Citizenship and Immigration to extend Taylor a grant of citizenship. Taylor became a Canadian citizen in a widely publicized ceremony on 24 January 2008.[21]

In contrast to the cool rationality of the legal arguments in *Taylor*, Taylor's extra-judicial campaign for his citizenship invoked the high-gloss romanticism that has come to characterize war bride discourse. Much of the appeal of the Taylor story derived from its nostalgic rendering of passion in wartime. In the media and the House of Commons, the origins of Taylor's citizenship claim were framed in terms of his parents being "caught in the throes of war."[22] Joe Taylor Sr went off to Europe, where he "met his English Rose and fell in love."[23] Jenny found herself pregnant, but Joe Sr, who wanted to do right by her, was denied permission to marry by his commanding officer.[24] Thankfully, Joe survived the D-Day invasion and returned to his beloved and their infant son. The dramatic saga was thus framed in terms of "the story of love and war, of passion and tragedy, of overcoming so many obstacles, of courage and strength in the face of adversity."[25] Indeed, the brevity of the marriage, Taylor Senior's violence toward his wife, and the facts that Taylor Junior had no contact with his father and had lived virtually his entire life outside of Canada were not included in the popular representation of the story.

On the indignation front, Taylor invoked the insult that the failure to grant him citizenship represented to his father's sacrifice for Canada. In his appearance before the Standing Committee on Citizenship and Immigration, Taylor recounted that his father had volunteered to fight for Canada and that the things he had seen in the war had ruined his life.[26] The pathos of his plea continued: "It is [Prime Minister] Harper who's supposedly in charge of a department that's taking bitter legal action against me to try to prevent me from even laying flow-ers on my father's grave in the Legion's Field of Honour in Port Alberni, British Columbia."[27] This rhetorical flight concluded with a public shaming: "I never imagined I would be treated like this by Canada, of all countries."[28]

Taylor's indignation also extended to the "arcane" morality that determined his citizenship on the basis of his parents' marital status. In many media inter-views Taylor referred to his shock that he was being denied citizenship on the grounds that he was a "bastard" – a term that also appeared in the Federal Court's judgment.[29] Indeed, representatives of war brides and members of the Standing Committee on Citizenship and Immigration were quick to speak against any dishonour in the out-of-wedlock pregnancies that had emerged from the extraordinary conditions of wartime and to condemn the continued application of old-fashioned notions of propriety in "this day and age."[30] War bride advocates argued that the wedlock rules reflect a "ridiculous, discrimina-tory, anti-charter ... provision in an outdated, anachronistic, dinosaur, Fred Flintstone, 1947 Citizenship Act."[31] But as we have already seen, this sensibil-ity of sexual tolerance ignores the political rationale that lay behind the wed-lock rules. Canada had worked assiduously to divest itself of responsibility for the extracurricular activities of its soldiers. As Taylor Sr's commanding officer allegedly claimed, "Canada is not in the business of producing widows and orphans" – or at least women and children for whom the Canadian govern-ment might have to take some long-term responsibility.[32] In the absence of a marriage, the sweetheart and progeny of a Canadian soldier were, effectively, nothing to Canada. And even when people married after the birth of a child, the child's status as "born out of wedlock" was not necessarily erased. My point here is not to defend the wedlock rules or the Canadian state's efforts to insu-late itself from the citizenship claims of children fathered by its armed forces personnel, but to observe that the wedlock rules had an explicit purpose with regard to defining membership in Canada. They were not simply an expression of conservative sexual mores.

Taylor argued that he was a lost Canadian on the basis of his father's Cana-dian citizenship (kinship) and his father's military service to Canada (contribu-tion to the country). The romance of war and the indignity of mistreating the offspring of soldiers by denying their claims to citizenship on the basis of prim morality were central to Taylor's campaign. But his story was also framed by his enthusiasm for and identification with Canada. On 24 January 2008, Taylor was granted citizenship in a ceremony of his own devising. He described his emotional reaction to the event as "feeling like he was getting married again."[33] When asked about his response to the special grant of citizenship, Taylor claimed, "It means a lot; it means I can come home to live,"[34] and when asked what it meant to him to be a Canadian, he effused, "It means everything to me. I mean, I've always believed I was a Canadian."[35] Taylor used the occasion of his citizenship ceremony to invoke a central trope of Canadian identity – multiculturalism – and the ceremony itself offered refracted echoes of the first Canadian citizenship ceremony, described in the previous chapter. The *Vancouver Sun's* account of the event noted that Taylor's guests included Hereditary Chief Adam Dick of the Kwagiulth First Nation, Roy Miki, a poet and former advocate for the Japanese redress movement, and Frank Wong, a Second World War veteran, all of whom had struggled with the Canadian government regarding their citizenship. But the story is not simply one of Taylor's integration into the multi-nationality of Canada. Rather, the description of the guests implies the hierarchy of Canadian identity: a hierarchy in which Taylor, officially the newest Canadian of the group, lays claim to the greatest proximity to Canadian authenticity. One segment of the article is illustrative:

> Flanking Taylor as he took the citizenship oath were Chinese-Canadian veterans including Frank Wong. Wong, Taylor's father and 14,000 Canadian troops landed on Juno Beach on D-Day in 1945. Both Taylor's father and Wong had been born here, but Wong wasn't a citizen because of his race. The act that gave Wong his citizenship, stripped Joe Taylor of his birthright. The veterans were there to bear witness to both being wrong.[36]

The journalist's language is revealing. While Frank Wong was born in Canada, the effect of the 1947 Act was not to restore his birthright but rather to establish his citizenship. By contrast, Taylor's loss is described not in terms of citizenship but in terms of birthright. The way this language maps onto the racial identities of the subjects reinforces the connection between whiteness and Canadian authenticity, even as the paragraph concludes by stating that the denial of citizenship, prior to 1947 for Wong, and post-1947 for Taylor, was wrong.

Joe Taylor's claim to citizenship thus rests on a connection to Canada established through blood and on the fact that his birth was the product of one of the most significant moments in the formation of Canada's national identity. In fact, Taylor's hailing of his father's wartime sacrifice brings the importance of the war forward into the contemporary moment, as Canada continues its project of national identity construction. Again, Taylor relies on an organic connection to Canada. He asserts that "he can come home," although the construction of Canada as "home" is, necessarily, a fantastical imagining. After all, Taylor had no relationship with his father, nor any lived experience of Canada. Nonetheless, his impassioned battle to reinstate his citizenship, while contested by the federal government in court, was unchallenged in the public forums of the media, the hearings of the Standing Committee on Citizenship and Immigration, and the floor of the House of Commons.

While less fully elaborated in the public record, a number of other citizenship cases of war brides and Canadian soldiers' children follow a similar legal and rhetorical track. Jackie Scott, for example, was born out of wedlock in England in June 1945.[37] Her parents, James Ellis, a Canadian soldier, and Winifred Lucy, a British citizen, were not permitted to marry by James's commanding officer; indeed, they did not marry until several months after she and her mother arrived in Canada in 1948. The long delay in their journey resulted from the fact that Scott was a sickly child and thus was denied permission to land until her health improved. Scott subsequently grew up in Canada, moving to the US with her own husband in 1972. She then applied for proof of citizenship in 2004, but was denied in 2005, on the grounds that, since she was born out of wedlock, she had inherited her citizenship from her British mother. She tried again in 2010, after the Conservative government had implemented a series of reforms to the *Citizenship Act*. These reforms extended citizenship entitlement to anyone born on or after 1 January 1947, on the basis of birth to a citizen parent (mother or father, regardless of wedlock status). Scott's application was again denied, this time on the grounds that "at the time [she] was born in 1945, neither of [her] parents was a Canadian citizen."[38] Since Canadian citizenship did not officially exist until 1 January 1947, the government argued, there was no Canadian citizenship from which to derive status prior to that date.

Mrs Scott subsequently filed an application for judicial review.[39] In addition to making arguments about the gender and marital status inequities of the decision denying her citizenship, Scott, like Joe Taylor, asserted the primacy of her claim to Canadian belonging as a person with both British origins and a connection to a significant episode in Canadian nation-making. She noted that the Canadian government had a long history of resisting the retroactive application of the wedlock provisions. As the legal adviser to the Secretary of State had warned in the 1970s, granting citizenship to children born abroad to unwed Canadian fathers would have negative consequences. Given Canada's participation in the Korean War, and peacekeeping activities in the Middle East and Cyprus, the adviser had warned, "You do not know what you would be sweeping up."[40] And while Scott's legal submission observes that such public references to Koreans, Arabs, and Cypriots as sweepings were reflective of a bygone era, the submission also goes on to note that the children of those foreign encounters had now received entitlement to Canadian citizenship under the 2008 legislative reforms. How is it, Scott's legal argument asks, that those (extremely foreign) children have a greater claim to Canada than "the children born out of wedlock to men who served Canada overseas in the Second World War, children born in Britain, Malta, Holland, Belgium, and the USA"?[41] As this statement again demonstrates, birthright citizenship claims work through what Richard Day describes as "the great chain of race" to tell us who the real Canadians are.[42]

Jackie Scott cuts a sympathetic figure. Another grandmotherly woman who passionately expresses her connection to Canada, her effect on the Canadian public is, as Bonnie Honig has described in a different context, to make Canadians feel desired and choice-worthy.[43] Why, after all, should she not be a Canadian when someone born a year and a half later would be granted that status? Joe Taylor received a special grant of citizenship, having lived in Canada for only four months, as an infant, so why should Scott be denied citizenship when she lived in Canada into her early adulthood? If the terms of the debate are framed in this way, noting the randomness of an imposed time frame and the highly discretionary application of the law, it does seem difficult to argue that she should be denied Canadian citizenship. But on the other hand, Scott has not lived in Canada since 1972.[44] Except for her encounters with the Canadian state regarding her citizenship, she has been disengaged from the operation of the Canadian polity for four decades. Indeed, in turning down her citizenship request, a CIC official noted that Scott had permanent resident status and so could consider applying for a grant of citizenship. Nonetheless, the CIC official advised, Scott would need to consider whether she met "the requirements for such a grant, including the requirement to have accumulated at least three years of residence in Canada prior to the date you apply."[45] Yet even in light of this pointed observation by a government official, Scott's sustained absence from Canada does not render her a "citizen of convenience" in the public or the political imagination. Her passion for Canada and her connection to a Canadian soldier give her, like Joe Taylor, a moral claim to Canadian belonging. The hallowed cord of birth, particularly when it is attached to her British heritage, her white racial identity, and a national symbol as powerful as the Second World War, overwhelms other arguments for inclusion based on one's relationship to the experience of Canadian governance.

Of course, Scott was denied citizenship twice in the 2000s, so it would be a mistake to discount the struggle entailed in her efforts to assert her Canadian belonging. Yet the political liability posed by Scott and others who shared her situation, and the incongruity of denying Canadian citizenship to the children of veterans – given the Harper government's penchant for sepia-inflected nationalism – proved unsustainable. The media storm that was gathering around Jackie Scott following her March 2013 application for judicial review seems to have been the triggering event for the *Citizenship Act* amendments of 2014. The government had explicitly intended to sanctify 1 January 1947 as Canadian citizenship's hallowed day, as we can see in their arguments before the Federal Court in *Taylor* and in the failure to address the citizenship claims of veterans' children in the 2008 round of legislative amendments. It seems likely that at least part of the rationale for that sanctification was a financial one. Since people born before 1947 are now senior citizens, their claims to social entitlements (i.e., pensions and health care) will increase in the years ahead. Thus, denying them citizenship would alleviate the demands they make on the public purse.

Ultimately, though, the symbolic force of the Second World War veterans and lineage would overpower austerity as a justification for citizenship entitlement. The 2014 amendments were, again, aimed primarily at tightening access to citizenship, and thus the Harper government still managed to underscore its commitment to exclusive membership in the Canadian club while extending citizenship to the children of veterans. There is a rich irony in this. Paul Martin Sr had argued in favour of a citizenship act as a means to articulate Canada as an inclusive nation but managed to *exclude* many children of war veterans in the process; the Harper government's efforts to make Canada more exclusive articulated a means to *reinstate* those children.

Willy van Ee's relationship to Canadian citizenship offers several additional layers of complication to this discussion of birthright, gender, race, identity, and national belonging. Van Ee was born out of wedlock to a Dutch woman and an Indigenous Canadian soldier father, and while van Ee's biological father had fully intended to marry his Dutch sweetheart, his intentions were thwarted by his own mother's disapproval.[46] After re-establishing himself on Manitoulin Island, the soldier married a local woman and raised two sons. Meanwhile in the Netherlands, van Ee's mother regrouped as well, marrying and having another eight children. Van Ee's childhood did not include revelations regarding his Canadian Indigenous parentage, and although he did not resemble his siblings, his distinctive features were "never an issue."[47] Details regarding his biological origins began to emerge when, in the 1960s, van Ee decided to seek his fortune in South Africa. The racial attentiveness of the officials at the South African Embassy led to a request for his birth certificate and subsequent revelations regarding his paternal origins. In his efforts to locate his birth father, he discovered that the man had died in 1972. Van Ee's overtures to his half-brothers were rejected, but he was able to establish relationships with his father's extended family and has visited Canada on several occasions. Van Ee asserts a spiritual tie to his father's Ojibwa heritage, and after his first visit to Canada, he built a totem pole at his home in Utrecht.[48] Van Ee received his Indian status card in 1986, but until 11 June 2015 he was denied Canadian citizenship on the basis of his birthdate and his birth out of wedlock. Had he been born out of wedlock to an Indigenous Canadian woman and a Dutch man, he would have inherited citizenship but not Indian status.[49]

Unlike Taylor and Scott, van Ee did not undertake judicial action to assert his right to Canadian citizenship, although he hoped he would eventually receive it since he "feel[s] Canadian."[50] And while his status card documents his blood connection to officially recognized "Indianness" in Canada, band membership is a separate process, distinct to local communities. Thus, while van Ee may be a Status Indian according to Crown-Indigenous Relations and Northern Affairs Canada, he would not necessarily be recognized as a member of his biological father's community. Willy van Ee's situation offers us a fascinating natural

experiment through which to consider how belonging and identity are constructed. It also raises difficult questions. Van Ee was born in the Netherlands,
and his Dutch community apparently lacks a strong racializing script through
which to make sense of his physical difference, or perhaps to see that difference
at all. This is not to say that race is inconsequential in the Netherlands, but
rather that van Ee did not manifest a presence that was racializable within the
given range of possibilities. In his encounter with the South African embassy,
and the twentieth-century South African project of racial governance, however, he was marked as deviating from white. But who is van Ee with regard
to Canada and Indigeneity in Canada? Upon discovering his paternal origins
and visiting his Manitoulin relations, van Ee expressed a spiritual connection.
Undoubtedly there is a significant psychological response to finding oneself
among a group of people with whom you share a strong resemblance. Indeed,
this power of resemblance is what makes those British war brides and their
white children so sympathetic to the majority white population of Canada. Yet
van Ee's life in the Netherlands has separated him from the experiences and
struggles of life in Canada generally, and life in Indigenous Canada specifically.
For van Ee, then, as for Taylor and Scott, my question is whether an extended
absence from those conditions necessarily obviates a Canadian and/or Indigenous identity, what degree of connection we might agree should be required
in order to assert and receive membership in the polity, and whether we could
reimagine the relationship between identity and political belonging in order to
take lineage out of the determination of political belonging altogether.

Belonging without Citizenship?

One final case involving national attachment and the children of Canadian Second World War veterans offers a slightly different perspective on birthright and
political membership. In the case of Paul Cornes, and undoubtedly many other
foreign-born Second World War children (including, apparently, rock'n'roll
legend Eric Clapton), Canadian citizenship is not their objective; rather, they
seek knowledge of their birth fathers and an official recognition of the inter-
connections of blood and nation.[51] As a representative story, Cornes's quest for
information regarding his biological paternity reveals a great deal about contemporary articulations of family and the inherent tensions between care and
lineage. And his representation of his connection to Canada raises important
questions about the challenges of delinking ancestry and citizenship.

Like Taylor and Scott, Paul Cornes was born out of wedlock in the UK, to
a British mother.[52] He grew up believing that the man who raised him was his
biological father, who was nonetheless obliged to adopt him in order to erase
the scourge of illegitimacy. In fact, his biological father was a Canadian soldier,
and his birth was the result of a brief affair. According to Cornes, the duplicity

surrounding his birth could have been the plot for an overwritten romance novel. In an effort to protect her British boyfriend from the truth – a boyfriend who was serving in Burma and was a very infrequent correspondent during his four years abroad – the young woman claimed that her pregnancy had resulted from a sexual assault. Despite the sense of shock and betrayal, the returned British boyfriend eventually decided to marry her anyway. Then, wanting to protect the young son from his complicated origin story, his parents maintained the ruse of the seamless, biologically related nuclear family. From Cornes's account, his mother went to her grave maintaining this story, and while his adoptive father never discovered the more banal circumstances that led to his son's birth, he did eventually concede the truth about his non-biological parentage. An aunt would subsequently reveal that Cornes's birth was the result of a straightforward wartime relationship with a Canadian serviceman.

Cornes's book laments the circumstances that gave rise to these complicated deceits, but he advances a special fury for the Canadian government's unwillingness to assist him in locating information about his biological father. In Cornes's view, this official resistance is tantamount to a denial of natural justice, a violation of a universal human right to know one's origins, and a black mark on Canada's humanitarian reputation.[53] He too invokes a hierarchy of blood-based belonging in Canada, asserting that biology trumps public service when staking a claim to national identity. "The war children possess clearly-defined Canadian genetic roots which, in many instances, could be as deep as, if not deeper than, those of the members of Canada's establishment who have presumed to determine their fate."[54] Cornes's resolve – ultimately, he succeeded in locating his Canadian roots, including his Canadian half-siblings – has provided him with a sense of his true identity, since "if you don't know your history, if you don't know your family, who are you?"[55] Cornes's investment in the truth is certainly understandable given the degree of deception that marked his upbringing. Yet his story also invites us to consider what constitutes the "truth" of origin stories. Anthropologist Marilyn Strathern has observed that the pursuit of one's "true" origin is a particularly Western conceit, as is the idea that a parental identity is formed through a single sexual act rather than a continuous process of involvement, care, and nurturance.[56] As Strathern notes, the more Euro-Americans know about the biological facts of procreation, the more they feel informed about the facts of kinship.[57]

In his efforts to understand the Canadian government's unwillingness to provide assistance to the children of Canadian veterans in locating their paternal origins, Cornes notes that the government limits access to the relevant documentation to Canadian citizens. In Cornes's view, this restriction attaches an unnecessary political dimension to lineage. After all, he maintains, he is not interested in citizenship, he just wants to know who his biological father is. Yet because of the logic of birthright citizenship – because lineage *is* political – Cornes finds himself in a catch-22. The Canadian government avoids the prospect of a birth-right citizenship claim by denying prospective citizens access to the information concerning the circumstances of their birth. Canada may have some long-standing interest in protecting its soldiers from the consequences of their sexual adventures, as Cornes alleges, but more than that, the Canadian state has an interest in protecting *itself* from the consequences of the sexual adventures of its soldiers. And while this is an undoubtedly confounding situation for genealogical researchers, it also provides eloquent testimony to the extent to which birth and political belonging are intertwined. Of course, thoughtful legislators could revise privacy and access to information law, as well as the *Citizenship Act,* in order to enable such research into origins without incurring the risk of citizenship – if, indeed, that risk is considered especially grave. Instead, reforms to the *Citizenship Act* in 1977, 2008, and 2014 have grudgingly expanded the reach of birthright, even for Conservative governments that have otherwise intensified their efforts at exclusion.

Conclusion

After long resistance, the Conservatives finally acceded to the citizenship claims of Second World War veterans' progeny with the passage of Bill C-24 in May 2014. Birthright citizenship is now granted to a person "born to a parent who, at the time of the person's birth, was employed outside Canada in or with the Canadian Armed Forces" (or the federal or provincial public service), without regard for the date of birth.[58] With this, Canada's long attachment to the patriarchal logic of wedlock and legitimacy provisions in the determination of citizenship for the children of its Second World War soldiers has been abolished. This legislative reform undoubtedly represents a triumph in the efforts to secure citizenship for lost Canadians and certainly represents an overdue correction to Canada's decades-long refusal to acknowledge at least the most obvious manifestations of its soldiers' sexual liaisons. In the process of the struggle, Canadians have been treated to full-throated arias of national devotion, as well as less tuneful anthems proclaiming the racial and ethnic origins of the "real" Canadians. Yet, as with the debates surrounding the original citizenship act, opportunities to consider the criteria for political membership beyond the standard categories of birthright and naturalization were squandered. Given the ideological temperament of the Harper Conservatives, this squandering is just as well. To the extent that the Conservatives did consider alternatives to birthright citizenship, they contemplated (albeit ultimately rejected) barring the children of refugees, tourists, and permanent residents from *jus soli* membership rather than engaging in a substantive debate on what it should mean to be a member of a political society and how that could happen. As these stories of the children of the Second World War illustrate – and as the examples elaborated in subsequent chapters will also show – birthright is a peculiar basis for a democratic polity.

Haunted as it is by blood relationship, birthright citizenship misrecognizes matter for what matters. The assignation of political belonging on the basis of criteria of birth, regardless of an individual's social connection to the polity, simultaneously invests blood with political meaning while depleting the substantive expectations for political belonging. If all it takes to be a citizen is birth to the right person on the right day, or on the right soil, the stakes of membership rely solely on chance rather than commitment, investment, or, more passively, being on the receiving end of governance. But perhaps this is where the work of nationalism and its blood-based trappings becomes necessary. If we can't rely on conscious commitment as the basis of membership in the polity, then emotional appeals to ancestry and the glory of the nation might be mobilized in the service of securing our commitment to the political community – and indeed, to our willingness to fight and die for it.

4

The Veranda of Citizenship:
The 1977 *Citizenship Act* and After

The previous chapters used the stories of the war brides and their children as a means to map the origins of Canada's *Citizenship Act,* outline some of the difficulties of the birthright provisions of the 1947 Act that pertained directly to their situation, and describe the resolution of those difficulties in 2014. This chapter puts us back in the middle of the *Citizenship Act* story and shifts the focus to a broader cross-section of Canadians impacted by the loss provisions of the act. As we will see, the concern with connection that animated sections of the 1947 Act found new formulations in the 1977 overhaul and beyond. In most respects, Canada's birthright citizenship provisions became more generous, and certainly more equitable. Yet the new act was also flawed, as became apparent in its encounters with the equality provisions of Canada's *Charter of Rights and Freedoms.*

As the political struggles and social unrest of the mid-twentieth century unfolded, it became increasingly apparent that Canada's 1947 *Citizenship Act* was unfit for contemporary circumstances. Parliamentarians grew frustrated with the cumbersome accumulation of amendments that had been grafted onto the 1947 Act. The report of the Royal Commission on the Status of Women had made a series of recommendations for changes to the *Citizenship Act,* and the arguments of civil and women's rights groups succeeded in persuading the public of the need to address racial and gender inequities. With the abandonment of a national preference immigrant selection process and the adoption of a point system in 1967, the final demise of the British Empire, Canada's definitively North American orientation, and Quebec's increasingly muscular nationalism, many parliamentarians felt that change was long overdue. In introducing Bill C-20 in the House of Commons in May 1975, Secretary of State James Faulkner observed that the 1947 Act, while progressive in its day, had "become complex and unwieldy, in certain respects illogical or not fully equitable, and somewhat out of tune with the times."[1]

After several delays, the Canadian government finally passed a new *Citizenship Act* in 1976. Coming into force 15 February 1977 (and so commonly known as the 1977 *Citizenship Act*), this pre-Charter overhaul of the *Citizenship Act* purported to advance the unequivocal equality of birthright and naturalized citizens and to remove the gender and wedlock provisions of the 1947 Act that had caused so much grief for the war brides and their children. It also reduced the discretionary powers of the minister, eliminated good character requirements,[2] reduced the residency requirement from five years to three, and replaced references to British subjects with citizens of the Commonwealth.[3] As would become evident almost immediately, however, the government's opposition to retroactive application of the new law created a host of new difficulties. For example, while the 1977 Act enabled children to inherit Canadian citizenship from either of their parents, regardless of their wedlock situation, this provision was not extended to children born before 15 February 1977. Thus, Canada's citizenship laws effectively divided the population according to age: people born before 1 January 1947, people born between 1 January 1947 and 14 February 1977, and people born on 15 February 1977 and after, with different provisions (including superseded laws) governing specific age categories. Subsequently, the 2008 amendments to the *Citizenship Act* eliminated the 1947–77 citizenship category, but they also implemented a post–17 April 2009 category for the second generation born abroad. And, as discussed in the previous chapter, the 2014 amendments extended birthright citizenship entitlement to people born prior to 1 January 1947, conceding that the first *Citizenship Act* no longer provided a bright line for the origins of Canadian citizenship. As Elizabeth Cohen observes, "the existence of temporal boundaries reminds us that rights derive not just from *who* we are and *where* we are but also from *when* we are."[4]

This chapter sets out the debate and terms of the 1977 *Citizenship Act*. The chapter after this will explore the interaction of the 1947 and 1977 Acts in creating a series of difficulties for people who were popularly understood to have a credible claim to Canadian citizenship. Chapter 5 engages situations that the public, courts, and parliamentarians have regarded as considerably more dubious – those involving criminality and security threats. The 1977 *Citizenship Act*, the debates that surrounded it, and the consequences of its enactment elaborate fascinating tensions and slippages in the norms that shape prevailing conceptions of citizenship. In its efforts to ensure that children can inherit citizenship from either of their parents, regardless of their wedlock status, we see a clear example of changes to the rules of birthright. There is evidence of significant equivocation in these discussions, particularly around the question of whether character qualifications and security clearances should be required for people to avail themselves of newly extended birthright entitlements. Birthright, after all, is presumed to protect people against such judgments and equivocations. One's national family, like one's nuclear family, is supposed to accept you regardless of your idiosyncrasies and foibles. Yet when legislators were presented with an opportunity to set the terms of inclusion, even among people purported to be "one's own" by virtue of criteria of birth, the temptation to selectivity surged.

This newly experienced consciousness of birthright citizenship as a set of rules – not like gravity at all, but instead a product of political design – might have opened a small opportunity to explore political membership more broadly. How is it, one might have been compelled to ask, that we accept the lazy, the vicious, the talented, and the brilliant among "us," but are so suspicious of the range of human attributes among "them?" How are they "them" and we "us?" Yet, rather than drawing a line from the rules that govern inclusion by birth to the rules that govern inclusion generally, the citizenship debate imposed a break, rerouting the discussion of membership to the bordered terrain of "insiders" and "outsiders" and reinforcing the blood-based bounds of belonging in the process. This structure of belonging and exclusion, in turn, framed the arguments of the lost Canadians, promoting an appeal to Canadian hearts and minds in which national attachment was most compellingly expressed in terms of organic, emotional, and familial connection to the country. As a result, the discussion of Canadian belonging was articulated in forms that had very little to do with the substantive political task of setting and exercising the conditions through which members of the polity make their lives together.

Bill C-20 – "A Gentle Invitation to Citizenship"

From our contemporary vantage point, the elder Trudeau government's aspirations for a revised *Citizenship Act* seem remarkably bold, asserting a positive conception of humanity over anxieties about diversity and security. The articulation of citizenship as a right rather than a privilege (or a duty), and the lauding of equality as the Act's paramount virtue, contrast sharply with the Harper government's efforts to "enhance the value of Canadian citizenship" by making it more difficult to acquire, and to cast a long, suspicious shadow over would-be Canadians entering the polity as newcomers rather than (citizen-bred) newborns. Trudeau the younger campaigned on the claim that "a citizen is a citizen is a citizen," but in office, his government's actions have been more mixed. In any event, the 1970s Parliamentary debate around retroactive application, residency, and dual citizenship made it clear that generous conceptions of human character were far from universal. And as fears of terrorism and international instability intensified over the subsequent decades, the Liberals too, would increasingly foreground security concerns over inclusion – even for people with a plausible case for birthright citizenship.

Gender Equality

The gender distinctions of the 1947 *Citizenship Act* were the most obvious weaknesses requiring amendment in the new legislation, a position that parliamentarians unanimously supported. In its 1970 report, the Royal Commission on the Status of Women (RCSW) had recommended that children born abroad be able to inherit citizenship from either of their parents, regardless of their wedlock status, and that the same provision apply to adopted children.[5] It had also recommended that Canadian women who had married non-British subjects prior to 1947, and thus had lost their British subject status, be entitled to regain Canadian nationality, and that the residency requirement for foreign spouses of Canadians – husbands and wives – be the same.[6] In the 1947 Act, foreign wives only had to acquire one year of residency before being entitled to citizenship, while foreign husbands required five years.[7] Finally, the RCSW recommended that either Canadian parent be entitled to apply for a born-abroad child's Canadian citizenship. Under the 1947 Act, this power had been limited to the "responsible parent" – the father, in the case of married parents, or the mother, if a child was born out of wedlock or if the parents were divorced (via custody).[8] All of these recommendations were incorporated into the 1977 Act, although in the case of Canadian women who had married foreigners prior to 1947, the restoration of their citizenship was not automatic. Concerned that such a provision might, in fact, jeopardize their existing national status in countries where dual nationality was not permitted, the Canadian government opted to require women to submit a letter of request for the resumption of their Canadian citizenship.[9]

Given all of the trouble and the serious gender inequities that would result from the failure of the 1977 Act to apply retroactively (with the notable exception of those pre-1947, Canadian-born wives of foreign nationals), the fact that the Canadian Advisory Council on the Status of Women (CACSW) supported non-retroactive application offers an object lesson in the difficulties of anticipating legislative consequences. During her appearance before the Standing Committee on Broadcasting, Films and Assistance to the Arts – the site of the committee hearings on Bill C-20 – Katie Cooke, the chair of the CACSW, was asked to share her views on the non-retroactivity of the proposed Act. While some committee members felt that all born-abroad children of married Canadian mothers should be deemed citizens, Cooke demurred:

> There could be ... endless administrative messes which would occur if one tried to put in that kind of retroactivity [automatic citizenship for the born-abroad children of Canadian mothers], and I have no idea what the legal consequences would be. We felt that at least rectifying the situation in 1976 was a positive step. If consideration can be given to providing for such persons to obtain their citizenship now by the mother's application at no cost, it would be nice but we did not ask for a retroactivity on that [sic].[10]

In Cooke's view, the vast majority of Canadian citizens would be acquiring citizenship by virtue of birth in the territory, so the number of people who would

benefit from the retroactive acquisition of citizenship would be, in her estimation, relatively low.[11] The CACSW was far more interested in ensuring that the
new *Citizenship Act* avoided any future exercise of gender discrimination; thus
it was willing to tolerate whatever gender inequality might persist for citizens
born prior to the enactment of the new legislation.

Public servants in the Secretary of State enthusiastically supported Cooke's
position. As noted in the previous chapter, the automatic entitlement to citizenship for children born abroad to unmarried Canadian men was particularly
concerning to the department. As the Secretary of State's Director of Legal Services, Lewis Levy, asserted,

> if we were to go back to provide a sort of retroactive catchall there, the government
> and the country would be in the position of having to accept as citizens all sorts
> of – perhaps this might sound a little farfetched but if you want to go back to say
> the Korean war or Canadian Forces policing expeditions in the Middle East or in
> Cyprus and so on, and assuming that some of the members of the forces may have
> been active, and more active than others and they had children, they would have a
> right to have them declared Canadians and bring them into the country.[12]

In the interest of addressing the RCSW's recommendations, parliamentarians
focused their gender equity gaze on women, and thus were concerned about
the ongoing exclusion of born-abroad children of married Canadian women.
The bureaucrats in the Secretary of State, however, understood gender equity to
include men as well, and regarded the application of gender equity to birthright
entitlement with a great deal of ambivalence. Concern about the citizenship
consequences resulting from the foreign sexual adventures of Canadian men
was only one articulation of this ambivalence. R.W. Nichols, the Citizenship
Registrar, offered a particularly tortuous demonstration of the logic used to
justify the citizenship resumption provisions for Canadian women who married foreigners when he came out against a retroactive citizenship mechanism
for the foreign-born children of Canadian women. As he explained it, "women
who married aliens prior to 1947 lost their Canadian citizenship, women who
married aliens after 1947 did not – so one group of women was denied the
citizenship granted to all other women. But since the born abroad children of
Canadian married women had never received Canadian citizenship there was no
equality issue."[13] Since the citizenship status of women who married foreigners
differed only by virtue of time, erasing the significance of time corrected the inequity.[14] That technicality aside, when the citizenship status of children differed
by virtue of the gender of their citizen parent, a retroactive equality provision
was apparently not even in the realm of possibilities. Men and women were
so profoundly different that an equal capacity to confer citizenship was, historically at least, beyond the horizon of possibilities, apparently unthinkable –

at least for the public servants. The bureaucracy's recommendation was to leave the inequities of the 1947 Act – for both married Canadian mothers and unmarried Canadian fathers – intact.

The parliamentary committee members were not persuaded – at least insofar as married Canadian women were concerned. At the 9 March 1976 meeting of the committee, Liberal MP John Roberts proposed an amendment to the Act to enable the born-abroad children of Canadian mothers to apply for citizenship within two years of the coming into force of the Act. Levy again warned that a consequence of this cleaving to equality should then logically extend to unmarried fathers as well, resulting in the inclusion of the illegitimate, potentially non-white, offspring of Canadian men, and could "make eligible for citizenship people who may have already been rejected by the Department of Immigration on valid grounds."[15] In other words, Levy implied, Canadians could give birth to bad people – people who, notwithstanding their birth tie to a Canadian, should be excluded from the polity. This is a remarkably bald expression of birthright as a product of law rather than nature, and as soon as it appeared, its unseemliness was challenged. Given the desire to address the recommendations of the RCSW, both Liberal and Progressive Conservative parliamentarians refused to heed the non-retroactivity advice, again, as it pertained to married Canadian women, insisting that the proposed amendment be crafted appropriately for inclusion in the legislation. Mr Levy continued his attempt to defend non-retroactive application, this time citing the origins of the anti-retroactivity precedent established by Justice Willis in his decision in the 1870 English case of *Phillips v. Eyre*, but Progressive Conservative MP Gordon Fairweather was having none of it.[16] "Let us retire Mr. Willis and his retroactivity to another age. That does not persuade me; it inflames me to find a way to get around him."[17] The text of the provision that was ultimately included in section 5 in the Act compelled the minister to grant citizenship to children born before the coming into force of the Act, if they were born abroad to a Canadian mother, were not entitled to be a citizen before the coming into force of the Act, and applied within two years of the coming into force of the Act "or within such extended period as the minister may authorize."[18] The Act, did however, retain the non-retroactive entitlement to citizenship of the born-abroad children of unmarried Canadian men.

Importantly, this extension of citizenship to the foreign-born children of married Canadian mothers was less automatic than it first appeared, and thus not parallel to the provision enabling Canadian women who married foreigners to resume their citizenship. In fact, people making claims under section 5 still had to undergo a security check and could be rejected if the Governor in Council felt that the extension of citizenship "would be prejudicial to the security of Canada or contrary to public order in Canada."[19] This security provision did not appear in section 5 of the Act, but much later, in section 18. There is no indication in the transcripts of the committee hearings or the parliamentary debate

that parliamentarians were aware of, asked for, or considered the consequences
of this limitation with regard to its differential treatment of the children of married Canadian men and women. In any event, the legislation ultimately did
incorporate the bureaucrats' concerns. There was no retroactive application
for the children of unmarried Canadian men, and the children of Canadian
women were subject to a security clearance. As we will see in the discussion
of the *Benner* and *Augier* cases in chapter 6, twenty years later, with the help of
the *Charter,* the security risk identified by the public servants and the power of
birthright would come into stark and highly contested relief.

Citizen Equality

Besides desiring to address gender equality in the new citizenship act, the Liberal government sought to ensure the equality of naturalized and birthright
citizens. It is important to emphasize here that while equality was the goal, that
objective only came into play once citizenship had been acquired. As Secretary of State Faulkner explained, citizenship was a qualified right, attainable for
those who complied with specific statutory requirements.[20] Technically, that
statement applied to both birthright and naturalized citizens, although the idea
that citizenship could be understood as a right was contested mainly in the
context of prospective candidates for naturalization. As the inclusion of section 5
suggests, in the context of a prospective birthright claim, parliamentarians generally regarded the extension of citizenship as a logical development. In the
context of birth in the territory or birth to a citizen parent, the articulation of
citizenship as a right made sense. By contrast, mobilizing the language of rights
to describe newcomers' citizenship claims was a great deal more controversial.

   The language of right, *qua* birthright, and qualification, or privilege, in the
case of everyone else, reveals how a presumption of the "nation as family"
divides the accepted from the suspicious, but also reveals what Bonnie Honig
has described as the xenophobic/xenophilic paradox of the role of the foreigner
in a settler society.[21] Honig's insights focus on the conceptualization of foreigners in the founding and maintenance of nation-states. Understanding the
discursive purchase of the foreigner is especially important in settler societies where foreignness is precisely the feature from which the nation derives its
character.[22] Honig, writing in the context of an immigrant America, observes
that foreigners are agents of national re-enchantment whose desire for membership regularly reinforces the choice-worthiness of the regime. Yet there is a
Janus face to this re-enchantment. This is the xenophobic attitude that casts suspicion on immigrants for "their" desire to get ahead, which might consequently
jeopardize "our" jobs and resources, and "their" supportive and culturally rich
communities, which, it is feared, might also breed social fragmentation and
extremism and thus threaten "our" way of life.[23]

The twin dynamics of creating a conception of the nation as family and reinforcing that conception through xenophilic and xenophobic iterations of the foreigner are readily discernable in the debate surrounding the 1977 *Citizenship Act*. With regard to the privileged position of the national family and xenophilia, Progressive Conservative MP Bill Jarvis's contributions to the parliamentary debate on second reading are apposite:

> It gives me particular pleasure to follow, in the debate, the hon. Member for Davenport (Mr. Caccia). I think many of my colleagues share the feeling I have. It is easy for me to understand the judicial import of this legislation and the techniques and logistics involved, but being Canadian by birth it is impossible for me to share the emotion which I am sure must be felt by the hon. Member for Davenport and those for whom Canada is their chosen country.[24]

One might detect a hint of wistfulness in this claim, yet the clarity with which Jarvis's remarks express the privilege and authenticity associated with birthright, a valuing of rationality over emotion, and the alignment of Anglo and southern European heritage with reason and emotion respectively, reveals a resplendent white, Anglo characterization of the authentic Canadian polity. Through the passion of Mr Caccia, the person positioned as a foreigner, the desirability of the settler society is reinforced, as is the line between belonging and aspiring, between host and guest, between authentic and artificial.

Several politicians were more circumspect with regard to the settler identities of Canadians and their relationship to newcomers. MP Gordon Fairweather acknowledged that "none of us can claim any special privileges about citizenship because all of us at one time or another came here from somewhere else,"[25] while Liberal MP Roderick Blaker observed that "it is perhaps we who are born here who too easily forget that the accident of birth has entitled us to one of the most valued and desirable citizenships on earth."[26] Blaker's familial warmth was expressed in his support for a generous immigration policy:

> Citizenship amounts to membership in the family called Canada, and it would seem to me that any new legislation would have to begin with the most basic consideration of all: shall we make it relatively easy or shall we make it relatively difficult for our brothers and sisters throughout the whole of humanity to join us in our Canadian family? I think we would want to do everything possible to enable others to join us and to share in the pursuit of a decent life in a nation which is one of the most fortunate on earth.[27]

Yet other parliamentarians did not draw the same ethical lessons from the vagaries of the birthright lottery. It was Progressive Conservative MP Howard Johnston's view, for example, that no "nation of this world is called upon to remedy the fate of any individual born elsewhere in the world. I just do not think that is a factor that needs to enter into a rational discussion of citizenship at present."[28] The hard borders of the state thus defined the bounds of compassion.[29] Articulating precisely the opposite view from Roderick Blaker, Progressive Conservative MP J.A. Maclean railed against an inclusive immigration policy, "Extremists" he claimed,

> say that people should be free to migrate at will and settle anywhere without hindrance, thereby benefitting from the natural and man-made advantages that exist in any particular spot on the face of the globe. I do not go that far. Perhaps the strongest argument that we are living in a global village is that we have global village idiots who try to suggest that is a viable situation for a country to espouse.[30]

In a similarly sceptical cast, Progressive Conservative MP W.C. Scott asserted that Canada was "already threatened by overcrowding ... a high level of unemployment ... [and] beset with tensions and animosities based on race, colour, creed, language."[31] In the face of so much difference, Scott felt that Canada was no more desirable than any other country, since it "has all the problems that exist in countries from which people would like to emigrate."[32] As far as Scott was concerned, Canada had reached the limit.

For some politicians, the occasion of renewing the *Citizenship Act* presented an opportunity to assert a pseudo-ethnic form of Canadian identity. One can observe the ethical dilemma in expressing such a desire in the Canadian context in Liberal MP Peter Stollery's suggestion:

> Is it not time in our existence as a country to say, as many other countries do – in fact, I think almost all countries, other than those in what was formerly known as the New World, because people were always coming here and changing the nature of it; but most countries – that there is something sacred about being born in a country. I think it is time we brought that to Canada – the concept that when you are born in Canada, you cannot lose that. That is an aspect of your life that goes with you, and that you take with you. I think that is a very important concept.[33]

If one situates this aspiration in the context of a desire to address the negative consequences of the 1947 Act's prohibition of dual citizenship, Stollery's argument for a lifelong claim to citizenship makes sense. Yet as a more broadly framed statement concerning birthright citizenship, Stollery's observation is riddled with assumptions regarding a preferred model of national attachment. It is not clear whether he is advocating that the sacredness of birth in Canadian territory be extended to a *jus sanguinis*, intergenerational claim for the children of Canadians, but his argument that birth in the territory is sacred, and that lifelong political membership should be a function of birth rather than consent, commitment, residence, or subjection to governance, is, or rather should be, a remarkable claim for an elected official in a liberal democracy. His muddled contrast of the change-ability of the New World with the implied stasis of the Old, and his apparent admiration for a kind of national perpetuity, reifies a form of national attachment associated with Europe while lamenting the dynamism of attachment in supposedly more purposefully constructed polities. This tension between what is necessarily a fantasy about the coherence of European forms of national identity and the presumed incoherence (be it good or bad) that emerges in settler societies leaves its traces throughout discussions of Canadian citizenship.

Residency

A central point of contention in the parliamentary debate around Bill C-20 concerned a shortening of the residency requirements for citizenship to three years from five. And while that debate did not directly concern birthright citizenship criteria, the claims made with regard to the knowledge of Canada that can accrue within a specified time, and the time required to assess whether a person is sufficiently law-abiding to be a Canadian citizen, play out against a largely unremarked backdrop of authentic, birthright Canadians for whom residency, suitability, and knowledge are not a matter for consideration – at least in the first instance. It was the Progressive Conservative position, for example, that the proposed shift to a shorter residency period was wrong-headed. This was most crudely expressed in the accusation that a reduced residency period was a vote-grab. By reducing the residency requirement, the Liberals could increase the number of its supporters eligible to vote – "immigrant" voters are historically inclined to vote Liberal – and help ensure the Liberals' success in the next election.[34] Some members suggested that immigrants should not be entitled to become citizens until they had witnessed at least one federal election, as a means to inform newcomers of the operation of the Canadian political system and to prevent overt augmentation of the electorate.[35] That said, even with Canada's generous immigration policy, the number of people with newly acquired citizenship each year, and their likely settlement in federal ridings that already had a high concentration of Liberal-voting immigrants, was more likely to augment the Liberals' popular vote in secure ridings than to affect the electoral outcome more broadly. Moreover, the fact that 25 to 30 per cent of the Canadian electorate had failed to vote in the federal elections of the postwar period suggests that a significant percentage of birthright Canadians had not been observing federal elections either.[36]

A modification of this concern regarding familiarity with the Canadian political system and the proposed attenuation of the residency requirement provided an opportunity to underscore the growing "foreignness" of immigrants to Canada. As Benno Friesen argued, even when the majority of immigrants to Canada were arriving from Commonwealth countries, they had to meet a five-year resi-dency requirement. With the broader range of immigrant source countries aris-ing from the shift to a point system in 1967, Canada could no longer rely on immigrants' knowledge of the Westminster form of parliamentary government, and thus, in Friesen's reasoning, shortening the residency requirement would be precipitous.[37] Of course, there is no requirement that birthright Canadians understand the Westminster system of government either, a situation lamented by NDP MP Andrew Brewin.[38] Tellingly, though, while Brewin felt it was unfor-tunate that native-born Canadians were not also obliged to demonstrate some knowledge of Canada, this observation was a mere talking point. Had he sin-cerely felt that a demonstrated knowledge of Canada should be a requirement for *all* Canadians, he might have proposed an amendment to that effect. Instead, for Brewin at least, the requirement that immigrants demonstrate knowledge of Canada served as an expression of xenophilia, in that it placed the informed foreigner alongside the ignorant native-born while nonetheless reinforcing the privilege of ignorance. For his part, Secretary of State Faulkner defended the shortened residency requirement with the argument that contemporary com-munications technology enabled people to acquire knowledge of Canada far more easily than had been possible for previous generations. In a remarkable observation, at least from our current wired vantage, Faulkner, speaking in 1975, asserted that

> we live in a society where highly sophisticated systems of telecommunications not only put us instantaneously in touch with events across the country but link us to events in the far corners of the earth and even beyond. The fact that such a wealth of information is so readily available to every potential citizen is a cogent argu-ment for the reduction of the waiting period.[39]

One might also note the inattention to the perspectives of Indigenous people regarding the settlement of their territories in the parliamentary debate. The impact of immigration on Indigenous peoples was simply not an issue for consideration, and invocations of the Canadian family and Canadian identity were silent on the place of Indigenous peoples within the political community. Intriguingly, the lone Indigenous MP of the day, and the first Status Indian to serve in Parliament, Len Marchand, supported a short residency requirement. Echoing his fellow Liberals, Marchand argued: "It must be a very difficult and emotional experience for people to decide to move from their homeland to another land. This is a very human experience, so I think that once mature peo-ple have made the mature decision that they want to become citizens of another country, why should we put them through the agony of having to wait five years?"[40] Whether or not this view was widely shared among Indigenous politi-cal organizations at the time does not seem to be a matter of public record.[41]

For the Liberals, a shorter residency requirement would signal Canada's willingness to welcome and include newcomers; in Secretary of State Faulkner's words, to "reach ... out to potential citizens of Canada to issue, on behalf of the Canadian community, a gentle invitation to citizenship."[42] For critics of the shortened residency requirement, Canada was at risk of cheapening citizenship and "making the whole process like that of a sausage factory."[43] The fact that birthright citizens did not have to meet a residency requirement, and thus, that for most Canadians the process of citizenship acquisition was virtually automatic, was, of course, not considered. Nor, moreover, did the argument for a shortened residency requirement include the important democratic principle of the consent of the governed – an entitlement to representation for virtually everyone who falls under the state's authority. Indeed, there was no mention of the democratic consideration that people who are subject to governance have a legitimate claim to a say in how they are governed.

Character

The abandonment of good character provisions was another instance in which the pursuit of equality for birthright and naturalized citizens played out, though this time in more explicit fashion. The character provisions of the 1947 Act had, in fact, been very rarely used as a basis to deny citizenship, though the numbers had increased during the "red scare" of the 1950s.[44] The Liberal government's view was that an assessment of character was "vague and indefinable" and, interestingly, "not applied to the native born."[45] In Secretary of State Faulkner's view,

> citizenship is not a reward for good behavior. It is not a prize to be awarded only to the more meritorious. The native born do all the things I listed a moment ago without any test of character. I have reached the conclusion that the broad character requirement in the present act is indefinable, unrealistic and unfair. As practiced in the past and in any known design, it punishes, sometimes wrongfully, human behavior not punishable by law. For these reasons, in Bill C-20 we have turned to the law. Instead of the nebulous phrase "good character", we have set down specific criteria which can be invoked without fear of abuse.[46] (5986)

More explicitly, character assessments were to be replaced with evidence of criminal convictions for acts that would fall under Canada's *Criminal Code* and *Narcotics Control Act*. Anyone charged with, on trial for, serving a sentence for, or paroled for an indictable offence or a false claim under the *Citizenship Act* would not be eligible for citizenship while those proceedings were ongoing and for the years required to meet the residency requirement.[47] Yet some Progressive Conservative parliamentarians regarded the abandonment of subjective character qualifications as ill-advised. Expounding a rabid anti-communism, Benno Friesen asserted that

> we have all too many examples in our country of people who have come here not for the welfare of Canada but for selfish or spurious reasons, not thinking of the good of our country at all. I am thinking especially of one who gained national notoriety about a year ago, a man by the name of Hardial Baines, an openly avowed Marxist. He came to this country 16 years ago, he is a landed immigrant, he applied for citizenship and was refused, but is still in the country. He openly speaks of the need for people to revolt against the capitalistic form of government [sic]. Are we to forgive that kind of man?[48]

Of course, it was precisely the exercise of these kinds of ideological preferences and majoritarian limits on freedom of thought and expression that had recommended the abandonment of character provisions in the first instance. Furthermore, the shift away from character requirements would also limit the most egregious expressions of racism as grounds for exclusion. One example of this slippage between character and racial preference can be seen in the concern expressed by Progressive Conservative MP Gordon Towers that, first, immigrants to Canada should be told that "we expect them to become good citizens because that is the only way in which an individual can justify his existence here" and then that "I sometimes wonder if Canada has that much [more] to offer other people than perhaps they have in their own country, because this is not a land where you can go out and pick a coconut or a banana, or an orange off a tree."[49] It seems unlikely that Mr Towers was referring to prospective immigrants from Florida or Southern California. Moreover, the fact that a substantive expression of good citizenship was not in fact required to justify the existence of most Canadians living in Canadian territory – birthright Canadians – seems to have eluded Towers.

Second Generation *jus sanguinis* Provisions and Dual Citizenship

Two additional features of the 1977 *Citizenship Act* reflected the shortcomings of the 1947 Act and also set up the conditions, or exacerbated difficulties, for Canadians with a birthright claim to citizenship after the 1977 Act came into force. These features were the recognition of dual citizenship and a requirement that the second generation born abroad – that is, people born abroad to a Canadian parent who had been born abroad – had to affirm their citizenship by age twenty-eight. The latter provision was felt particularly keenly in the Mennonite community, as I will elaborate in the next chapter. Dual citizenship has given rise to a paradoxical discourse in which the loyalty and commitment of some dual citizens is questioned, inciting debates about the duty owed to them by the Canadian state in situations of international crisis or encounters with foreign legal systems. In other situations of dual nationality, though, Canadian expatriates are celebrated for their contributions to international culture, sport, politics, and humanitarianism.

Patrick Weil has observed that a country's preference for *jus soli* or *jus sanguinis* has been historically rooted in its migration patterns.[50] Countries of emigration have often sought to maintain the connection between the state and "the people," a situation in which *jus sanguinis* enables this connection over distance and time. For countries characterized by immigration, by contrast, a desire to ensure the inclusion of newcomers, and thus to be able to impose duties upon them, provided the governing logic for a *jus soli* citizenship regime.[51] The idea of citizenship as a right to be claimed on the part of prospective members themselves, as opposed to a duty demanded by the state, is, according to Weil, a post–Second World War phenomenon.[52]

Under the 1947 Act, Canada's *jus sanguinis* citizenship provisions were focused on the first generation born abroad. Under the terms of the first *Citizenship Act*, a Canadian born abroad was required to make a declaration of his intention to maintain his Canadian citizenship by the age of twenty-two, and, if also holding citizenship in a country that permitted renunciation, divest himself of that second citizenship.[53] As well, if a naturalized Canadian subsequently lived abroad for a period of six years, she would automatically lose her Canadian citizenship status.[54] The notion of citizenship as a duty owed can thus still be detected in these limitations. Intriguingly though, these provisions were already subject to modification in 1953, with retroactive application to 1 January 1947, when the Canadian government amended the *Citizenship Act* by extending the age to declare citizenship for born-abroad Canadians to twenty-four and the period of residence abroad required to trigger the loss of citizenship for naturalized Canadians to ten years.[55] The 1977 Act subsequently did away with any loss provisions for the first generation born abroad as well as loss provisions related to residence abroad for naturalized Canadians, requiring instead that a second-generation born-abroad Canadian make an application to retain citizenship by age twenty-eight and reside in Canada for one year prior to the application date or establish a "substantial connection with Canada."[56] The inclusion of this more robust *jus sanguinis* provision received virtually no attention by parliamentarians, except in general terms, such as those cited by Mr Stollery with regard to the achievement of an independent Canadian identity and the need for a lifelong retention of Canadian citizenship to bolster the country's distinctive nationality. The discussion also included one prescient, but unheeded, observation that a mechanism should be devised to inform born-abroad Canadians about their need to affirm their desire for citizenship by the mandated age limit.[57]

Despite the easing of restrictions on *jus sanguinis* citizenship acquisition included in the 1977 Act, Canada had not become a country of emigration. As we have seen, parliamentarians were quite divided over whether Canada should be espousing a policy of openness or whether it should be imposing heightened restrictions on citizenship acquisition. This discussion was situated in a larger context in which Quebec sovereignty was very much front of mind in the Canadian political imaginary, regionalism was intensifying, the idea of Canada as multicultural was gaining traction, and Indigenous peoples were articulating their own political claims and identities in response to their long and devastating experience of assimilationist colonialism. The issue of how membership in the Canadian polity should be defined was thus entangled in arguments about the character of the Canadian polity itself. Residence, lineage, duties, rights, unity, and diversity were central concerns in the struggle to define the contemporary national project.

If the growing political saliency of Canada's complex identity was only weakly expressed in the context of *jus soli* provisions, that complexity received a far livelier rehearsal in the context of the debate over whether to permit dual citizenship. Bill C-20, in its initial form, did not include a provision for dual citizenship. Rather, the Secretary of State asked the House of Commons Committee on Broadcasting, Films and Assistance to the Arts to consider proposing an amendment to the Act in this regard.[58] In 1973, as new citizenship legislation was being contemplated, Canada's Federal Court had ruled, in *Ulin v. Canada*, that in fact, Canada's *Citizenship Act* did not require applicants for citizenship to renounce their prior citizenship. There was a regulation to this effect associated with the legislation, but in Justice Noel's view, a requirement of renunciation was a much more substantive expectation than what would reasonably be included in the regulatory details. Renunciation, in his view, demanded an explicit statutory provision in the Act itself.[59] Since the Act did not explicitly contain a renunciation provision, all that was required to become a citizen, in Justice Noel's interpretation, was to take the oath of allegiance to Canada.[60] As a consequence of this decision, naturalized Canadians could, in fact, hold multiple citizenships. By contrast, Canadians who took out citizenship in another country were generally deemed to have lost their Canadian citizenship.[61] The resulting situation created an inequity in which, as MP Symes argued, *jus soli* Canadians had a weaker claim to Canadian citizenship than naturalized Canadians:

> [It] seems very unfair ... that it affords to aliens a right denied to natural-born Canadians. An alien coming to Canada does not have to renounce his former citizenship; yet you are saying that if a Canadian moves out of the country he must do so. I think that is unfair and inconsistent ... [The minister] stated that the people really being affected by the automatic loss clause are native-born Canadians, and that in order to make the law completely fair and to retain the present clause, aliens would have to be required to renounce their former citizenship before obtaining

Canadian citizenship. The Minister, quite rightly, acknowledges that this is just impossible to do; there is no way of forcing aliens to renounce their former citizenship.[62]

And while it was certainly true that the citizenship situations here were unequal and unfair, the accompanying insinuation that the hierarchy of entitlements was absurdly tilted away from *jus soli* Canadians and toward naturalized foreigners signals the persistence of a conception of legitimate belonging rooted to birth in the territory, despite the Secretary of State's laudable ambitions in pursuit of citizen equality.

Historically, dual citizenship was not favorably regarded because of its association with split allegiances. Since, as we have seen, citizenship is often analogized to family and to marriage, the possibility of dual membership invoked the spectre of infidelity or polygamy, "a condition utterly at war with the logical, spiritual, emotional and psychological presuppositions of communities [thus conceived]."[63] Furthermore, if the prospect of a non-metaphorical war lay on the horizon, then citizens with divided loyalties – particularly if those loyalties were unallied – posed serious difficulties for the state. As well, some objections have been raised with regard to the prospect of dual citizens voting in more than one national election, thus granting them more democratic rights than a sole-country citizen. As the Canadian debate around dual citizenship suggests, though, by the 1970s, such concerns were being eclipsed, or at least strongly challenged, by efforts to address inclusion and even possibly to profit from the international connections of global citizens.[64] Progressive Conservative MP Mark MacGuigan remained on the singular nationality side of the debate, primarily as a bulwark against the vigorous patriotism of the United States. For MacGuigan, dual citizenship, like the shortened residency requirement, cheapened Canadian citizenship. He felt that if Canadians were able to hold US citizenship as well, their Canadian citizenship would be swamped, overridden by the deliberately cultivated American spirit that was designed "to persuade people to retain American citizenship at whatever cost and to absorb whatever people from other countries come to live in their country."[65] In the absence of dual citizenship, Canadians living in the US would be better able to withstand the onslaught of American culture. By contrast, Gordon Fairweather, who moved the amendment to include dual citizenship in the Act, argued that enabling dual citizenship would reflect a "mature understanding of ourselves."[66] In the end, the amendment carried.[67]

Conclusion

The equality impetus that was so central to the 1977 *Citizenship Act* was remarkable in many ways, and particularly so in light of the twenty-first century's political discourse in which the idea of citizenship as a right has been replaced by growing suspicion of immigrants and an obsession with security via controls over borders and national membership. Yet despite its impressive democratic foundations, the fact that the 1977 Act did not apply retroactively and, thus, maintained gender and marital status inequities for people born before 15 February 1977, as well as diverse regimes for loss provisions and *jus sanguinis* citizenship acquisition, meant that these inadequacies in the Act were almost immediately apparent. Moreover, since some Canadians (those born on 15 February 1977 and after) did benefit from equality, while older Canadians did not, the inequities of the previous Act only became more apparent. It was not merely that one might wish for a more equitable law and mobilize to persuade one's representatives to take action. That more equitable law was already on the books. The problem was that it was inapplicable to the vast majority of Canadians. The following chapters will offer a vivid demonstration of the consequences of this peculiar state of affairs.

5

Lost to Canada by Ordinary Means

For all the good intentions that had motivated the *Citizenship Act* of 1977, its weaknesses, and especially its lack of retroactive application, would become increasingly burdensome for subsequent Parliaments. By the mid-aughts, this burden had been cast as the phenomenon of the lost Canadians, gaining a particularly sharp political edge through the implementation of the passport requirements of the Western Hemisphere Travel Initiative (WHTI) in 2007. While many Canadians had quietly encountered the inconstancies of the *Citizenship Act* prior to the WHTI's enforcement, the necessity of holding a passport to cross the Canada–US land border (formerly dispatched with a driver's licence or birth certificate) brought the distressing news to a growing number of (presumed) Canadians applying for passports that their citizenship was in some doubt or even granted in error. As these stories gained media attention, the Conservative government of Stephen Harper faced growing pressure to correct what were popularly regarded as legal outrages, most notably in situations involving people who had been born in or lived all or most of their lives in Canada, and who even voted.

We have already explored the citizenship struggles of the war brides and their children – challenges that demonstrate the simultaneous operation of the pre- and post- 1947 citizenship regimes. Yet their difficulties provide only a partial illustration of the range of provisions that created lost Canadians and the powerful connections among lineage, citizenship, and national belonging that lost Canadians, generally, can invoke. The 1947 Act's prohibitions against dual citizenship, the operation of the wedlock provisions, and citizenship affirmation requirements of the 1947 and 1977 Acts affected a wide range of people, people I describe here as "ordinary lost Canadians," whose life circumstances lacked the particular drama and ethical purchase of wartime sacrifice but whose love of country, hard work, and embodiment of Canadian values would ultimately compel legislators to pursue reform. The fact that these citizenship difficulties could emerge through no fault or wilful act on the part of the individual, and could involve the arbitrary exercise of state power to suddenly deny citizenship, sometimes despite previous confirmation, inflected these non-military stories of lost Canadians with a comic book morality and a clear case for justice. They provide rich fodder for an analysis of the workings of birthright citizenship and the substance of Canadian belonging.

In this chapter, I explore the challenges posed by the coexistence of distinct citizenship rules emerging from the non-retroactive application of the 1977 *Citizenship Act*. More specifically, I examine three, sometimes conflated, categories of loss: those resulting from ongoing gender discrimination within the *Citizenship Act*; cases involving foreign citizenship acquisition by a responsible parent; and the challenges posed by the age twenty-eight affirmation requirement. All of these examples invoke the kinship basis of the Canadian state and advance a vision of the "authentic" Canadian replete in masculinity, racialized whiteness, and the moral worthiness of the exalted subject. The evidence I present here is drawn from court cases, legislative debates, and parliamentary committee hearings around the Liberals' Bill C-18 (2002–3), and subsequent legislative hearings on the *Citizenship Act* under the Conservative government of Stephen Harper, as well as media reports. As noted in the previous chapter, the inadequacies of the 1977 Act became apparent quite quickly, yet very little substantive action was taken until 2008. The Mulroney government (1984–1993) issued a lofty promise for a new citizenship act in 1987, a promise that ultimately foundered on the shoals of the national unity agenda.[1] The Chrétien Liberals (1993–2003), in a much more security-focused guise, introduced and ultimately let lapse three separate revisions to the *Citizenship Act*. The most significant attempt was Bill C-18, which included extensive cross-country hearings on the proposed bill, and which brought lost Canadians to the attention of parliamentarians for the first time. As their difficulties with the *Citizenship Act* continued under the Harper government and intensified with the WHTI, lost Canadians and those who argued on their behalf before the Parliamentary Standing Committee on Citizenship and Immigration, grew increasingly polished and persuasive. Moreover, their virtuous desire for Canada provided a fascinating counterpoint and an important brake on the conflation of citizenship discussions with security, and thus with threat.

The Persistence of Gender Inequities

Because the 1977 *Citizenship Act*'s gender equality and wedlock provisions were not retroactive, it should hardly have been surprising that challenges emerged to the ongoing regime of gender and marital status discrimination in citizenship determination. In 1981 the Federal Court heard the case of *Re: Chute*.[2] This case involved the citizenship of a child, Jesse Chute, born in 1975, in Houston, to a Canadian father (Douglas) and American mother (Margaret Bliss).[3]

The parents were cohabiting but unmarried, since Margaret had been married previously and, as a Catholic, was prevented from remarrying within her faith community.[4] The couple also had two younger children who did have Canadian citizenship, since their daughter was born in Toronto in 1976 and their youngest son was born in New Zealand after 15 February 1977 (in 1978).[5] Douglas had attempted to register young Jesse as a Canadian at the Dallas consulate after the new *Citizenship Act* was passed, but was not permitted to do so, because, as an unwed father to a child born before 15 February 1977, he was not considered the child's responsible parent. At the time of the court hearing, the family was living in Toronto, where Douglas held a position as a tenure-track professor. Jesse and Margaret had permission to reside in Canada until 4 April 1981, and thus were considered visitors.[6]

In this case, Douglas was really up against the strict letter of the law – a law whose inequities had clearly been recognized by the 1977 Act, but which, nonetheless, did not apply to his son Jesse's case due to his birthdate. Douglas was unable to adjust his personal life to fit the requirements of the law, since his partner would not marry him; she also refused to consent to his formal adoption of his son – a strategy that had been proposed to the couple in order to bring Douglas into a formal legal relationship with Jesse, and thus enabling Douglas to mobilize the provisions of section 5(2)(a) of the *Citizenship Act* to apply for permanent residence for his son and subsequently for citizenship.[7] Margaret resisted the adoption option because she had lost custody of a child born to her marriage and did not want to risk a similar outcome if her relationship with Douglas fell apart.[8] The judge noted that this was a weak argument at law, as custody would be determined on the basis of the best interests of the child. Since the father was acknowledged on the birth certificate, adoption was unlikely to provide him with any additional rights of custody "in the event that other circumstances indicated that the mother was the person to have such custody."[9] By implication, then, while Douglas would have parental standing in the family law context of a custody determination, that standing did not extend to his ability to pass on his citizenship to his son.

Again, we see that birthright citizenship and the family are products of law, but that depending on the law's objective, these definitions may not align and may even act at cross-purposes. We also see the extent to which birthright citizenship law assumes a gendered social order that is remarkably resistant to disruption. None of the rules of citizenship determination pertained to Jesse's commitment to Canada, to the fact that Canadian law directly affected his capacity to live his life, or even to his character (dubious as character may be as a basis for citizenship determination). Rather, Jesse's lack of citizenship was a function of the Canadian state's desire to protect itself from the membership claims of foreign-born children of unwed Canadian fathers. Parliament knew that this approach to birthright citizenship was anachronistic, even if some public servants did not, and while legislators had found a means to temper the legal prohibition against retroactive application for the children of married Canadian mothers born before 1977, the children of unmarried Canadian fathers were a bridge too far.

It was clear that Justice Walsh was deeply sympathetic to the family's plight. Walsh noted the financial hardship associated with paying kindergarten fees for Jesse that amounted to more than 10 per cent of Douglas's annual salary and that were being imposed as a result of Jesse's status as a visitor.[10] Had Jesse been "residing" in Canada, he could have attended kindergarten without cost. Nonetheless, Justice Walsh adjourned the appeal, finding that he could not recommend that the minister exercise his discretionary power to grant citizenship under section 5(4) of the *Citizenship Act* since it was not clear to him that he was empowered to overturn the citizenship judge's earlier refusal to make that recommendation.[11] And, moreover, he was not persuaded that the minister would heed the court's recommendation in any event. "[E]xperience in the past has shown that such recommendations are seldom if ever acted upon, placing Judges of this court in the invidious position of having recommendations, made after the hearing of an appeal, rejected at the executive level of government which creates an undesirable situation."[12] This refusal to act must have been a harsh blow indeed to Douglas Chute. Ultimately, these citizenship challenges proved untenable, and the family returned to the United States.[13]

Retroactivity after the *Charter*

Without the equality provisions of the *Canadian Charter of Rights and Freedoms* (which did not come into effect until 1985), Douglas Chute was unable to persuade the court that he should be entitled to pass his Canadian citizenship on to his son. By 1992, though, the gender and marital status inequities that had been retained in the 1977 *Citizenship Act* were increasingly difficult to defend. The case of *Glynos v. Canada*[14] was an important breakthrough in this regard, for it exposed a tension in the judiciary regarding the consideration of *Charter* arguments around gender equality while also revealing a thorough inattentiveness to the retroactivity arguments that had been considered in Parliament in the development of the *Citizenship Act* of 1977. Subsequent decisions, however – as we have already seen with regard to *Taylor* and will briefly survey in this chapter as well – would find other means to reinstate the prohibition against retroactive application.

In a citizenship regime in which connection and (future) contribution were the bases for membership, the case of Jason Glynos would have been a "nobrainer." A young man, educated at Cambridge and residing in Vancouver, he embodied the normative form of an ideal Canadian. Yet when his mother sought Canadian citizenship for her sons, Byron was granted citizenship, while Jason was denied.[15] Jason was born in 1967 in the United States to married Canadian parents. Thus, he began his life as a dual citizen; Canadian and, because he was born in the US, also American. In 1970, though, his father took out American citizenship, and as a result, Jason and his younger brother Byron were understood to have lost their Canadian citizenship in the process.[16] In 1985, when their mother Anita applied for citizenship documentation on behalf of her sons, she was informed that her children were no longer Canadian citizens. She subsequently succeeded in securing citizenship for Byron under section 5(2)(a) of the Act (for he had been admitted to Canada as the minor child of a citizen).[17] Citizenship for Jason, though, who was by then eighteen and thus an adult, was denied. In response to Anita's correspondence with the ministry arguing for her elder son's citizenship entitlement, the Secretary of State responded that 5(2)(b) of the Act – the provision that enabled the minister to grant citizenship to a person born abroad to a Canadian mother before 15 February 1977 – did not apply to Jason, since in the Secretary of State's interpretation, this provision was only applicable to persons who had never been citizens.[18] Since Jason had been a Canadian at birth, this technicality could be used to deny his eligibility.

Given the patent unfairness of this outcome, Anita and Jason decided to launch legal proceedings in September of 1989, shortly after Jason had returned to Canada from his studies in the UK. At this time, he was attending law school at the University of British Columbia.[19] The grounds for their action addressed the Secretary of State's interpretation – or the true construction – of section 5(2)(b) of the Act, as well as raising a *Charter* challenge on the basis of gender and marital status discrimination regarding the capacity of married women to transmit their citizenship. But since Jason was now living in Vancouver, as the proceedings unfolded he soon became eligible to resume citizenship under section 11 of the Act, for, having ceased to be a citizen, he had been lawfully admitted to Canada as a permanent resident, and had been resident for one year. At trial, the judge agreed with the government's argument that the issue of Jason's citizenship was now moot, since, having met the residency requirement, the government was willing to grant Jason citizenship if he were to apply.[20] Persuaded by the government's position, Justice Walsh held that since Jason Glynos was already entitled to Canadian citizenship, the case was really about the "determination of a women's rights issue"[21] and that "the time of the Courts is too valuable to spend it in deciding hypothetical issues, merely because of their possible future consequences in other cases when no such issue needs to be decided in the present case."[22] For Justice Walsh, Parliament was the proper venue to resolve the issue of the ongoing gender discrimination in the *Citizenship Act,* even if the federal government had argued in the context of the case at bar that invoking discriminatory gender and marital status provisions on people born before 15 February 1977 was a reasonable limit on *Charter* rights.[23]

In any event, the Federal Court of Appeal was not persuaded by the mootness argument and did find that the *Charter* arguments should be heard. In Justice Décary's view the issue before the court was whether or not Jason was entitled to be granted Canadian citizenship by virtue of his mother's Canadian citizen-ship.[24] The fact that other provisions of the Act might be accessed to address his citizenship evaded the central issue of the gender and marital status provisions that continued to determine the birthright citizenship eligibility of people born before 15 February 1977.[25] Justice Décary effectively chastised Justice Walsh of the Federal Court, noting that "the Trial Judge appears to be blaming [Anita Glynos]" for her interest in "seeking to correct long-standing discrimination against Canadian women."[26] Décary then turned to the parliamentary record to build his argument that the government's objective in passing the 1977 *Citizenship Act* had in fact been to redress the discriminatory treatment that had been visited upon women in the 1947 Act.[27] Yet it appears that Justice Décary read the deliberations of the Standing Committee on Broadcasting, Films and Assistance to the Arts with his own perspective in mind. As we observed in the previous chapter, the committee's deliberations involved considerable dis-cussion regarding the retroactive application of citizenship to the children of married Canadian mothers. Rather than a blanket extension of citizenship to the born-abroad children of Canadian mothers, legislators chose a much more moderate accommodation, granting time-limited access to citizenship by appli-cation and on the basis of a security check. Yet in *Glynos*, Justice Décary held that "the legislator intended that *anyone* born to a Canadian mother at *any time* prior to the enactment of the Act and who had been adversely affected by the former Act's discriminatory provisions was to be entitled to receive citizenship under subsection 5(2) [my emphasis]."[28] Ultimately, the court held that Jason was eligible for a grant of citizenship on the basis of a birthright entitlement, as he was the son of a Canadian mother.

While Justice Décary's ruling in *Glynos* was sorting out Jason's citizenship situation, several additional opportunities emerged to test and nuance Justice Décary's interpretation of 5(2)(b) of the *Citizenship Act*. In the context of the category of "ordinary" lost Canadians, subsequent refinement would be exacted with regard to the Canadian citizenship status of people born before 1 January 1947. In *Crease* (1994)[29] and *Wilson* (2003),[30] for example, a birthright claim to Canadian citizenship for born-abroad children on the basis of a Canadian-born mother was denied because the plaintiffs were born before the coming into force of Canada's first *Citizenship Act*. In both these cases, the government argued – and the court agreed – that while the plaintiffs' mothers had been born in Canada, the women would have been British subjects rather than Canadian citizens. And, indeed, since both mothers had married foreign nationals before 1947, they had also lost their Canadian citizenship by virtue of marriage. Since Canadian citizenship did not exist prior to 1 January 1947, and the women themselves were not Canadians, these women had no Canadian citizenship to pass along to their children.

While the court cases discussed above were certainly significant in the lives of the plaintiffs and in establishing legal precedent, their details have been confined to the judicial record. It would take the efforts of advocates for lost Canadians, appearing at parliamentary hearings and speaking to the press, to translate the dry technicalities of the *Citizenship Act* into the lived experiences of would-be Canadians and, most importantly, to frame those experiences as a political liability. As we have seen, the political force of the citizenship appeals launched by war brides and their children relied primarily on the moral purchase of wartime sacrifice and heroism. By contrast, the "ordinary" lost Canadians invoked a populist argument regarding the inanity of rules and the hard-heartedness of the people who enforced them. Importantly, this focus on Orwellian bureaucracy gave rise to calls for better rules, but it also created space for affective invocations of the "natural," and thus unassailable or at least uncontestable, connections among children, their parents, and the nation-state. This argumentative mode was highly successful, at least in Parliament and the media, since it mobilized an apparently democratic basis for membership in connection and commitment, but did so on the basis of birthright and familial attachment to the state, rather than a democratic logic focused on a right to participate in the structures and processes through which one is governed.

Citizenship Loss through a Responsible Parent

One of the most significant categories of "lost Canadians" was created by the 1947 Act's provision that minor children were presumed to have lost their Canadian citizenship if their responsible parent took out citizenship in another country. This was the situation for Jason Glynos discussed above, but the legal strategy that he and his mother deployed emphasized the gender inequity of the rule that prevented married Canadian women from passing on their citizenship rather than the inequity of the loss provision itself. For Don Chapman, the leading voice of the lost Canadians, the wrong of the Act lay in the loss of citizenship if one was in fact born on Canadian soil. We have already canvassed the various ways in which the *Citizenship Acts* of 1947 and 1977 established birthright entitlement through the patriarchal norms of the married, heterosexual family. These elements are characteristic of the loss provisions as well. Yet in the case of Don Chapman, the citizenship story is in many ways notable less for the legal technicalities that rendered him a lost Canadian than for the rhetorical strategies he mobilized successfully to justify his entitlement to the Canadian polity.

Don Chapman is a central figure in the story of the lost Canadians as he has been their primary champion, appearing before Parliament on numerous occasions, assisting many individuals in advancing their cases with political representatives and public servants, and keeping their stories in the public eye through a self-published book and a website and as a reliable, quotable source for journalists.[31] And while Chapman's parliamentary testimony often waxes hyperbolic (comparing the situation of lost Canadians to the cultural genocide visited upon Canada's Indigenous population, racial segregation in the US, and the Holocaust), his determination to pursue legislative change was undeniably instrumental in bringing about statutory reforms.[32] Chapman's advocacy on behalf of lost Canadians emerged from his own situation. He was born in Vancouver in 1954, shortly after which his family moved to the US, where his father acquired US citizenship in 1961.[33] Chapman attested that he was unhappy about his loss of Canadian citizenship even at the tender age of five and that he had been fighting to reclaim his citizenship since his late teens, although the public record does not clarify why he did not succeed.[34] Under the 1947 Act that governed Chapman's situation, there was an opportunity for a child who, having lost citizenship in this way, could petition to have his citizenship reinstated at age twenty-one.[35] Given the ardour with which he made his arguments, perhaps it is not surprising that parliamentary committee members chose not to ask him why his earlier attempts had not succeeded.[36] He has subsequently raised a family in the US and works as an airline pilot based in Arizona. In addition to his indignation regarding his own loss of Canadian citizenship, Chapman has expressed considerable fury with regard to his inability to pass on Canadian citizenship to his children.

In Chapman's appearances before the House of Commons he often made the case for his Canadian citizenship by conflating lineage with commitment to Canada.[37] Chapman invoked a Nova Scotia ancestor, William Alexander Henry, who was a Father of Confederation.[38] He pointed to the fact that his ancestors had co-founded the Universities of St Francis Xavier and Toronto.[39] He observed that collectively, his family had donated millions of dollars to Canadian charitable institutions, and that a library at the University of British Columbia bore his father's name.[40] He also noted that his father had served in the Canadian military.[41]

This expression of commitment to Canada, which relies explicitly on kinship, also makes claims to authenticity. Chapman's recurring testimony before the House of Commons standing committee often invoked "common sense" understandings of what identities made for a Canadian and what identities led to suspicion. From Chapman's enumeration of his heritage of attachments, it was clear that he felt the work of his forbears entitled him, a person who made his living as an airline pilot based in Arizona, to be a Canadian. Indeed, he frequently contrasted his "impeccable" history with that of government officials. In a story in the *Vancouver Sun,* for example, Chapman was quoted thus:

"We started this fight when Paul Martin was prime minister and Joe Volpe the minister of citizenship and immigration. Think about the irony – the minister was a foreign-born son of an enemy in World War II [Italy] challenging [me], the son of a Canadian hero of World War II."

"Even when the Conservatives came to power," Chapman quipped, "the ironies continued." "At one time, Vic Toews, who's a Mennonite from Paraguay,[42] was handling the file as minister. He was telling me I wasn't a Canadian."[43]

The fact that both Volpe and Toews had dedicated themselves to public service in Canada was completely discounted in this reasoning. For Chapman's case to be persuasive, it is not the acts of the current generation that should matter, but those of the fathers. Chapman's statement also invokes a particular ethnic rationale for his claim to Canadian citizenship. Unlike the enemy Italian or the born-abroad member of a religious minority, Chapman's father was, supposedly, a "proper" Canadian, a status that can be derived from the fact that he fought on the winning side. It was obvious, apparently, that these familial contributions supported the son's claim to citizenship, as evidenced by the citation of a CBC news story that described Chapman as "as Canadian as you can get" in the Standing Committee on Citizenship and Immigration's December 2007 report to the House of Commons.[44]

Chapman's argument in support of his citizenship claim collapses kinship and ethnicity while papering over the significance of these rationales through the assertion of a demonstrated commitment to Canada. This liberal sleight of hand (the same one that replaces kinship with consent in the story of the social contract) is evident in Chapman's response to the 2008 amendment to the *Citizenship Act* that denied citizenship to second-generation children born abroad. In one of the few instances in which a member of the House of Commons Committee on Citizenship and Immigration challenged Chapman, Liberal MP Jim Karygiannis asked Chapman whether his loss of Canadian citizenship had rendered him stateless – a concern that arises from the second-generation rule. Chapman replied that the United States had "taken pity" on him. But the benefits of that pity aside, it was his view that

> all countries of the world are starting to redefine who belongs in their countries and who doesn't. You see it in Holland, Australia, France, Germany, all over. Eventually under the current system, if you don't put some stop to it somewhere, it might happen that everybody in the world ends up as a Canadian citizen. Just out of common sense, you have to start establishing some attachment to the country, somewhere and somehow. All countries are grappling with this.[45]

Chapman's ability to argue for limiting Canadian citizenship even while invoking his entitlement to that citizenship on the basis of his white, Canadian heritage, and not to be challenged to demonstrate his own commitment, distinct from that of his forefathers, is illustrative of the naturalization of kinship and ethnicity in the Canadian national identity. As noted above, Chapman had resisted using the Canadian immigration system to regain his citizenship on the grounds that Canadian citizenship was his birthright and that acquiring citizenship on his own behalf would not enable him to pass that citizenship entitlement on to his children. The significance of the retroactive application provision in the 2008 amendments to the *Citizenship Act* is that it enables formerly lost Canadians to confer their status on their children, although it limits the *jus sanguinis* citizenship claim to the first generation of children born abroad.[46] And it was this detail that lay at the crux of Karygiannis's challenge to Chapman. For Karygiannis, as for Chapman, the capacity to pass on one's citizenship to one's kin was central. In Karygiannis's case, he was concerned that his foreign-born daughter could have a child outside Canada and thus that his grandchild would not be a Canadian. Indeed, under the 2008 amendments, second and subsequent generations born abroad are prohibited from claiming Canadian citizenship, except as immigrants, unless the effect of the rule is to render an individual stateless.[47]

Don Chapman offers a kind of hyper-representation of birthright and belonging. This hyperbole usefully illuminates otherwise assumed elements of the argument for citizenship. Family is tied to the nation-state. The rules of kinship that make citizens are imbued with ethnic identifications that enable the marking of some people as authentic and "old stock," while others are perpetually new. Of course, Chapman was only one of many thousands of people who lost their Canadian citizenship by virtue of the actions of their responsible parents. Many of those people have undoubtedly embraced a new national citizenship with perhaps only passing interest in their childhood affiliation with Canada. Yet such was the strength of Chapman's argument that he succeeded in persuading the Conservative government and Parliament to reform the *Citizenship Act* and extend Canadian citizenship to everyone who had been born in Canada after 1 January 1947 regardless of their current relationship to the country, or, as we will discuss in the next chapter, their criminal record. One is left to ponder whether Chapman's lobbying would have had the same persuasive force had he been not quite "as Canadian as you can get." Moreover, even with Chapman's success in attaining a more comprehensive provision of birthright citizenship acquisition, cases continue to arise in which the Canadian government seeks to exclude people with birthright citizenship claims.

Wedlock, Affirmation Requirements, and the Arbitrary Acts of the Sovereign

The last two cases I want to consider, one argued in court, the other in the court of public opinion, involve the peculiar situation of a group of Mennonites. In the 1920s, approximately six thousand members of the Mennonite faith who had settled in Manitoba and Saskatchewan relocated to Mexico in response to the Canadian state's efforts to impose educational standards, including English-language instruction, on their children.[48] Economic hardship and religious disagreements then compelled some of the descendants of these families to return to Canada, believing, as they did, that they were Canadian citizens.[49] In fact, as Royden Loewen argues, some of these families tracked back and forth between Canada and Mexico as well as other countries in South America, all the while holding fast to their belief that their Canadian citizenship was secure.[50] For their part, Canadian authorities seem to have been highly inattentive to the finer points of citizenship determination for Mennonite children born abroad, at least until the 2000s. This lax disposition understandably reinforced the itinerant Mennonites' belief that they retained their citizenship in Canada. One can appreciate their ensuing dismay when the Canadian government increased its vigilance and began denying passport applications and renewals of citizenship certificates on the grounds that previous documents had been granted in error. According to these newly attentive citizenship officials, many of the Mexican-born descendants of these Canadian-born Mennonites did not qualify for birthright citizenship since they were born out of wedlock. Because Mennonite couples were married in church weddings that were often not registered with the Mexican state, and because a legitimate marriage is a function of the state, these church weddings did not in fact constitute a lawful marriage. Even when these couples later registered their marriages with the Mexican authorities, the Canadian government continued to hold that any children born prior to this official registration were born out of wedlock.

What, exactly, is to be gained from upholding the original wedlock provisions of a century-old statute, provisions that have since been revised, given some degree of retroactive application, and later rejected altogether? At least part of the rationale seems to lie in a desire to place a limit on the intergenerational transfer of citizenship, so that people born abroad are obliged to enhance their birthright entitlement with a demonstration of substantive connection to the country. As we have seen, the 1947 and 1977 *Citizenship Acts* both included provisions that managed the *jus sanguinis* inheritance of citizenship, requiring either the first or second generation born abroad to affirm their connection to Canada in their early adulthood. The provisions of the 1947 Act were evidently not uniformly enforced, a situation that supported the understanding that the born-abroad descendants of Canadian Mennonites were in fact Canadian citizens. Moreover, the fact that many of these people moved back to Canada indicates that they regarded themselves as having an attachment to the country and were seeking to (re)establish productive working lives in Canada. Their cases gain a special poignancy since the Canadian government has granted citizenship certificates to many of these people. They only learn that the wedlock status of their parents or grandparents has disqualified them from Canadian citizenship when they have subsequently applied for a passport renewal or a new citizenship certificate or have attempted to meet the citizenship retention requirements by affirming their citizenship before their twenty-eighth birthdays.

The case of *Veleta v. Canada (Citizenship and Immigration)*[51] provides a vivid demonstration of how the shifting rules of birthright citizenship can maroon people in uncertainty and, because of the state's sovereign power to determine membership, can create conditions in which basic tenets of fair process are not simply disregarded but considered irrelevant in the first instance. This case also highlights the risks of both under- and over-inclusiveness in *jus sanguinis* citizenship provisions. *Veleta* involved the citizenship of four children, born between 1993 and 2001 outside of Canada. They claimed citizenship on the basis of their father Jacob's Canadian citizenship. Jacob had also been born outside of Canada, as had *his* father, David. The claim to Canadian citizenship began with the children's great-grandparents, Peter and Anna, who had both been born in Canada but moved to Mexico and married there, in a church wedding, in 1924.[52] Their son David was born in 1933. The great-grandparents obtained a civil registration of their marriage later on, in 1937.[53] However, as noted above, in the 2000s, at least, the Canadian government had not viewed this civil registration as affecting the "out of wedlock" status of David's birth.

Earlier, though, the Canadian government had been more inclined to recognize David's Canadian citizenship. In fact, he had applied for a citizenship certificate in 1966, and that certificate records 27 September 1957 as the date of his citizenship, since that was the effective date of an amendment to Canada's *Citizenship Act* that extended the status of legitimacy back to a child's date of birth, if the parents had eventually married.[54] David moved to Canada in 1967. His son Jacob, however, was not born in Canada, although he too received a citizenship certificate, in 1982.[55] These efforts to obtain the formal documents of Canadian citizenship on behalf of both David and Jacob indicate some understanding of the need to affirm their desire to maintain citizenship, although it is not clear whether they were fully compliant, or, again, whether the Secretary of State was especially attentive to the rules at the time of their initial applications. David applied for a renewal of his citizenship certificate in 2001, and that was granted.[56] It was not until his grandchildren attempted to obtain *their* citizenship that the citizenship of David and Jacob became an issue.

The case was first heard as a request for judicial review of a citizenship officer's refusal to grant Canadian citizenship to these children, on the grounds that their grandfather had been born abroad, out of wedlock, and thus was not a Canadian citizen and could not pass on citizenship to his son or to his grandchildren. At trial in 2005, Justice Mactavish relied on the *Naturalization Act* of 1914 to determine that at the time of David's birth, children could only inherit citizenship from their fathers, and only if they were born in wedlock.[57] Furthermore, Canadian citizenship was only vested in people who were *British* subjects immediately prior to the coming into force of the *Citizenship Act* of 1947. Thus David, born out of wedlock, and in Mexico, and thus a Mexican citizen under that country's *jus soli* provisions, was not a British subject immediately prior to the coming into force of Canada's *Citizenship Act*. Since the grandfather was not a Canadian citizen, he could not pass that citizenship along to his son Jacob, nor Jacob to his children.[58]

It was not until the appeal hearing that the information regarding David's acquisition of a citizenship certificate in the 1960s was revealed, as well as his residency in Canada since 1967. The court was particularly concerned that neither David nor Jacob had been informed by the Ministry of Citizenship and Immigration that their citizenship was being denied, noting that "it was surprising, at the very least, that Jacob ... was given no formal notice that he was no longer considered a Canadian citizen."[59] When the government's lawyer was asked about this lack of formal notice, he responded that it was "standard practice for the [Ministry] not to formally notify persons of the loss of their citizenship, but rather to wait until such persons either requested a certificate of citizenship or the issuance of a passport before informing them."[60] The court then requested the statutory or regulatory authority for this practice.[61] After the hearing, Citizenship and Immigration provided the regulations that govern how people submit their documents for renewal. The court, however, did not find evidence that this process had been applied to either Jacob or David. Since both Jacob and his children had relied on David's status as a Canadian citizen for their claim to citizenship, it was clear that establishing David's citizenship was the first order of business and that the appeal of the citizenship officer's negative decision should be redetermined in Federal Court.[62] And so ends the judicial record of the Giesbrecht Veleta case. As it turned out, the Department of Citizenship and Immigration came to an out-of-court settlement with the family, and all involved subsequently received their citizenship certificates.[63] However, the remaining legal and procedural issues were unresolved, and, indeed, remain so, despite the 2008 and 2014 amendments to the *Citizenship Act*.

Johann Teichroeb's situation follows a similar pattern, though in the end, his case was resolved as a result of media attention and public pressure rather than a more sheltered set of court proceedings. Teichroeb's predicament was especially compelling because, unlike most of the cases discussed in this chapter, he had lived almost all of his life in Canada. And though he had no family history of wartime service to call upon, as a young, God-fearing family man trying to make an honest living, he characterized a morally upstanding Canadian as well as most people.

Johan Teichroeb was born in Mexico, in 1980, to Canadian parents (or at least parents who thought they were Canadian) of Mennonite faith. Moving to Canada at the age of six months and having lived there continuously since then, Teichroeb affirmed his desire to retain his Canadian citizenship before his twenty-eighth birthday as per the requirements of Canada's *Citizenship Act* that applied to people born abroad after 14 February 1977.[64] Confirming his citizenship status was particularly important to Teichroeb as he worked as a trucker and frequently crossed the Canada–US border.[65] In 2003, however, Teichroeb received a letter denying his citizenship status. A diligent immigration officer had discovered that Johan's great-grandfather, who had emigrated from

Canada to Mexico, was married in a church wedding in Mexico but had not had his marriage registered with the Mexican state. As a result, Canadian law considered Johan's grandfather to be illegitimate and thus unable to claim the citizenship of his father or pass on Canadian citizenship to his daughter, Johan's mother.[66] Citizenship and Immigration subsequently informed Teichroeb that his previous citizenship documents "had been granted in error" and that his citizenship was being revoked.[67]

Andrew Telegdi, a Liberal Member of Parliament, responded to this case with outrage: "What the hell is the government doing checking out the marital status of ... grandparents? They say they don't have the resources to process immigration applications faster but they have the resources to keep track of the genealogy of Mennonites of all people."[68] As it turned out, the Canadian government does have dedicated resources for tracking Mennonite ancestry, as revealed by an immigration officer who appeared before the standing committee. Rose Anne Poirier noted that "at the case processing centre ... we have a series of family trees. If you want to refer to them as a genealogical tool, we have an in-house system that we use on a regular basis to help us facilitate applications coming from people from the Mennonite community."[69]

Johan Teichroeb was a particularly sympathetic figure because he was a hardworking man supporting a young family. He had dutifully complied with the citizenship regulations yet he had still fallen victim to the heavy hand of the Canadian state. In his emotional testimony before the House committee, Teichroeb outlined how the ministry's decision had cost him his job and his house, that his wife had become severely depressed, and that he had been obliged to rely on his extended family for financial support.[70] Moreover, Teichroeb's religious affinity to a Protestant sect renowned for its commitment to community service and a quiet, simple life underscored the injustice of his treatment at the hands of the Canadian state.[71] Evidently the Canadian government recognized the political threat this case posed: Teichroeb's citizenship was restored four weeks after his story was reported in the national media.[72]

As William Janzen has noted, however, one-off resolutions to these cases do not provide an adequate or just approach to the predicaments in which these Mennonites – or anyone else who may be similarly situated – find themselves.[73] Johan's siblings, cousins, and even second cousins may also believe they have Canadian citizenship. They may hold citizenship certificates and passports. Yet as these stories of citizenship reassessment become more widely known, many people are choosing not to seek clarification of their citizenship status for fear that their citizenship will be denied. For many people it is safer to simply continue using their existing citizenship certificates, which by all appearances seem permanently valid. Not until 2007 were citizenship certificates issued with a stamp indicating that the holder was required to affirm their citizenship by age twenty-eight.[74] The Canadian government did eventually attempt to rectify the situation by repealing the affirmation requirement and ending *jus sanguinis* citizenship acquisition for the second generation born abroad after 17 April 2009. Yet a small, highly technical bit of trouble remains.[75] Because of the way in which the amendments were structured to fit with existing provisions of the Act, a group of second-generation born-abroad people born between 15 February 1977 and 17 April 1981 are still subject to the affirmation requirements and the loss provisions. This is because the 2008 and 2014 amendments to the *Citizenship Act* have reinstated citizenship to everyone who was born a Canadian before 15 February 1977 and lost their citizenship (other than through renunciation), while the requirement for second-generation born-abroad Canadians to affirm their citizenship was repealed, covering everyone who had not yet reached the age of twenty-eight when the provision came into force.[76] A gap remains for people born on or after 15 February 1977 who had already reached the age of twenty-eight when the revocation of the requirement came into force. It is highly unlikely that any legislative drafter would have noticed this anomaly, given the many intricacies surrounding the definition of a Canadian, but for those few people who find themselves in this unfortunate position – located in citizenship limbo and fearing that efforts to clarify their status will be expensive, complex, and potentially unsuccessful – this anomaly is highly salient.

In (largely academic) debates about citizenship acquisition, birthright citizenship in either its *jus soli* or *jus sanguinis* forms is often lauded on grounds of clarity, simplicity, natural logic, and certainty.[77] Resistance to more consensual proposals for state membership determination, inclusion based on residency, or subjection to governance is advanced on grounds that such principles are subject to revision, with the risk that vulnerable populations may be targeted for revocation through the force of majoritarian populism. More conservative proponents of birthright appeal to a logic of shared cultural values that emerge from shared origins, a claim that imbues national borders with a unique capacity to constrain the norms that govern human interaction. Yet as the stories discussed in this chapter clearly indicate, birthright is, itself, a product of rules – always political, variably enforced, and, at least in the Canadian case, highly changeable.

Nonetheless, even if the reality of birthright citizenship determination has virtually nothing to do with the will of the individual, proponents of birthright citizenship are frequently seduced by the forces of connection and contribution as means to shore up its argumentative force. Don Chapman and Johan Teichroeb used commitment to Canada, albeit in differing ways, to provide the justifactory leverage for the restoration of their Canadian citizenship. Successive secretaries of state and ministers of citizenship and immigration have also underscored the need for a demonstration of national commitment as an element of Canadian citizenship acquisition (*qua* the affirmation requirements for *jus sanguinis* Canadians), and commitment requirements received extensive consideration in the meetings of the parliamentary standing committees. Yet ultimately, the 2008 amendments to the Act abandoned the affirmation requirement for the second generation born abroad, and an automatic birthright entitlement was further extended in the 2014 amendments. At root, criteria of birth are what determine who shall be a Canadian. The closest approximation of an expression of commitment is required from those second-generation born-abroad children who would be rendered stateless as a result of the amendments. In this instance, in order to acquire citizenship, these people must be under twenty-three, must have lived in Canada for three of the four years prior to application, must always have been stateless, and must not have been convicted of various terrorism-related offences.[78]

Conclusion

Jacqueline Stevens concludes her exploration of kinship and the state with the following observation: "Political societies develop birth practices so as to provide a connection between the current population and those of the past and future, via laws and related regimens of intergenerationality."[79] It is the rules of kinship that constitute a political society, that make birth something more than a mere biological feat, and in this process of meaning-making so too is politics made.[80] The resistance to this observation, despite the abundant evidence in its favour, gives rise to the question of what will to power, and profound human desire, maintains the fantasies of the naturalness of family and the non-familial grounding of the liberal-democratic state. Since kinship is central to all political societies, including liberal democracies, one might ask how it has come to be that liberalism nonetheless eschews its familial groundings even while projecting these origins onto "barbaric," culture-bound others. But most importantly, it raises the question of whether more democratic and emancipatory rules for political belonging might emerge if we were willing to acknowledge the political character of kinship.

The emergence of the lost Canadians on the political agenda provided an opportunity for Canada to confront the politics of kinship and the meaning of national belonging. The responses included indignation, embarrassment, demonstrations of worthiness framed in terms of industriousness, and the imbrication of familial history with the tropes of Canadian national mythology. Citizenship was restored for some people and laws were amended. But aside from explorations of the consequences of specific kinship criteria, the broader question of what kinship *does* was left untouched. Of course, for such a project of interrogation to have real meaning it would need to extend beyond the borders of a single nation-state. Examining the prerogatives of membership would require some difficult thinking about the very existence of nation-states. While it seems unlikely that our commitment to our kin will disappear, we might at least begin to think about the politics of that commitment and how and whether it might be otherwise. In the next chapter, we will consider the tricky situation of political membership-as-kinship in the face of claims to belonging infused with criminality and security concerns.

6

Security and Birthright Citizenship Determination

Canada's remarkably complex history of birthright citizenship determination belies our commonsense intuition that birth in the territory or birth to a citizen parent is – or at least should be – a straightforward path to political membership. As previous chapters have demonstrated, birthright citizenship laws have been used to deny citizenship to people with robust and sustaining ties to Canada, as well as to grant citizenship to people with virtually no substantive relationship to the country but a strong claim to ancestral heritage. As evidence of the injustices of birthright citizenship denial accumulated, so did the political liabilities. Tellingly, though, the rhetorical and normative heft of these membership claims was most keenly observed in the context of (more-or-less) model Canadians: people (or the children of people) whose achievements, aspirations, and ancestry embodied the Canadian nation-state. In this chapter I turn my attention to the interaction of the rules of birthright citizenship and a host of much trickier characters: people deemed to pose a security threat due to criminality or, more rarely, treason or terrorism. While we might be aghast at the prospect of the Canadian government denying citizenship to the senior-citizen daughter of a Canadian soldier, we are, perhaps, more circumspect in the face of a foreign-born convicted murderer claiming citizenship on the basis of Canadian parentage. This conundrum succinctly demonstrates the challenge that birthright citizenship poses in a liberal democracy. On the one hand, some might argue, birthright citizenship should be automatic and inalienable;[1] on the other, and in the face of an affront to the security of the polity, one might replace duty for birthright and argue that criminal behaviour, and certainly treasonous behaviour, breaches the terms of membership.

This chapter explores two categories of security and citizenship entanglement: individuals with criminal records born abroad to a Canadian parent; and, more speculatively, dual citizens accused of treason, various terrorism-related offences, or fighting for the enemy (what was section 10 of the 2014 amendments to the *Citizenship Act*). The courts' decisions in these cases complicate the security narrative as well as the conceptualization of national threat

and belonging. In each of the cases I consider, security issues provide a rationale for prohibiting citizenship entitlement – the right to citizenship, at its
most basic level. Shifting from the liberty, privacy, and due process interests
that have generally been the focus of analysis in the security-versus-rights lit-
erature, the cases I examine, again, involve gender and marital status equality
as well as the principle of retroactive application as the basis for birthright
citizenship determination. Equality, blood, and national belonging combine
in these cases, demonstrating the power of the sovereign in a distinctive register – as limited by equality rights but also actively articulating citizenship
as a privilege, bestowed by the patron state.[2] Conceptions of foreignness and
entitlement collide with patriarchal lineage to confound Canada's national
mythology of consent-based political membership and inclusive diversity.
And despite the silencing effects rendered by appeals to "national security" – a
depoliticizing move known as "securitization" – persistent public concern with
equality and belonging has ensured an ongoing conversation about citizenship
for Canadians charged with terrorism offences.[3] Courts and governments have
certainly attempted to justify limits on equality and to reconfigure citizenship
as a privilege contingently conferred and revocable, rather than a right automatically granted once a membership claim based on birthright or naturalization has been determined. In the cases I consider, however, these efforts have
met with uneven success.[4]

Citizenship in the Security Context

As we adjust our analytical lens to foreground security and blur the rules of
birthright, it quickly becomes apparent that the subjects in focus are exotic
creatures – "bad hombres," hostile strangers, or "dangerous, internal foreigners."[5] These images reveal that threats to the nation are marked by difference,
that danger arises from something "outside" and "inauthentic," a formulation
that has the useful nation-building effect of drawing the line between "us" and
"them." As Janine Brodie observes, security discourses *produce* the nation; they
are integral to the "cultivation of the idea of a national community, and the
articulation and re-articulation of national subjectivities."[6] As security discourses express the national identity, concepts of outsiders and foreignness are
expressed and politicized by various actors, with the follow-on effect of framing
issues of democratic rule and citizenship. In other words, foreignness works as
"a site at which the anxieties of *democratic* self-rule are managed."[7] By locating
threats in the space of the foreign, and thus outside the national community,
citizens can understand themselves as secure among "their kind," as people who
are law-abiding, in contrast to risky, foreign others. And when the Canadian
government has made mistakes – misidentifying "one of us" as "one of them,"
as it did in the extraordinary rendition of Maher Arar to Syria – the country's

democratic and multicultural values have had to be very publicly and ceremonially reset.[8]

The connections among "us" are also reinforced through familial metaphors. "Homeland security," the "family" of Western nations, and the post 9/11 rendering of the Canada–US relationship as "brotherly" are iterations of connection that evoke common ancestry, ethnic homogeneity, and shared values.[9] Indeed, the processes that racialize and familialize the national "we" intensified and shifted throughout the war on terror. Canada's official discourse of multiculturalism has always overlain a hierarchy of belonging in which people of European, but especially English and French, descent claim greatest proximity to "authentic Canadianness," but this hierarchy has appeared in new forms since 2001.[10] The Conservative government of Stephen Harper, in particular, invoked a normative form of national attachment that insisted on an exemplary love for the country and that harboured a deep suspicion of those who were seen as taking advantage of Canadian citizenship. The juxtaposition of the government's treatment of the lost Canadians with the Canadians evacuated from Lebanon in 2007, who were denigrated as "citizens of convenience," provides one example of how this dynamic of belonging has played out.[11]

As I have already suggested, the interaction of security concerns (whether understood as everyday criminality or as threats to the nation-state) with the rules of birthright citizenship determination adds complexity to the meaning of the Canadian national identity. In this context, the risks posed by the incorporation of the foreign, or at least badly behaving, other within the national family collapses the distance between "them" and "us." First, the "foreign other" may, but for a technicality, be "one of us" – and not so foreign after all.[12] Second, the risks associated with that person mean that their potential citizenship could incorporate various forms of bad behaviour as part and parcel of the national family. This concern is most pronounced in the figures of the "home-grown" terrorist and, increasingly, the white supremacist, but it also tracks through serious albeit more common criminal behaviour. Thus, the confrontation between national security and birthright citizenship determination evinces a struggle between excluding real or potential risk as anathema to the national character on the one hand, and taking responsibility for all members of the community, regardless of their morality and misdeeds, on the other.

There is an additional distinction worth noting here. When citizenship and national security come together, the debate focuses on the threat posed by an organized force or set of ideas to the integrity of the nation-state as a whole. In cases involving criminality, the more specific threat, the individualized, embodied form of the human-as-criminal, determines the extent to which cultural anxieties of belonging and the national character are expressed. This distinction is especially apparent in the consequences of amendments to the *Citizenship Act* made in 2008 and in 2014. To reiterate, in 2008, amendments to the Act extended citizenship to everyone born in Canada or to a citizen parent after 1947, regardless of the sex or wedlock status of the parent. The 2014 amendments abandoned the sacredness of the 1947 bright line for the existence of Canadian citizenship. These amendments, as we have seen, affected a wide range of people, some of whom were criminals. Moreover, these amendments brought an end to adjudicative efforts to find exclusionary exceptions for some difficult cases. It seems likely that the Harper government, with its "tough on crime" ideological commitment, would have shrunk that net of inclusion if it had been legally feasible, but evidently it was not. Nonetheless, under the guise of "strengthening Canadian citizenship," the 2014 amendments focused directly on dual citizens, including birthright citizens, who committed national security offences (with the definition of those offences being, arguably, quite broad). In these cases, the affront to the state was deemed so grave as to merit revocation and exile. While that punishment was clearly to be meted out to individuals, the banishment of the human also constituted a banishment of the ideas that motivated him. In such cases, rehabilitation and reintegration were simply inconceivable. Regular criminals, then, who met the technical rules of birthright, and thus lineage, were entitled to citizenship. People with dual citizenship, including birthright citizens, who engage in terrorist activities broadly defined, however, were to find themselves on the fast track to expulsion. Audrey Macklin provides a powerful illustration of this dynamic. She notes that the 2014 amendments

> permit[ted] the Minister to revoke the Canadian citizenship of a dual citizen sentenced to five years for the *Criminal Code* offence of "providing, making available, etc., property or services for terrorist purposes." It would not, however, permit the Minister to revoke the citizenship of Canadian Forces Colonel Russell Williams, a dual citizen of Canada and Britain, who was sentenced to two concurrent life sentences for sexual assault, forcible confinement and murder of two women committed while an officer in the Canadian Armed Forces.[13]

To be clear, Macklin is not advocating for the revocation of Colonel Williams's Canadian citizenship; rather, she is observing that the distinctions between the societal harms of terrorism and other serious crimes are, perhaps, not so great after all. From that perspective then, revocation and exile (or banishment) should be off the table for anyone deemed a citizen.

As the courts have struggled with Canada's rules of birthright citizenship in the context of these security decisions, they have ultimately opted to strengthen birthright on the grounds of equality. One might read this outcome as an acknowledgment that the anomalies of the birthright provisions in Canada's *Citizenship Act* were simply errors in need of fixing. Once properly robust criteria were established, birthright would act as the straightforward means of citizenship determination that we commonly understand it to be. On the other hand, this is a very peculiar outcome when one considers that this extension of birthright happened in the context of membership determinations for some rather nefarious characters. If we think that birthright should be inclusive enough to override considerations regarding the membership suitability of badly behaving people, what is it exactly that we feel lineage does? And why does its absence (or possibly its attenuation through dual citizenship) make even law-abiding people who otherwise desire to be part of the political community more excludable? These are confounding questions in the Canadian context since we generally conceive of membership in this liberal-democratic state as non-ethnic, that is, as non-kin-based. Yet as the security examples discussed below clearly indicate, familial attachment expresses the norm of membership from which exceptions are subsequently drawn.

The remainder of the chapter examines two categories of security/citizenship encounters. The first category includes people who would be categorized as lost Canadians, with the added complexity of a criminal record. The second group, which only touched one person before the J. Trudeau Liberals revoked the law, involved a birthright Canadian with dual citizenship who had been convicted of terrorism offences. My research draws primarily from the judicial record, embellishing this discussion with material from House of Commons debates and media reporting. My findings reveal that equality arguments have been surprisingly successful in overcoming national security concerns in the context of birthright entitlement to citizenship. The larger question, though, of how it is possible to consider birthright citizenship and equality without noticing their profoundly paradoxical relationship, is markedly absent from these cases.

Criminality and Birthright

The first case I want to explore is unique among those canvassed in this volume. Rather than a demand for inclusion, the case of *Re: Drinnan*, heard in 1982, involved a failed attempt to *renounce* Canadian citizenship.[14] Eric Drinnan was born in Regina in 1950 to Canadian citizen parents. At six months of age, he was adopted by a Canadian father and an American mother and moved to the US, where he grew up, married twice (both times to an American) had two children, and enlisted in the US army. As part of his enlistment he was required to swear an oath of allegiance to the US, which, he argued before the court, included a renunciation of his Canadian citizenship. He was honourably discharged from the military in 1972. Subsequently he moved to Canada and committed a serious criminal offence that landed him in the Saskatchewan Penitentiary in Prince Albert. While confined there, he sought to be deported to the US on the grounds that he was a US citizen. Both the citizenship judge and the Federal Court judge denied Drinnan's claim of US citizenship. The US consul general in Winnipeg had provided a letter indicating that while Mr Drinnan had been adopted by an American mother and had "lived in the U.S. for an extended period, he neither entered the United States as an immigrant nor did he ever apply for naturalization as an American citizen."[15] As far as this US government official was concerned, Drinnan had been a Canadian citizen since birth, and remained so. The official did acknowledge that Drinnan's military service had included an oath of allegiance to the US, but that oath did not equate to naturalization.[16] The same official further noted that Drinnan's military service would entitle him to expeditious US naturalization but for his "present status," that is, his incarceration for a criminal offence in Canada. Ultimately, Federal Court Justice Smith held that Drinnan was not a US citizen or national, which made it impossible for him to renounce his Canadian citizenship, since he had no other citizenship to claim.

The arid text of this judgment – unlike *Benner* discussed below, for example – provides no sense as to whether the Canadian state might have been interested in pursuing Drinnan's deportation. The Americans were certainly clear that they would not be extending a generous interpretation of their citizenship laws to include him. Moreover, the court record omits a lot of important details. We do not know *why* Drinnan wanted to renounce his Canadian citizenship, nor do we know the nature of his crime. Nonetheless, the court's refusal to grant Drinnan's renunciation illuminates a number of complex features surrounding birthright citizenship and the significance of statelessness. How is it that the Canadian state finds itself claiming Drinnan as a member when he has spent the majority of his adult life in the US (residence), served in the US military, swearing allegiance to the United States in the process (connection), and, in addition to committing a serious crime in Canada, clearly does not wish to be a Canadian? It is only the happenstance of his birth in Canada to Canadian parents – parents to whom he has had no connection since his infancy and whose ties to him were severed through adoption proceedings – that makes him a Canadian. And these birth criteria subsequently oblige the Canadian state to uphold his membership, since the polity of his choosing will not acknowledge his membership claim – again, despite an adoptive American mother, American wives and children, and US military service – because his criminal act in Canada marks him as unworthy of belonging to the US state. Because the US will not claim him, Canada cannot abandon him, regardless of his expressed desire to quit the Canadian polity. Even if one does not want to be a member, there is no leaving without a place to go.

Is this any way to run a political community? Advocates of birthright citizenship might argue that Drinnan's situation is the exception that proves the rule. After all, statelessness is among the gravest of human situations – it is to be without status. In the absence of the broad membership principles of birthright, states could exercise an excessive selectivity, leaving vast populations without representation, rights, or entitlements. But if the lack of state membership is, indeed, such an unconscionable way of being in the world, then why offer birthright citizenship as the solution? To do so is to invoke a fetish of the innocence of infants and a familial logic of eternal forgiveness that beg the question rather than answering it. If the political community is prepared to accept everyone with a lineage or territorial birth claim (in all their specificities), regardless of their interest in the polity itself, why not be open to people with an interest but *no* birth claim?

In many ways, the case of Richard Bell provides a mirror image to that of Eric Drinnan. Heard more than a decade later, *Bell v. Canada (Minister of Employment and Immigration)* (1994, 1996) involved a man born in Australia in 1960, out of wedlock to an Australian mother and a Canadian father.[17] He came to Canada with his mother in 1967, and his biological parents married in 1968. He was granted permanent residence in 1968. In 1971, his biological father adopted him, a process required at the time in order to legitimize the child under Alberta's *Child Welfare Act*.[18] Bell's father did not subsequently register the child's birth for the purposes of obtaining Canadian citizenship, believing, presumably, that the adoption itself would have achieved this outcome. Bell's citizenship then came into question when he ran afoul of the law and was ordered deported by the Immigration and Refugee Board in 1985. A series of stays were granted, but in 1992, the stay was cancelled due to Bell's breach of conditions, including a subsequent conviction for dangerous driving and failure to attend court.[19] Bell then appealed the IRB's order on the grounds that he was not deportable, for he was a Canadian citizen rather than the permanent resident the IRB had determined him to be.

The trial court agreed with Bell. In a rather idiosyncratic reading of the wedlock provisions of the *Citizenship Act,* and disregarding precedent (*qua Chute*), the court found that regardless of wedlock status, a child born to a Canadian father *or* mother was a Canadian.[20] Moreover, the judge ruled, Bell was also entitled to citizenship by reason of his adoption, through which "his birth was legitimized and his adoptive father was a Canadian citizen."[21] The judge came to this conclusion by virtue of her reading of the *Citizenship Act* rather than her interpretation of Alberta's *Child Welfare Act*. Regarding the Alberta law, she found that adoption rendered a child a "legitimate and natural or 'birth' child of his Father" but that contrary to Bell's argument, the legal fiction that turned adoptive parents into natural parents did not extend to transforming Australia into Canada – it did not "address the child's birthplace or confer citizenship."[22] However, because Bell had a Canadian father, both when he was born out of wedlock and when he was adopted, he was entitled to become a Canadian citizen as of 15 February 1977. The adoption provisions of the *Child Welfare Act* could not make a *jus soli* citizen out of a child born abroad, but the *Citizenship Act* could identify a Canadian father and – by virtue of Canadian parentage expressed through the legal processes of adoption and thus legitimation – a *jus sanguinis* (blood-based) citizen.

Unsurprisingly, the Federal Court of Appeal had a different interpretation. In the absence of a *Charter* argument that might have required some consideration of the gender discrimination surrounding parentage and citizenship determination, Justice Strayer (interestingly, himself an architect of the *Charter*) held that Bell's birth out of wedlock meant he had no birthright claim to Canadian citizenship.[23] Citizenship was strictly a matter of federal jurisdiction. As Justice Strayer noted, "the requirements of the Citizenship Act as to place of birth and status of the parents at the time of birth are very specific, and cannot be read to incorporate subsequent changes of status prescribed by provincial laws for provincial purposes."[24] The appeal was thus allowed, and Richard Bell, despite his long-established Canadian life, including a Canadian wife and child, and only weak ties to Australia, was deemed subject to deportation. The technicalities of the citizenship rules – technicalities whose inequities had been recognized and corrected in law two decades prior to Bell's hearing in the Federal Court of Appeal – nonetheless provided the court with an additional and potent sanction against the criminal behaviour of a person whose circumstances of birth (timing, marital and citizenship status of parents, location) could be used to mark him as a non-member.

For Drinnan and Bell then, birth and criminality imposed strict limits on their political membership. Drinnan couldn't leave and Bell couldn't stay.

Benner – Dangerous, Married Canadian Mothers

The ability of the court to draw on the opportunities presented by the non-retroactivity of the *Citizenship Act* to enhance the potency of criminal sanctions for certain precariously situated people began to weaken with the Supreme Court's decision in the case of *Benner*.[25] Mark Benner was born in 1962 in the United States. His mother was Canadian and his father was American. Benner was separated from his parents in childhood and eventually located his mother in Toronto in 1986.[26] According to the Federal Court of Appeal, Benner lived in Canada under at least two pseudonyms, he had committed a number of serious crimes, and at the time his citizenship case was heard in Federal Court, he was serving a prison sentence for manslaughter.[27] He was deported prior to receiving a positive decision from the Supreme Court of Canada in 1997.

Unlike Bell's, Benner's citizenship argument made use of the equality provisions of section 15 of the *Charter*. Benner conceded that he was not born a Canadian citizen, as was clear from the terms of the 1947 *Citizenship Act* that pertained at the time of his birth. Nonetheless, he was entitled to apply for citizenship through the provision in the 1977 Act (section 5(2)(b)) that enabled persons born abroad before 15 February 1977 to be granted citizenship on the basis of

the Canadian citizenship of their mother, on application. He made this application in 1987. The equality issue arose because people who claimed citizenship
through a Canadian father did not have to undergo a security check or swear an
oath, whereas those applying on the basis of their mother's Canadian citizenship did have to undertake these additional requirements.[28] Not surprisingly,
given Benner's colourful criminal history, his application was rejected because
he failed the security check.

Benner's equality argument did not persuade the justices of the Federal Court
and the Federal Court of Appeal. In denying Benner's application, the justices
offered a variety of reasons, the most significant being either that section 15 did
not apply to an act that predated the *Charter* (no retroactive or retrospective
application) and that had, in any event, corrected the discriminatory treatment
for people born after 15 February 1977; or that the violation of section 15 equality rights performed by the *Citizenship Act* could, nonetheless, be saved by section 1 of the *Charter* as a reasonable limit on rights and as being "demonstrably
justified in a free and democratic society."[29] Other, more contorted reasons for
denying Benner's equality argument included Justice Marceau's argument that
there was no discrimination based on sex in 1947 and that the law's provisions
were simply a reflection of contemporary attitudes.[30] And even if one conceded
that there was sex discrimination, that discrimination affected the parents, not
the child.[31] Both sons and daughters of Canadian mothers married to foreign
fathers were treated the same way. Following this logic, and since a third party
could not bring a claim for discrimination, Mark Benner lacked standing. For
the lower courts, Mr Benner's criminal record and the risk he thus posed to
Canadians were sufficiently egregious to override the broader gender equality
issue. As Justice Letourneau witheringly summarized Benner's claim, the appel-
lant "submits that criminals born outside of Canada to a married Canadian
mother ought to be treated in the same way as criminals born outside of Canada
to a Canadian father. These criminals ought to be granted citizenship and you
cannot grant it to one category, those with a paternal link, and not to the others
who have a maternal link."[32]

The Federal Court of Appeal decision in *Benner* also offers a brief survey
of the legislative rationales for distinguishing between Canadian mothers and
Canadian fathers in the provisions offering this grant of citizenship to people
born outside of Canada between 1 January 1947 and 14 February 1977. In short,
the oath and security requirements would aid in establishing allegiance to Canada, thereby ensuring the security of the nation and the safety of the people.[33]
Justice Linden conceded that, while it would have been preferable to apply the
oath and security check to children of Canadian men as well, to do so would
have derogated from existing rights.[34] In a classic articulation of negative liberty,
Linden asserted that the integrity of the liberal-democratic state is upheld when
the law maximizes the freedom of individuals rather than mandating a pledge

of fealty and expectations of good behaviour, however salutary those expressions might be. And adding a bit of patriarchal icing to that liberal-democratic confection, Justice Linden nonetheless maintained that the distinction between maternal and paternal lineage "was not a significant incursion into the equality rights of [maternal lineage claimants], but it allowed the government to pursue the pressing and substantial objectives of the relevant provisions of the *Citizenship Act*."[35]

Justice Letourneau also examined the parliamentary record to explain the decision to draw a line between people born before and after 15 February 1977. In Letourneau's reading, Parliament had chosen to respect the national, international, and individual implications of retroactive legislation:[36]

> For instance, one could lose his foreign nationality if his country of origin did not allow its nationals to have a double nationality. One could avoid compulsory military service. In other words, one could be relieved of duties imposed by his country of origin or could become, by virtue of a new nationality imposed upon him, subject to all kinds of obligations that he does not necessarily want.[37]

As noted in chapter 4, however, the record of committee discussions clearly indicates that public servants rather than legislators were more keenly attuned to the legal principle of non-retroactivity. In any event, this set of considerations represents a telling conflation of birthright and consent-based conceptions of citizenship. According to Letourneau, the retroactive awarding of citizenship would be imposed without choice – although one can also imagine a provision, rather like the one under consideration in the case at bar – in which people could choose to apply for that citizenship or not. But Letourneau also observed that law emerges out of custom and consent.[38] This observation would seem to raise the question as to why membership in a polity, and particularly a democratic polity, is a matter of status and imposition rather than purposeful agreement, individual choice, and consent. Yet Letourneau did not entertain this question, opting instead to regard Benner as an alien and hence subject to the choices of the sovereign.

In weighing the balance between equality and security in Canadian citizenship law, Canada's Federal Courts, even in the 1990s, clearly held that security was a more significant virtue. The justices of the Supreme Court, by contrast, regarded Benner's equality claim rather more favourably and overturned the lower courts' rulings. The Supreme Court dismissed the argument regarding retrospective application, holding instead that the 1977 *Citizenship Act* had contemporary effects and thus that Mr Benner's situation did involve a rightful *Charter* claim.[39] The critical time was not when the person *acquired* a particular status but rather when that status was held against that person or disentitled the person to a benefit.[40] The Supreme Court also rejected the argument that the discrimination in the *Citizenship Act* did not apply to the children of Canadian mothers married to foreign husbands, with Justice Iacobucci stating that Mark Benner was the primary target of the sex-based discrimination and thus that he possessed the necessary standing to raise it.[41] In Justice Iacobucci's judgment, it did not matter whether historical circumstance or gender stereotypes provided the rationale for the differential treatment of the children of Canadian mothers and Canadian fathers, since the ultimate effect of the legislation was "to suggest that, at least in some cases, men and women are not equally capable of passing on whatever it takes to be a good Canadian citizen. In fact, it suggests that children of Canadian mothers may be more dangerous than those of Canadian fathers, since only the latter are required to undergo an oath and security check."[42] This concern, it might be noted, aligns with the anxiety about the potential citizenship demands of unwed foreign women and their children, who, as we saw in *Taylor*, also inspired some of the thinking behind the non-retroactive effect of the 1977 *Citizenship Act*. Clearly the reproductive and thus citizenship-producing activities of women abroad, Canadian or foreign, was a site of regulatory angst.

Having established that the sex-differentiated entitlement to pass on one's citizenship constituted a violation of equality rights, the Supreme Court could have, as Justice Linden did in the Federal Court of Appeal, nonetheless decided that the security interests of the Canadian nation constituted a reasonable limit on those rights. The Supreme Court did not take this view. While the justices acknowledged that the security and national allegiance objectives of the legislation were pressing and substantial, they did not see an inherent connection between these objectives and the discriminatory means used to realize them.[43] In particular, the justices were unmoved by the argument surrounding the negative effects of retroactive entitlement to citizenship, not only because it was unclear why this effect would be worse for children of Canadian mothers than children of Canadian fathers, or than for children born after 1977 regardless of their Canadian parentage, but also because citizenship based on lineage has never been imposed automatically.[44] Rather, a parent could choose whether or not to register the birth of a foreign-born child with Canada. The Supreme Court justices also noted that their decision could have re-established gender equality by imposing the security check and oath on all applicants, regardless of the sex of their Canadian parent. Ultimately though, because a security check and oath were not required of people born after 1977, the Court felt that the chosen path of abolishing the requirements interfered "far less with the overall legislative scheme introduced by Parliament."[45]

At the level of the Supreme Court, one would not expect concern with the details of Mr Benner's particular bad behaviours, since the Court's interest lies with the principles of the law rather than the facts of the case. Undoubtedly Mark Benner did not fit the model of the ideal citizen, but in the broader context of Canada's national values of citizenship and how that status should be acquired, the democratic principles that governed the law of lineage rather than Benner's personal virtues and vices were what mattered. One might note again, the perverse imbrication of democracy and birthright that makes it possible to craft the sentence "the democratic principles that govern the law of lineage."

Augier – Danger and Unwed Canadian Fathers (Redux)

While *Benner* mobilized the *Charter* to contest the security provisions required of foreign-born children of married Canadian women to establish their citizenship, the case of *Augier v. Canada (Minister of Citizenship and Immigration)* revisited the capacity of unwed Canadian men who had children with foreign women to pass on their citizenship. *Augier,* heard in 2004, involved a request for judicial review of a refusal to grant citizenship to Gideon (Glenn) McGuire Augier, born in 1966 in St Lucia to a St Lucian mother and a Canadian father.[46] Since Augier's parents were unmarried, he was not entitled to Canadian citizenship. Augier moved to Canada in 1970 as a permanent resident and has lived in Canada ever since. His application for a grant of citizenship was denied in October 2001. In responding to the request for judicial review, the Federal Court held that the immigration officer had been correct in denying citizenship to Augier, but also found that the relevant section of the *Citizenship Act* (section 5) violated the equality guarantees of section 15 of the *Charter* by discriminating on the basis of marital status and gender (in this case, the fact that Augier's unmarried father could not pass on his citizenship), and thus that these provisions were unconstitutional.[47]

The outcome of this review was relatively predictable, given that it took place with *Benner* as precedent, but it might also be noted that the case was heard during the intensified national security regime of the post-9/11 moment. Moreover, Augier's criminal involvement was at least as brightly hued as Benner's. Indeed, Augier had been convicted of fraud, he was a suspected member of a forgery ring, and he acknowledged his involvement with Russian organized crime in running immigration scams in Belarus, Ukraine, and Russia.[48] And in 2008, when a Canadian investigative news program began examining Mr Augier's rich background several years after the Federal Court ruling, his father's identity also appeared to be in question.[49] Nonetheless, in the strict terms of the constitutionality of Canada's *Citizenship Act*, the Federal Court held that Augier should be entitled to claim citizenship on the basis of his father's Canadian citizenship and regardless of his parents' marital status. It would be up to a new citizenship officer to determine whether the evidence supporting the identity of Augier's father was sufficiently persuasive.

Since *Augier* established that the marital status distinction in the *Citizenship Act* was unconstitutional, how do we make sense of the Federal Court of

Appeal's subsequent decision in *Taylor* discussed in chapter 3? In that case, the court distinguished both *Benner* and *Augier*, holding that the application of the *Charter* to legislation that had been repealed (the 1947 *Citizenship Act*) would give the *Charter* retrospective effect that it cannot have, and that, even if Taylor was defined as a Canadian citizen under the 1947 Act, he was subject to its loss provisions, having lived outside of Canada for six years and not having registered his intention to maintain his Canadian citizenship by the age of twenty-four.[50]

Legislative Fixes

The courts' rulings in *Benner* and *Augier* did trigger some political efforts to amend Canada's citizenship legislation, although tellingly, security concerns continued to shadow the discussion. In 2004, under the minority Liberal government of Paul Martin, an opposition-sponsored private member's bill was passed that restored citizenship to yet another category of "lost Canadians" – people born in Canada whose "responsible parent" took out citizenship in another country between 1947 and 1977. As discussed in the previous chapter, minor children acquired the new citizenship of their fathers, if their parents were married, or their mothers, if their parents were not married. Prior to amendment, the *Citizenship Act* required citizenship applicants in this category to reside in Canada for one year and undergo security and criminal checks. The amendment dispensed with these safeguards, providing an automatic right to citizenship.[51] Given that the debate surrounding the bill took place in the wake of the *Benner* decision, and in clear sight of the prospect that dubious characters could lay claim to Canadian citizenship, it is intriguing that the bill's sponsor, a Member of Parliament from a notoriously "tough on crime" political party, dismissed the security concerns as "scaremongering."[52] By contrast, the Parliamentary Secretary to the Minister of Citizenship and Immigration expressed concerns about the lack of safeguards for medical inadmissibility, the lack of need to show a demonstrated commitment to Canada, the risks of permitting hardened criminals to enter Canada after a long absence, and the necessity for heightened scrutiny of citizenship applicants "in this day of border security and … the alliances of people with certain groups."[53] Despite these objections, the bill passed.

The inadequacy and inconsistencies in Canada's rules of birthright citizenship came to a head in the lead-up to the imposition of the passport requirements of the Western Hemisphere Travel Initiative (WHTI). As of 1 June 2007, Canadians and Americans have been required to produce passports, rather than drivers' licences or birth certificates, in order to cross their shared border. In the process of applying for those documents, many people discovered that their long presumed Canadian citizenship was in question. And, not surprisingly, most of these people, and certainly those profiled in the media and who appeared before the Parliamentary Standing Committee on Citizenship and Immigration, were fine, upstanding characters with an admirable love for Canada. Some of these people were categorized as "Benner babies," referring to their exclusion from Canadian citizenship through the same rule that had affected Mark Benner, but the reference certainly did not extend to the criminal dimensions of his case. The public incredulity that emerged around these "lost Canadians" finally compelled the Conservative government of Stephen Harper to implement more thorough-going amendments to the *Citizenship Act*, including, as discussed earlier, the elimination of the 1947–77 category of citizenship and the reinstatement of citizenship for anyone born in Canada, or to citizen parents, who had not personally renounced their citizenship. And with regard to the risk of "what might be swept up" into the Canadian fold as a consequence, the Parliamentary Committee's report on the matter offered a laudable and logical perspective:

> The Committee is of the view that lost Canadians who have a significant attachment to Canada should not be subjected to [security] checks at all as a precondition to being granted citizenship ... It would be consistent with the idea that granting citizenship to lost Canadians is about correcting their status to reflect that these people have been Canadians all along, as opposed to looking at them as new candidates for citizenship. If any lost Canadian with a significant connection to Canada is a criminal or a security threat, that person should be viewed, morally speaking, as a Canadian criminal or security threat.[54]

In short, the birthright rules of membership in the Canadian state, that is, in the Canadian national family, meant that the shortcomings and inadequacies of particular family members would simply have to be accepted.

Border Towns

The remaining case in the category of lost Canadian criminals is that of Robert Clark. Clark's family lived in a small town in Manitoba near the Canada–US border. Since the nearest maternity ward was on the American side, Robert Clark was born in the US. Clark, born in June 1947, had spent his entire life in Canada, and his parents were "natural born" Canadians, but his conviction for drug possession and trafficking resulted in an investigation of his citizenship status. When it was discovered, in 2006, by an official of the Canadian Border Services Agency (CBSA), that Clark's birth had not been registered in Canada, the official issued a deportation order.[55] Clark then made a successful request that the deportation order be stayed, pending an application for judicial review of his citizenship status.[56] Robert Clark's siblings faced the same citizenship difficulties, but when the family's story became public, the Minister of Citizenship and Immigration offered his brothers a special grant of citizenship. Clark's situation was undoubtedly aided by the media attention that was focused on the lost Canadians at the time that his deportation order was issued. And indeed, the report on the lost Canadians published by the Parliamentary Standing Committee on Citizenship and Immigration explicitly mentioned Robert Clark's situation, stating that deportation was for *foreign* criminals.[57] By contrast,

> Mr. Clark, and others like him, are Canadians in every sense other than the purely legal. The Committee believes that it is unfair for the government to take advantage of a legal anomaly, which denied him citizenship. It is unfair to Mr. Clark who is suffering twice for his crime – punished by the criminal court in proportion to his crime, and now facing indefinite banishment from his home of 60 years. And it is unfair to the United States, whose connection with Mr. Clark was random, fleeting and should remain inconsequential.[58]

Telling here is the committee's statement: "in every sense other than the purely legal." What, after all, would it mean to be a Canadian in any sense other than the legal one? The standing committee's statement invokes a Canadian ethnicity and a claim to lineage that may strike many Canadians as odd, given the widespread preoccupation with a purported lack of national identity that is common among those who comfortably inhabit normative Canadian-ness. But regardless of the various contradictions in Canada's civic *cum* ethnic nationalism, the committee's broader point that the Canadian government should not be relying on highly contested technicalities to deport people whose character is not to the government's liking is certainly valid. Birthright citizenship law is a very blunt tool for the management of crime and national security. Clark's situation was finally resolved when the *Citizenship Act* was amended in 2008. As a person born after 1 January 1947 to citizen parents, Robert Clark was automatically entitled to Canadian citizenship, without a security check, upon application.

The Terror of Dual Citizens

The second category of security and citizenship – dual citizens convicted of terrorism-related offences – has primarily been considered in Parliament and in academic and public debate, with only one person, Zakaria Amara, having had his citizenship revoked on these grounds. Amara's citizenship was subsequently reinstated when the terrorism provisions were repealed in 2017. The contours of the discussion highlight important fault lines in the debate over the meaning of citizenship – as an inalienable right or a revocable privilege. In Canada's 2015 election, the Liberal Party's insistence that "a citizen, is a citizen is a citizen" triumphed over the Conservatives' position that the worst kind of people (dual citizens convicted of terrorism) forfeit their citizenship. Less well-appreciated, however, is that the overwhelming majority of the security cases engaging citizenship considerations – indeed, virtually all cases of contested citizenship – play out on grounds of whether a person is a citizen in the first instance, rather than whether their lawfully obtained citizenship should be revoked.[59] Canadian governments, be they Liberal or Conservative, seemingly have no qualms about challenging the existence of citizenship status – naturalized or birthright – as a prosecutorial and bureaucratic strategy.[60] Nonetheless, for people facing a challenge to their Canadian citizenship, there is little to distinguish between "citizenship granted in error" and "revocation." The experience of loss of status is the same. For these people, "a Canadian, is a Canadian is a Canadian" misses the point altogether.

My argument throughout this book has been that birthright citizenship appears to confer an unassailable claim to political belonging, but that when we look at the evidence it turns out that birth, blood, and kinship are the product of rules, which are subject to interpretation. It is this interpretive effort that is engaged in contestations over the existence of citizenship and that we have considered thus far. Revocation, at least as a process, is different. It begins from the shared understanding that citizenship exists and then determines whether delineated grounds for removal from the political community have been met. This is a sharply defined issue of whether a state can disavow those it once claimed, whether the manner of one's citizenship acquisition affects vulnerability to disavowal (naturalized vs birthright; dual citizens vs sole citizens), and what grounds would trigger such a disavowal. And it was onto this terrain that the Conservative government of Stephen Harper chose to march in its insistence that citizenship is a privilege rather than a right.

The *Strengthening Canadian Citizenship Act* (Bill C-24) envisioned citizenship revocation for dual citizens who were convicted of

- treason or high treason under section 47 of the *Criminal Code*;
- a terrorism offence as defined in section 2 of the *Criminal Code* (This section includes offences such as financing or participating in a terrorist group, including leaving Canada to participate, facilitating an activity, giving instructions, or harbouring someone likely to commit a terrorist activity);
- aiding the enemy, in battle or as a prisoner of war; *and/or*
- espionage or communicating safeguarded or operational information.[61]

Notably, and especially in light of the government's arguments against retroactivity in *Taylor*, these provisions *were* retroactive. Indeed, as we will see below, they seemed purposefully designed to apply to members of the Toronto 18, a rather hapless terrorist cell that had planned to detonate three fertilizer bombs in downtown Toronto in the summer of 2006. Moreover, except when it came to adjudicating a situation in which the person charged had served in an armed force fighting against Canada, the authority for revocation lay solely with the minister, having given notice and received written representations.[62] In the situation of armed conflict, the minister was obliged to seek a Federal Court declaration confirming that the person had served in an enemy service; that declaration would then constitute the citizenship revocation.[63] As a result of revocation, the person would be deemed a foreign national but could not be rendered stateless. Canada's obligations under international law meant that even people who had been convicted of the most egregious offences to the polity had to be guaranteed political membership, regardless of what the Conservatives might have desired. But if, in the end, Canada had to claim them, traitorous terrorists would first have to demonstrate that they held no other citizenship. The onus of proving statelessness rested with the person making the claim.[64]

These provisions provoked considerable debate and conjecture about their constitutionality. Equality of citizenship was a central concern in this debate, and more precisely that Canadians with an additional nationality should be treated the same way as single-nationality Canadians. At the time, Craig Forcese noted that the Conservatives had not amended the equality-of-citizenship provision in section 6 of the *Citizenship Act,* which guarantees equal treatment to all Canadians whether they were born in Canada or not. This set up an incoherence in the law, since dual- and single-nationality citizens would be treated differently. Read through a different lens, the section 6 equality guarantee meant that both birthright Canadians and naturalized Canadians with dual citizenship could have their Canadian citizenship stripped from them. Yet practically, the vast majority of dual citizens were, in fact, people who were born outside of Canada and had obtained their Canadian citizenship through naturalization.[65] Using figures from 2011, Forcese observed that "subjecting everyone with dual nationality to the possibility of revocation of citizenship would single out 2.9% of the population for a special peril, and more than three quarters of those people are new Canadians."[66] Moreover, many of those new immigrants are racialized. In the especially charged context of terrorism and its association with Islamic extremism, the Conservatives' revocation provisions reinforced Islamophobia.

The Conservative government's hostility to Muslim immigrants, and its particular instantiation in the revocation provisions of the *Citizenship Act,* were boldly illustrated during the 2015 federal election. The Conservative campaign emphasized the party's commitment to a narrow, homogenizing version of Canadian values. Their platform included a proposal to establish a "barbaric cultural practices tip line" through which presumably "old stock," well-behaving Canadians could snitch on the "foreign" behaviour of their presumably new and racialized neighbours. The implementation of the revocation provisions of the newly amended *Citizenship Act* further advanced this political strategy. In journalist Paul Wells's recounting, the Harper government was spurred to act after a campaign speech in which Liberal rival Justin Trudeau unequivocally stated his intention to repeal the revocation provisions and other contested elements of Bill C-24 upon election, emphasizing the unfairness of revocation through ministerial fiat.[67] Trudeau had insisted that "the idea of imposing a radically different penalty, depending on whether or not your family was born in Canada or not, goes completely against a rule of law and a respect for justice that I know Canadians expect."[68] Trudeau acknowledged the egregiousness of the behaviour that the revocation provisions addressed but insisted that severe consequences already existed for people who committed terrorism or acts of war against Canada. A penalty that relied on the creation of two classes of citizenship was, in Trudeau's view, un-Canadian.[69] Healthy applause greeted Trudeau's remarks, but according to Wells, "hours after Trudeau spoke, Zakaria Amara became the first Canadian to have his citizenship revoked under the auspices of Bill C-24."[70]

In Wells's view, the timing of the revocation was no accident, and it was especially bold because of the well-established practice that governments refrain from significant political decisions during election campaigns.[71] Removing Amara's Canadian citizenship became a means to up the ante in a hard-fought electoral contest. The Conservatives imagined that twinning its hard line on revocation with the figure of the terrorist plotting to detonate bombs in Canada's largest city would be unassailable in political debate, yet Trudeau managed to pivot from this dog whistle to underscore Canadians' commitment to multiculturalism and to brand the Harper Conservatives as fear-mongering. Ultimately, Trudeau's "sunny ways" won the day.

And what of Zakaria Amara himself? In 2006, when he was arrested for plotting an elaborate terrorist scheme to detonate three bombs in downtown Toronto, he was twenty years old, a husband and father.[72] The objective of this scheme was to provoke the Canadian government to remove its troops from Afghanistan. Born in Jordan and having immigrated to Canada as a youth, Amara had had little success in post-secondary education; he was working at a gas station and had become obsessed with *jihad*.[73] He would eventually recruit seventeen other people to assist him with his plans, but virtually from the outset, the group was infiltrated by law enforcement agents. Throughout the planning, training, and acquiring of materials, the group's actions were known, and often directed, by those agents.[74] And while eighteen people were initially charged, only four men were ultimately convicted. Amara pled guilty and was sentenced to life in prison.

Amara was not an especially skilled terrorist; that said, his plans were elaborate and lethal. But the psychiatric report included in the court record also reveals a young man deeply remorseful for his actions and for the damage he had done to his family and community. Was his regret sincere? Does personal remorse matter in a context framed by an ideological/religious threat to national security? Perhaps not, but it does point to an underlying humanity that the Harper government was simply unwilling to countenance and that is almost definitionally absent from discussions of terrorism. With the tool of revocation in hand and an election in the balance, revoking Amara's citizenship was a strategic card to play, a symbolic eviction of the ideas of the Islamic state from Canada. The Conservatives were only too anxious to play it. And therein lies the cautionary tale for a law of revocation. As critics argued, the severe consequences of removing a person's citizenship should require strict procedural safeguards, and preferably the constitutional protection of due process. Mere ministerial discretion or an unappealable court order place disproportionate power in the hands of the state without appropriate protections for the affected party. Because revocation is not a criminal penalty, in that it does not confer a fine or a direct form of imprisonment, it has not been regarded as requiring the same legal safeguards for the person facing the action. Nonetheless, as Craig Forcese argues, when revocation becomes a consequence for various criminal activities (beyond fraud in its acquisition), it crosses into the domain of the punitive, and that is certainly how revocation was envisioned in Bill C-24.[75] In such circumstances, Forcese continues, the courts may find that revocation serves as a punishment designed to redress "the wrong done to society at large" and thus requiring the protections of section 11 of the *Charter* – the presumption of innocence, the right to a fair and public trial before an independent tribunal.[76] This punitive consequence could also trigger rights guarantees surrounding the onus of proof and the unfairness of placing the burden of proving statelessness on the person facing revocation. In short, if revocation is included in a state's citizenship laws, significant safeguards are necessary to ensure that its use is highly constrained.

One further issue here, and one that also applies to people who are found to have held their Canadian citizenship in error, is that if deportation follows from revocation, there has to be a receiving state. It is difficult to fathom what would induce a country to accept a convicted terrorist and whether Canada could be assured that the person whom they were deporting would not be subject to additional forms of punishment that Canada otherwise decries in various international forums. Whether it should be possible for the state to cast out a citizen whose acts have grievously harmed the political community is not easily resolved. At a minimum, the answer to that question requires a sustained debate in which political point-scoring is not the central motivation for the law.

Conclusion

The Canadian case law and the political debate that unites birthright citizenship and security display a complex dynamic of claims and resistance to belonging, as well as instrumentalism and principled commitments to equality. As the cases I have discussed demonstrate, the courts and Parliament have struggled to resolve the tensions this dynamic creates, sometimes insisting that democratic values be moderated in light of national security concerns, and sometimes insisting that national security can only be realized if those democratic values are fortified. It is important to emphasize that the applicability of equality arguments to national membership is only obvious, if unevenly determinative, for birthright claims to citizenship. The power of the sovereign to determine the state of exception, and thus to compromise liberal rights, is fully operational in Canada's interactions with immigrants and refugees.

The Canadian state understands its social responsibility to punish and rehabilitate "its own," but this dynamic involves a process of reintegration that sustains the reliance on an inside/outside logic. That said, while Canada does not exile its criminal nationals (or at least, not currently), the Canadian government has worked assiduously to deny citizenship to incarcerated individuals when contested cases emerge, and it regularly deports long-time permanent residents with criminal convictions. When the opportunity to disavow membership presents itself, the Canadian state is enticed to seize it. Birth and blood do provide security against that enticement when birthright can be established, but in the challenges to security of citizenship, we see a deeper truth: that political membership is fundamental to our capacity to act in the contemporary world. Ultimately, we determine the terms of membership. The easy association of birth criteria with a kind of natural inevitability may assist in reinforcing the strength of a birthright claim, but only as long as we agree that it has that power and that this protective quality of birthright citizenship is worth the related harms – around exclusion, inequality, racism, and sexism – to which it also gives rise. If we refocus our lens from the (false) solidity of birth criteria to the fundamental significance of political membership, it may be possible to envision security *with* inclusion.

7

Reproductive Technologies and "Maternity Tourism"[1]: *Jus sanguinis* and *Jus soli* Redux

Babies: innocent, vulnerable, full of potential; the embodiment of national futurity. They are the hope and promise of all that we might be, the latent solution to the messes we have created, or inherited and failed to fix. Babies are, as Conservative Minister of Citizenship and Immigration Monte Solberg, once stated, "clean slates."[2] While all of the cases in this book so far have engaged situations of *jus sanguinis* and *jus soli* birthright citizenship claims, this chapter focuses on two timely contexts in which the political debates surrounding the worthiness of children to be citizens – as distinct from adults with birthright citizenship claims – have almost nothing to do with the children themselves. Instead, the focus is on the identity, behaviour, and intentions of their parents. For children born abroad to Canadian citizen parents with the assistance of reproductive technologies, and children born on Canadian soil to non-citizen parents, political concern is focused on assessing (potential) connection to the nation-state. In the absence of a capacity to demonstrate that connection directly, kinship serves as a proxy, though in different and sometimes paradoxical ways. Until July 2020, children born abroad with the assistance of reproductive technologies had to have a genetic/biological relationship to a Canadian parent in order to be considered Canadian, even when the genetic donors were anonymous. Connection, in these cases, is in the blood. Birth in the territory is supposed to do similar work. That is, children born on Canadian soil, regardless of the citizenship status of their parents, are Canadians unless their parents work for a foreign government and enjoy diplomatic immunity.[3] Yet increased attention on foreign women giving birth in Canada has led to concerns about "maternity tourists," whose lack of connection to Canada and presumptively self-serving motivations are alleged to undermine the meaning and integrity of Canadian citizenship. Class politics, racism, and sexism combine to define foreign and non-resident mothers who give birth in Canada as immigration queue jumpers who are gaming the system by acquiring a birthright insurance policy in the form of their children. Tainted kinship thus renders these children unworthy of Canadian citizenship, despite their birth on the soil.

Considering the citizenship of actual babies, in contrast to the citizenship of the now adult progeny of Canadian soldiers and other mobile Canadians, and criminals (who were once babies),[4] shines an especially bright light on the deep contradictions of birthright citizenship in consent-based liberal democracies. On the one hand, birth offers the promise of a clear and simple entitlement to citizenship. If you meet the criteria, you acquire citizenship; there is no consent, no demonstration of worthiness. You are a human, born under certain conditions, and citizenship results. Yet when the opportunity presents itself, we cannot resist the invitation to demand more. In situations in which "nature" does not provide cover for the law's work in making families, parentage must be determined, giving rise to opportunities for judgment. Are the parents genuinely connected to Canada, and thus worthy? Do they "belong"? Are they seeking an advantage for their children that is somehow too crass, too instrumental, for a "proper" citizen? What burdens will these children and their relatives impose on Canada? Does Canada's *jus soli* citizenship acquisition undermine the integrity of Canadian citizenship altogether? Birthright citizenship protects against quixotic political decisions, until it doesn't; equality rights guaranteed by the rule of law are challenged by judgments of worthiness and ensuing privilege. Ultimately, debates around citizenship determination for children in these circumstances circulate around the morality, motivations, and affiliations of the parents and/or a desire for procedural simplicity.

These debates offer yet another opportunity – related to but distinct from those encountered in previous chapters – to consider the relationship between political membership and kinship. As elsewhere, these adjudications are entwined with understandings of race, gender, and class, often paradoxical and heavy with selective amnesia. Clearly, a secure citizenship is centrally important to human dignity, to the capacity to function in the contemporary world. Birthright citizenship provides the promise of security, but as I have been at pains to point out, and will argue here again, that promise is illusory.

Citizenship, Babies, and Reproductive Technologies

Parentage is centrally important to the determination of *jus sanguinis,* or derivative, citizenship. And while we generally envision that assignation to be straightforward – that biology does the work and the law reflects biology – it turns out that the situation is more complicated. In fact, the law makes parents. Prior to the advent of genetic testing, the formal status of marriage and husband served as a proxy for biological proof of paternity. This delineation reflects the widespread legal principle (in the English common law tradition, in the Napoleonic Code, and in Sharia law) that a husband is the father to any children of his marriage (*pater est quem nuptia demonstrant* – father is to whom marriage points).[5] The law has historically been less concerned with defining mothers, since birth itself was seen to do the work. Thus, while men needed the law to bring them into a parental relationship with children, women became mothers naturally.

Canadian law has variably conferred citizenship depending on one's relationship to legitimacy – whether one's Canadian parent was a married father or an unmarried mother. And, as we have seen with the illegitimate children of Canadian soldiers in particular, the state has used this framing of parentage, and the regulation of marriage, to control access to Canadian citizenship. These criteria operate within a monogamous, heterosexual model of family formation.[6] With the legal recognition of same-sex relationships, and the advent of reproductive technologies, however, this assignation of parental status based on presumptive procreative contributions has been confounded. Partners (same and different sex) who access surrogacy or who make use of sperm, egg, and embryo donation all complicate the scene of kinship formation in which the fiction of biological relatedness provides the foundation for parentage.

At the level of domestic law, Canadian provinces have steadily implemented reforms to accommodate the complicated parentage determinations that have emerged from the use of reproductive technologies. British Columbia permits the recognition of three parents (e.g., lesbian partners and a biological father), and Ontario and Saskatchewan law will recognize up to four parents who have formulated their parenting arrangement prior to conception (e.g., a lesbian couple, a gay couple, and the exchange of their respective genetic and biological contributions).[7] Alberta and Manitoba limit parental status to two people, but surrogate mothers can sign over their parentage rights through a court declaration and sperm donors do not carry a paternal presumption.[8] Quebec has undertaken a review of its parentage provisions though so far without legislative uptake.[9] Canadian law prohibits commercial surrogacy, and in cases of altruistic surrogacy, those Canadian provinces that recognize this form of assisted reproduction assign parentage to the birth mother in the first instance. In Alberta, BC, Nova Scotia, Ontario, and Saskatchewan, the transfer of parentage between a surrogate and an intended parent happens through an expedited legal process.[10] Provinces also differ regarding whether or not intentional parents require a gestational and/or genetic link to the child. In provinces without surrogacy provisions, clearly a gestational link is necessary. In provinces that do have surrogacy provisions, Alberta and Nova Scotia require a genetic link, whereas BC, Ontario, and Saskatchewan do not.[11]

While parentage is a provincial responsibility, the federal government mobilizes its own definitions as they pertain to laws within federal authority – including in the *Citizenship Act*. The regulations to the *Citizenship Act* define "parent" as the father or mother of a child, whether the child was born in wedlock or not, and include an adoptive parent.[12] Relatedly, the Act's definition of "child" relies on a "common sense" that pertained prior to the legal recognition of same-sex relationships and the advent of reproductive technologies: a child "includes a child adopted or legitimized in accordance with the laws where the adoption or legitimation took place."[13] The emphasis on legitimation is notable here. As we have seen in previous chapters, the fact that a child was born outside of marriage has been used on many occasions to deny Canadian citizenship, even when these children were subsequently legitimated through the marriage of their parents. And then there is the concept of legitimacy altogether. Provinces and territories have uniformly removed legitimacy criteria from their family law statutes, yet those criteria live on in the *Citizenship Act,* telegraphing the centrality of marriage to Canadian citizenship, in a context in which families have become increasingly diverse.

Notably, the word "genetic" does not appear within these definitions of parent and child. Yet until July 2020,[14] the instruction given to citizenship and consular officials in an operational bulletin was that "children born abroad through assisted human reproduction (AHR) and/or surrogacy arrangements undertaken by Canadian intending parents are not eligible for Canadian citizenship by descent when no genetic lineage to the Canadian parent can be established."[15] Intriguingly, this categorical statement is preceded by a description of the contemporary status of Canadian parentage law: "the determination of whether a person is a 'parent' is not merely dependent on a genetic link between the biological parent and the child, but also based on evidence of intention to parent and demonstration of parentage as displayed by the existence of a legal parent/child relationship."[16] At least in the context of this operational bulletin, parentage is understood as "biology plus." This assertion is intriguing because of what it demonstrates about the interaction of citizenship and parentage. First, in the absence of this insistence on intention as well as genetic relationship, an enterprising Canadian could set himself up abroad and make his sperm – and Canadian citizenship – available to anyone willing to have him recognized as the father. Second, "biology plus" is not, in fact, an accurate rendering of Canadian parentage laws. In fact, people can be deemed parents without a genetic link to a child (e.g., a married heterosexual couple who used donated gametes and a surrogate). Sometimes parentage is *only* about the "plus." And of course, in the Canadian domestic context, children derive their citizenship from birth in the territory. In the absence of Canadian soil, and in the transnational operation of Canadian sovereignty, basic principles of domestic family law are disregarded, and it is the genetic relationship (or the visual appearance of a genetic relationship) that matters. The bulletin does include provisions for discretionary processing, including issuing a temporary resident permit to enter Canada and a subsequent application for humanitarian and compassionate permanent residence, or, alternatively, an application for a grant of citizenship as a "special case."[17] As Minister Marco Mendicino noted in 2020, "the process was more cumbersome … It was not only unjust but also an unneeded additional source of stress and uncertainty for couples who should be focused on the excitement of starting their new family."[18]

The Federal Court of Appeal ruling in *Canada (Citizenship and Immigration) v. Kandola* (2014), while no longer current, is an object lesson in the lengths to which judges can go to rigidify the process of citizenship determination.[19] *Kandola* involved a child born in India to her gestational Indian mother and her Canadian father, whom the court refers to as her guardian. The father sought Canadian citizenship for his child, but his application was rejected on the grounds that he was not genetically related to his daughter. The decision was appealed to the Federal Court, where the father prevailed, and subsequently to the Federal Court of Appeal, where he lost. In fact, the child is not genetically related to either of her parents, but her mother gave birth to her and her parents are married. In Indian law, then (as in the law of every Canadian province and territory), the child was born in the context of a marriage, her gestational mother is regarded as her "natural" mother, and her father is the husband of her mother.

The parents were forthright with Canadian officials about the circumstances of their child's birth, and the consular official followed the explicit instructions of the operational bulletin, finding that the child was not a Canadian because she was not genetically related to her Canadian parent.[20] The family received advice to consider adoption, an option that was not, in fact, open to them since the adults were already legally recognized as the child's parents in India. One cannot adopt one's own child. Alternatively, as the Operational Bulletin discussed above advised, officials suggested applying for a temporary resident permit in order to gain access to Canada and then seek a permanent resident permit on humanitarian and compassionate grounds or a discretionary grant of citizenship.[21]

In Federal Court, Justice Blanchard rejected the Ministry of Citizenship and Immigration's narrow reading of the definitions of child and parent. Although he too repeated the fiction of biological relationship that attends *jus sanguinis* definitions of citizenship, and thus determined that the child could not make her claim on that basis, he felt that the child's right of citizenship was, in fact, conferred by the *Citizenship Act* because her birth was legitimated. In his reasons, Justice Blanchard cited section 2 of the *Act,* which, as noted above, provides that the definition of child "includes a child adopted or legitimized in accordance with the law of the place where the adoption or legitimating took place."[22] And furthermore, section 3(1)(b) of the *Citizenship Act* declares that a person is a citizen if the person was born outside of Canada after 14 February 1977 and at the time of his [*sic*] birth one of his parents was a citizen.[23] Justice Blanchard's reasoning thus returns us to the role of law rather than biology in defining parentage. Ironically, by drawing attention to the provisions surrounding legitimation in establishing definitions of parent and child – a concept that is now regarded as archaic in Canada's domestic parentage law – the court was able to reinvigorate a social definition of familial relationships.

This judgment was subsequently appealed and overturned, in a split decision, at the Federal Court of Appeal. Concerning the issue of legitimation,

Justice Noël, writing on behalf of his colleague Justice Webb, held that the term "legitimized" required a prior state of illegitimacy in order to acquire meaning. Because the child was born to married parents, this prior state did not exist.[24] Turning then to the definition of child, the Court held that the French wording of the act should apply. The English word "parent," in Justice Noël's assessment, carried a latent ambiguity.[25] The French phrases "née d'un père," or "née d'une mere" were preferable, since in his view (and that of CIC), there was no other way to understand the words "née d'un père" except that the father contributed to the child's genes.[26] Of course, prior to the advent of genetic testing, when a birth in the context of marriage turned husbands into fathers, "née d'un père" would indeed have meant something other than genetic contribution, an argument that was elaborated by Justice Mainville in dissent.[27]

The terrain got a bit rougher when considering the meaning of "née d'une mere" (although this was not an issue in the case, since the child's mother was not a Canadian). Since both genetic and gestational mothers could claim to have begotten a child, the French text was less instructive. And worryingly, Justice Noël noted, in a context of assisted reproduction, neither the genetic nor the gestational mother might be able to confer derivative citizenship if, as the federal government insisted, a "parent" is restricted "to a person who has begotten (father) or borne (mother) a child and who is genetically related to the child."[28] While the parties did not raise a *Charter* issue in their arguments before the court, Justice Noël noted that there might well be a section 15 (equality) argument here, in the unequal treatment of children of Canadian citizens depending on the manner of their conception.[29] Presumably there would also be a gender equality argument regarding the unequal capacity of men and women to convey citizenship to their children in the context of reproductive technologies and birth abroad. Indeed, the implication of the federal government's argument was that Canadian women who use certain forms of reproductive technologies and give birth, have a female partner who gives birth, or engage a surrogate to have a child abroad, may lack the ability to pass on their citizenship altogether. And, indeed, this was the case for Laurence Caron in her efforts to gain Canadian citizenship for her son – born in the Netherlands to her Dutch partner.

While the federal government found a sympathetic ear in the Federal Court of Appeal for its arguments regarding the narrow genetic definition of fatherhood in the citizenship determination of children born abroad, they were rather less successful in their efforts to insist that the law required "biology plus." In Justice Noël's view, the Operational Bulletin had no legal foundation, leaving him to conclude that paragraph 3(1)(b) of the *Citizenship Act* only provided for the acquisition of derivative citizenship to a child with a genetic relationship to a Canadian.[30] Justice Noël regarded the automatic grant of derivative citizenship – of *jus sanguinis* – as exactly parallel to the operation of *jus soli*. Thus, a child born abroad with an X or Y chromosome from a Canadian is a

Canadian full stop, just as a child born on Canadian territory is a Canadian, full stop. His reasoning ran as follows:

> A mother who comes to Canada with the strategic view of giving birth and conveying citizenship on her child achieves this goal the same way as a mother who gives birth in Canada in the normal course. Similarly, a Canadian parent who conceives a child with no intention to parent confers citizenship upon the child at birth in the same way as a parent who assumes his or her parental responsibilities. In short, paragraph 3(1)(*b*) ... is totally divorced from family law considerations.[31]

This is an extraordinary claim. There is, after all, no gene for Canadian-ness. One is a Canadian by virtue of the criteria of birth articulated through the law. Paragraph 3(1)(b) describes the acquisition of derivative citizenship as a function of the citizenship of one's parent; and parentage, as this discussion has been at pains to point out, is fundamentally the purview of family law considerations.

In any event, as Justice Noël noted, this rigid adherence to genetic relationship in the interpretation of the *Citizenship Act*'s definition of "parent" – to the "begetting," in the context of men – means that "a Canadian donor conveys that right like any other Canadian procreator."[32] Thus, the Court offered the federal government a cautionary warning – Canadian sperm waves a flag, and, in the citizenship context, genetics is proof enough to establish fatherhood and Canadian nationality. And while the federal government had an opportunity to address this issue in timely fashion, given that revisions to the *Citizenship Act* were before Parliament at the time of the judgment, they chose not to do so.[33]

A decision by the Quebec Superior Court in July 2020 revised this narrow genetic interpretation of a parent and child in a *jus sanguinis* situation.[34] In the context of a more citizenship-friendly and pro-LGBTQ Liberal government, the denial of citizenship to the Netherlands-born son of a Canadian woman and her Dutch partner on the grounds that his Canadian mother was not the birth mother was incongruous. Interestingly, though, the government did go to considerable lengths, at least initially, to try to avoid reforming the interpretation of "parent" as requiring a genetic relationship. Early efforts to have the refusal of citizenship reconsidered were unsuccessful. It was only after Laurence Caron was able to attract the attention of Canadian media, and the help of the Court Challenges program, that her efforts to gain citizenship for her son on the basis of her parental status began to gain traction.[35] The first effort to settle the case came through an offer of citizenship via ministerial discretion.[36] Caron turned this down, since it did not address the broader equality principle of citizenship entitlement for the born-abroad children of same-sex parents and parents using assisted reproduction. Subsequently, the Ministry of Immigration, Refugees and Citizenship suggested that she apply for citizenship for her son on humanitarian and compassionate grounds.[37] Caron regarded this suggestion as offensive and completely inappropriate, since it implied that her son was in some way in need of the benevolence of the Canadian state rather being entitled to citizenship as of right.[38] She did note that this grant would have entitled any of her born-abroad grandchildren to Canadian citizenship – a situation that does not pertain in birth abroad as of right, due to the second generation cut-off rule. In her view, though, it would be up to her son to determine the importance of his connection to Canada and govern himself accordingly.[39] Ultimately, her efforts succeeded, and despite the government's various attempts to settle the matter quietly and in a manner limited to their son, when the case was finally heard before the Quebec Superior Court, the Attorney General was supportive of Caron's claim, advocating in favour of an interpretation of parent that would include the non-biological partner of a same-sex couple.[40] In the wake of the decision, the Minister of Immigration, Refugees and Citizenship commended Caron and her partner: "Canada is grateful to them for the courage and strength they have shown in righting this wrong."[41]

The corrective of *Caron* is critical, but before we breathe a sigh of relief and move on, it is worth considering the implications of insisting on genetic relationship as the basis for national belonging. In the first instance, the privileging of genetic relationship tells us that Canadian blood is what makes a Canadian. And the implication of shared blood is a nation of people who are "of the same stock;" people whose blood ties them together with the common fate of the political society. This language of blood invokes a racial logic at the heart of birthright citizenship.[42] It is a discourse of national purity, or at least coherency, that echoes distressingly with other familiar and diabolical instances of insisting on blood as the basis of belonging. Of course, an insistence on genetic relationship to a Canadian as the basis for derivative citizenship does not create an ethnically or racially homogenous population (whatever that would be), but the insistence on genetic relationship as a claim to national membership does signal a certain cleaving to identity that can, at least according to some Canadian officials, be known in the blood. Until *Caron*, the Canadian state was at pains to ensure that when citizenship and family law collide, there was a simple, and highly illiberal, test for belonging. It's in your veins.

Of course, the other way to become a Canadian by birth is to be born on Canadian soil. In many ways, this seems like the most secure path to citizenship. Its origins are deep, having long provided a reliable method for formal incorporation of settlers within the Canadian nation-state. Yet it is this very reliability that makes Canada's *jus soli* citizenship the target of citizenship reformers who regard the robustness of this citizenship guarantee as, in fact, compromising the integrity of Canadian citizenship. According to this logic, handing out citizenship to anyone born on Canadian territory is a sign of a devalued citizenship. The possibilities and limits of reforming Canada's *jus soli* citizenship rule thus bring us to the second circumstance of the citizenship of babies, involving children born in Canada to foreign mothers – cases of so-called maternity tourism.

Jus soli Citizenship for Canadian-Born Children of Foreign Mothers

As noted at the beginning of this chapter, when foreign mothers give birth in Canada, political debates surrounding the worthiness of their children to be citizens have almost nothing to do with the children themselves. Instead, the debate around whether to grant citizenship to *all* children born on Canadian soil, regardless of the citizenship status of their parents, circulates around long-standing practice and a desire for procedural simplicity on the one hand, and on the other, the morality, motivations, and affiliations of parents and the costs of these children to Canada's social benefit system.

In the Canadian context, the stereotypical maternity tourist is an affluent Chinese woman using health care services in Vancouver or Toronto. That said, some reporting has noted other source countries for maternity tourists. A CTV report from 2016, for example, cited a Toronto immigration consultant who described two types of maternity tourism clients. According to him, one group includes "wealthy individuals, often from European countries who want a 'second passport' for their children and are able to pay anywhere between $10,000 and $20,000 to deliver a baby in Canada . . . Others are from poor, crime-ridden countries who want to provide security for their children and hope that their Canadian babies can provide an anchor in the country for the rest of the family."[43] Rich Europe and a desire for options, especially for post-Brexit Britons, is contrasted with "poor crime-ridden countries."[44] The insinuation is that women from "poor crime-ridden countries" desire to *settle* in Canada. Their pursuit of citizenship for their children is then juxtaposed with an "insurance" passport – and is laden with threat.

The representation of Asian women who give birth in Canada splits the difference between insurance and prospective threat. Their behaviour, like that of the European women in the CTV story, is read as motivated by a desire for a safety citizenship, but, as we will see, it accrues an additional, racialized layer of judgment that reads their actions as self-serving and unpatriotic. Prospective settlement through queue-jumping is identified as a primary concern, but rather than being linked to poverty and criminality, for Asian women it is, in the first instance, the costs to the health care system of giving birth in Canada and competing for space in maternity wards, and, later, the prospect of their children attending university at domestic tuition rates and then sponsoring their family members as immigrants to Canada, that raises the ire of critics. Clearly, race, class, and gender are strong subtexts in these arguments.

To be clear, "maternity tourism" is not a real problem in Canada (or anywhere, I would argue). Statistics Canada reports that between 2006 and 2016, the percentage of births to non-resident women ranged from 0.06 to 0.18 per cent of total births annually (233 to 699 babies).[45] And while the accuracy of these data is disputed, even the highest estimate reports the rate as 1.2 per cent of total births, (4,099 births in 2018).[46] Moreover, the reasons why a non-resident[47] may give birth in Canada are various – they may be Canadians who normally reside abroad, international students, or temporary foreign workers, for example. The numbers are minuscule, and appropriately, the actual policy response has been negligible. Nonetheless, the inadequacy of the data, the media's pursuit of attention-grabbing stories, and nationalist, nativist, and other motivations have ensured that *jus soli* citizenship acquisition by the children of foreign mothers has at various times attracted an impressive volume of sound and fury.

The lure of the maternity tourism dog whistle raises the question of what, exactly, the "problem" is. In the contestation over the worthiness of these children to belong, we learn, again, what Canadian nationals view as the basis for *anyone* to be a Canadian citizen. Unsurprisingly, it is not merely a genetic relationship, as the Federal Court of Appeal would have had it, but rather connection, reciprocity, and a shared history – or at least a commitment to the values that particular stories of Canadian mythology invoke. The motivations of the mothers are regarded as at best a disingenuous, instrumental attachment to Canada, at worst as fraud. As for the babies, their futurity, hope, and promise are tainted from the outset. Rather than being positively envisioned as eventually contributing to Canada, these children are inexorably cast as the inheriting agents of their mothers' malfeasance – as a conduit to undeserved citizenship for the whole family.

Context

The prospect that non-Canadian women might mobilize the possibilities of Canada's *jus soli* citizenship provision by giving birth in Canada has sporadically emerged as a political issue in tandem with similar panics in other Anglo-American democracies and *jus soli* countries, and in response to political developments in Canada and, especially, Asia. Notably, concerns about maternity tourism are synchronous with anxieties around the impact of foreign (read: Asian) investors driving up real estate prices and creating an affordability crisis in key Canadian housing markets.[48] Canadian governments are directly implicated in this phenomenon, having incentivized investment with the promise of a fast track to citizenship through the business immigration scheme. In 1986, at a time when Canada (BC in particular) was experiencing a significant recession, Citizenship and Immigration Canada established an investor stream in its immigration program.[49] Anticipating the handover of Hong Kong from the

UK to China in 1997, the program set out to encourage foreign investors – predominantly from Asia – "with abundant capital, personal funds of more than a million dollars, as well as a history of successful entrepreneurial activity in their homelands," to invest in Canada in exchange for permanent residency and eventually citizenship.[50] The specifics of the program changed over the decades, but it was very successful in attracting "high net worth individuals" from across Asia to invest in Canadian real estate, especially in Toronto and Vancouver.[51] It was much less successful in generating new businesses and employment.[52]

As distinct from "maternity tourists," these investors – men, primarily – were understood in terms of what they could potentially do for Canada – create jobs for others and provide tax revenues to the state.[53] And although they did not deliver on that promise through business development and employment, they certainly made a significant contribution to the property values of established homeowners and to Vancouver's property tax base.[54] Indeed, even as the problem of housing affordability intensified, "growth coalitions" of real estate developers and investors countered measures to limit their profitability, underscoring the benefits of high real estate values to the tax revenues of governments and the equity stake of existing homeowners.[55] This strategy succeeded for more than four decades. In 2014, Vancouver ranked as the second least affordable housing market in the world; only Hong Kong surpassed it.[56] And when the BC government finally decided to act, in 2016, it did so through a foreign buyers' tax, effectively blaming outsiders for its own policy failure. Instrumental rationality is thus celebrated when it is Canadian governments that are seeking wealth and enhanced economic opportunities vis-à-vis the contributions of foreigners. Yet those same governments, and Canadians themselves, are quick to absolve themselves of responsibility and mobilize racist tropes of greed and selfishness when the logic of those policies is fully realized. Anti-Asian sentiment has thus been inflamed by a narrative that displaces accountability for a lack of housing affordability from Canadian governments to racialized foreigners. The spectre of pregnant Asian women arriving in Canada to secure citizenship for their infants thus adds fuel to an already incendiary mix of racial and class tensions.

The concern with maternity tourism first appeared on the Canadian political agenda in 1994, in the midst of a constitutional crisis, the promise of a second Quebec sovereignty referendum, and, again, the impending handover of Hong Kong from the UK to China. Among a number of proposed reforms presented under the title *Canadian Citizenship: A Sense of Belonging*, the Liberal-led House of Commons Standing Committee for Citizenship and Immigration recommended amending Canada's *Citizenship Act* so as to limit *jus soli* citizenship to the children of Canadian citizens and permanent residents.[57] Notably, the arguments supporting this change were effectively the same in the mid-1990s as they were two decades later. For example, Richard Nolan, a senior official in Citizenship and Immigration, invoked the queue-jumping argument in his testimony before a Commons committee. Asked to comment, from a departmentmental perspective, on why the *Citizenship Act* needed to be revised, he stated: "Probably the major driving force is the fact that a person can be in the country for less than three days and get their citizenship. It's something I think we all find offensive, but it's now allowable under the act."[58] Of course that is not, in fact, how *jus soli* works. Nolan seems to be collapsing the citizenship status of foreign parents into the citizenship status of their newborn children. And while that citizenship status does provide those children with a future opportunity to sponsor their parents as family-class immigrants, that process is neither automatic nor straightforward. In any event, three subsequent, but unsuccessful, Liberal attempts (1998–2003) to amend the *Citizenship Act* did not propose to alter its *jus soli* provisions.[59]

The idea of abolishing *jus soli* citizenship re-emerged in the 2010s when revelations of "maternity hotels" and reports of foreign women giving birth in Canadian hospitals sparked further popular and political debate. The Conservative Harper government very seriously contemplated such an amendment in 2012–13[60] as part of a package of reforms to Canada's citizenship and immigration laws that were designed to "strengthen Canadian citizenship," often by denigrating foreign others.[61] In a secret briefing acquired by a former senior immigration official under a Freedom of Information request, and subsequently made public, Citizenship and Immigration Canada (CIC) recommended that *jus soli* be limited to the Canadian-born children of Canadian citizens and permanent residents, despite an admitted lack of data on the extent of the problem.[62] In fact, the memo noted that "while the limited data available suggests that the incidence of children born in Canada as a result of maternity tourism may be small, anecdotal information indicates that the problem could be more widespread."[63] Anecdotes were, indeed, a prime mover, and despite additional consultations, were never offset by concrete data.[64] The motivation for the change was threefold: to ensure that children who acquire citizenship by birth have a connection to Canada; to strengthen program integrity; and to protect the value of citizenship.[65]

The briefing goes on to lay out the various options and considerations in implementing the change. And while the higher virtues associated with the integrity of the Canadian nation are consistently repeated as worthy policy objectives, the briefing also raises the likelihood that this citizenship reform proposal could founder at the level of bureaucratic processes and in the context of the division of responsibilities between the federal government and the provinces and territories. Since provinces and territories issue birth certificates, these documents also serve as first-order citizenship papers, since to be born in a province or territory is to be a Canadian. The citizenship status of the parents is not a matter of consideration. If citizenship was to be restricted to the babies of citizens and permanent residents, hospitals and registries would bear additional responsibilities in acquiring the parents' citizenship status and recording both the birth and citizenship information of the child.

The briefing noted that these requirements might also lead to increased incidences of "fathers of convenience." And while the document describes this phenomenon as a situation in which "a non-Canadian/non-permanent resident woman ... claims that the child's father is a citizen or permanent resident," one might imagine a lucrative business opportunity offering up Canadian men will-ing to loan their paternity for a fee.[66] More seriously, one might also observe the presumption that a mother seeking a safe citizenship for her child by giv-ing birth in Canada would be willing to extend her "fraudulent" behaviour by falsely identifying the father. Immorality is, again, readily presumed, and the role of the family in ensuring good citizenship is underscored.[67]

According to the briefing, the added work of citizenship verification could result in error, inconvenience, data access issues to confirm permanent resi-dency status, and – most worryingly – added cost to the vast majority of parents who are Canadian citizens.[68] CIC was also concerned that this process could, in fact, make it *more* difficult to remove failed refugee claimants. If the Canadian-born children of these people were delayed in acquiring appropriate citizenship documents either because of an inability to access citizenship documents from their parents' home country, or in a case of statelessness, the parents would have a claim to postpone their repatriation.

Despite the challenges in overcoming these technicalities, the briefing none-theless recommended that the minister seek policy approval in principle to limit *jus soli* citizenship to the children of citizens and permanent residents, provide for children who would otherwise be stateless, and seek Cabinet approval to consult with the provinces and territories on implementation.[69] According to a former CIC official, the Province of Ontario may have been instrumental in putting an end to the proposed change.[70] With 37 per cent of Canadian births, Ontario would bear a disproportionate burden for the new policy. Responding to federal consultations, Ontario officials noted that there "is not enough evi-dence to justify the effort and expense for such a system-wide change."[71]

Readers might note that this consideration of *jus soli* citizenship was hap-pening in the midst of the "lost Canadian" controversy. While the Conserva-tives had resolved some of those matters with their 2008 reforms, critical issues remained, particularly regarding the citizenship of Canadians born prior to 1947. Given that context, it is especially notable that the complexities of retro-active application and two-tiered citizenship were not included in this policy briefing. In any event, the Conservatives chose not to proceed with limiting *jus soli,* at least not in their 2014 reforms to the *Citizenship Act.* According to then Citizenship and Immigration Minister Chris Alexander, "we have to make sure we get it right in a way that doesn't disrupt the vast majority of Canadians who are having their legitimate births in hospitals, but does detect and deter those cases where our generosity is being abused."[72]

As it turned out, the Conservatives would not be afforded the opportunity to realize their *jus soli* limitation objective before they were defeated by the

Liberal Party in the 2015 federal election. Nonetheless, the issue remained on their agenda, with the passage of a non-binding resolution to end "birth tourism" at its party convention in August 2018.[73] The resolution was sparked by a petition of a mere 8,568 signatories, initiated by a Richmond, British Columbia, resident, Kerry Starchuk, and supported by her Conservative Member of Parliament, Alice Wong, who insisted that the problem of "maternity tourism" was "rampant" in the riding.[74] Indeed, foreign women's demands on the resources of the Richmond Hospital were alleged to be depriving access to maternity beds for Canadian women.[75] As with the 1994 recommendation, the 2018 resolution proposed limiting *jus soli* citizenship to the children of citizens and permanent residents.[76] Notably, while the Liberal Party had authored the standing committee's recommendation in the 1990s, a different set of political calculations prevailed in 2018. The J. Trudeau Liberals owed much of their 2015 electoral success to a message of inclusion. "A citizen, is a citizen is a citizen" had been a campaign mantra and a clear differentiator between the two main party rivals. In response to the 2018 Conservative policy vote, Prime Minister Trudeau's then principal secretary, Gerald Butts, described the Conservative resolution as "a deeply wrong and disturbing idea."[77] Tellingly, the Conservatives made no mention of the resolution in their party platform for the 2019 federal election.[78]

In a particularly illustrative description of the events precipitating the Conservative Party's 2018 adoption of its resolution to limit *jus soli* citizenship to the children of citizens and permanent residents, the *Christian Science Monitor* outlined the story of Kerry Starchuk's discovery of a "maternity hotel" in her Richmond neighbourhood. Richmond, a city attached to Vancouver with a long-established Asian community, has been at the centre of the maternity tourism phenomenon. In the news story, the journalist describes Starchuk attempting to deliver a plate of cookies to her new neighbours – who turned out to be two pregnant women, a man and a toddler.[79] "The meeting began her personal battle against 'birth tourism,' where wealthy mothers like the ones she encountered next door pay to give birth, get citizenship for their babies, and return home."[80] Race and class then intersect in this story, as Starchuk, who presents as white, is described as a part-time house cleaner who "insists [that] her position is not anti-Chinese or anti-immigrant but is about rules and values, especially in a region where foreign wealth and capital have changed the face of communities."[81] When queried about the effect that maternity hotels were having, substantively, on her own citizenship, Starchuk insisted that "it does undermine me, because I'm trying to build community and welcome my neighbors to the neighborhood . . . And then I find out it's not a single-family home where there's going to be a new family but an international, underground birth-tourism hotel . . . It's like selling citizenship."[82]

Starchuk is clearly invoking criteria of deserving/undeserving through which her local identity is contrasted with globalism, her desire to welcome her new neighbours is counterposed to a presumed disregard for the character of the community, and her offer of baked goods meets a failed reciprocity of "selling citizenship." As Sunera Thobani explains in a different but related context, such arguments articulate the nation in negative terms – *against* the presence of migrants – and in doing so, they perform boundary-drawing work, communicating the substance and limits of Canadian national identity.[83] This story is also, of course, profoundly gendered. Pregnant, foreign women are represented as using their reproductive powers for their own selfish ends, while the Canadian citizen is insulted when her feminized demonstration of (national) hospitality encounters strangers doing strange things.

The journalist goes on to note that Starchuk's position is part of a broader pattern of anti-Asian behaviour, given that she is well-known in her community for her campaign to mandate English on business signage.[84] Nonetheless, she succeeded in persuading her Conservative Member of Parliament to champion the citizenship issue on behalf of the constituency, after Starchuk established the aforementioned online petition advocating for limitations on *jus soli* citizenship.[85]

As might have been anticipated, the 2018 Conservative convention's discussion surrounding the proposal to limit *jus soli* citizenship included appeals to a shared sense of national identity. One delegate asserted, for example, that "Justin Trudeau would tell you that Canada has no nationality and I think everybody here would disagree with that. I think our nationality runs in our culture, our land, our blood from Juno Beach to Vimy Ridge. We have a culture, we have a nationality, there's no reason to arbitrarily hand out citizenship to whoever happens to be on vacation here."[86]

This commentary echoes Starchuk's affrontedness at the presumptively instrumental behaviour of her foreign neighbours and shares its work of boundary demarcation. In this invocation of blood and history, though, we see an explicit ethnicization of Canadian identity in the invocation of blood and ancestry and, thus, a clearer articulation of racial anxiety. According to this logic, the capacity to transmit citizenship is inherent in parental heritage and inculcated in a prescribed version – a white version – of national culture.

It should also be noted that the Conservative Party resolution to limit *jus soli* citizenship to the children of citizens and permanent residents only succeeded by a narrow margin and that other racialized Conservative Party members spoke out against the motion. Deepak Obhrai, for example, argued that "any person who is born in Canada by law is entitled to be a Canadian; we cannot choose who is going to be a Canadian and who is not going to be a Canadian. This is a fundamental question of equality."[87] *Jus soli* citizenship *is* a question of equality and the never quite realized promise of inclusion that national membership carries. But even then, equality finds its limit at the borders of the nation-state.

Assessing the Concern

The spectre of foreign parents leveraging Canada's *jus soli* provisions to secure citizenship for their children does strike many Canadians as wrong. A public opinion poll conducted in the spring of 2019 found that only 24 per cent of Canadians felt that a child born in Canada to a woman on a tourist visa should be granted citizenship.[88] Interestingly, support for citizenship jumped to 55 per cent for a child born to two parents on work visas – signalling that the economic contribution of parents is a relatively persuasive justification for political membership – at least for their children.[89] Moreover, the political traction of the "maternity tourism" phenomenon was such that the Liberal immigration minister announced that his department had commissioned further research "in order to get a better picture of the scope of this issue and its impacts on Canada."[90]

So, what, exactly, is going on here? Despite the fact that birth provides the foundation for political membership, it is clear that connection and contribution are understood as fundamental features of citizenship. These substantive dimensions of citizenship are expected to emerge from the infant citizen, primarily as a function of their long-term presence in the polity. The demonstrated commitment of their parents to the political community – because of their own citizenship, or at the least some period of time living and working in Canada – serves as a proxy guarantee of that future commitment. In the absence of that connection or commitment, Canadians are aggrieved that "outsiders'" are accessing the Canadian political community for nothing. But are they?

Non-Canadian parents who give birth to a child in Canada do not acquire a "right to remain," freedom from deportation, or expedited access to citizenship, at least, not in the short term. Furthermore, a Canadian-born child may be obliged to leave the country if her non-Canadian parents are deported, giving rise to concerns about the robustness of the citizenship guarantee for children in such a situation.[91] Applications for a deportation stay might be made on humanitarian and compassionate grounds in such cases, but there is no guarantee that a stay will be granted. Thus, it will be very difficult for the children of foreign mothers to remain in Canada, and while the children's birth in the country certainly gives them more life options once they reach adulthood, the fact that they will spend their formative years abroad will undoubtedly affect the exercise of those options.

If the aim of giving birth in Canada is a future citizenship for the parents, that objective has to be placed in the context of the Canadian state's requirements for family sponsorship. Once the child reaches the age of majority, she will have to reside in Canada and find work, at which point she may be able to provide a pathway to citizenship for her parent(s) through a family sponsorship application. Nonetheless, from the perspective of the parent, this is a very long gamble. Indeed, as part of the Harper government's strategy to increase economic-class immigrants and reduce the family-class, family sponsorship requirements became considerably more demanding. A Canadian applying to sponsor a parent is required to earn an income at least 30 per cent above the low-income cut-off, and the tenure of their sponsorship obligation has been extended from ten to twenty years.[92] These reforms were justified as a means to limit the fiscal impact of these family-class immigrants and protect against alleged abuses of the social welfare system.[93] Notably, the J. Trudeau Liberals maintained these regulations.

In the broader context of the maternity tourism debate, then, the accusation that foreign women are selfish takers who abuse Canadian generosity without a thought to benefiting the Canadian common good is both factually overstated and dangerous. Take, for example, the claim by Andrew Griffith, a former high-ranking official in the Ministry of Citizenship and Immigration Canada, that foreign women who give birth in Canada are committing fraud. He asserts that "it is ... important that the motivation behind discussion and debates on birthright citizenship not be labelled as racist, xenophobic or anti-immigrant. The fundamental issue remains fraud and misrepresentation, not discrimination."[94] It is telling that Griffith feels the need to assert that objections to maternity tourism are not racist, but a matter of illegality or immorality. The fact is that it is not fraudulent for women – regardless of citizenship status – to give birth in Canada, and that it is not a misrepresentation to keep silent about one's pregnancy, since pregnancy is not a basis on which to deny entry. Nonetheless, the clear inference is that these women are acting both immorally and outside of the spirit of the law, that they are taking a citizenship for their children to which they are not entitled, and that they are "transgressors, undercutting the authority of the state in their movements and flexible use of citizenship."[95] Moreover, we can see that the charge of law-breaking or immorality is a cover for race since "maternity tourism" is necessarily a function of a structure of global inequality in which it is racialized people who are most negatively impacted by their lack of access to privileged citizenships, even for affluent people in authoritarian regimes. It is neither fraudulent nor a misrepresentation for a pregnant foreigner to give birth in Canada. By contrast, the furor over the practice and the proposal to eliminate *jus soli* citizenship in response is definitely racist, since the issue arises as a wholly disproportionate response to the actions of racialized women.

The heated debate around foreign women giving birth in Canada, then, illuminates what it means to be a Canadian. Inclusion comes from connection and commitment, for which birth is a quixotic proxy. In the absence of a substantive national attachment, the social expectation, if not the legal one, is that you "wait your turn," especially for racialized people. With whiteness as the default racial identity of Canada, and with multiculturalism as a means to reinforce it, national belonging is especially challenging for racialized Canadians, who are inherently positioned as "internal foreigners" or, in Mae Ngai's phrasing, "alien citizens."[96] Despite generations of settlement, "the foreignness of non-European peoples is deemed unalterable, making nationality a kind of racial trait."[97] In an economy of race and worthiness, then, racialized Canadians are compelled to assert their proximity to the nation. To do otherwise would risk the legitimacy of their inclusion in the Canadian multicultural nation and potentially damage their "solidified-yet-always-insecure position" in Canada's racial hierarchy.[98]

In a remarkable illustration of this dynamic in the maternity tourism context, Chinese Canadian journalist Jan Wong offered a withering indictment of foreign women who give birth in Canada and the *jus soli* provisions that extend citizenship to their children. Writing in a popular Toronto lifestyle periodical, Wong begins her article by congratulating herself for "winning the jackpot in the lottery of life":[99]

> Thank you, revered ancestor, for your wisdom in choosing Canada. My grandfather, Hooie Chong, came here as a coolie in the 1880s to build the Canadian Pacific Railway. Once it was complete, he paid a special tax to stay on and continue working, as a laundryman. Later, he paid triple head taxes to bring over my grandmother, their son and his wife.[100] Family lore has it that Grandfather Chong was the 10th Chinese person to become a naturalized Canadian (albeit without the right to vote).[101]

The piece goes on to deride those who would "actively seek to [jump] the immigration queue," avoiding the hardship, strife, and oppression to which her family was subjected.[102] Wong also berates the Canadian government for enabling foreigners to take advantage of Canadian citizenship and gain entitlement to a range of benefits – from schooling to clean air and water, to the absence of famine and civil war. Such advantages, one surmises, are limited to lottery winners. She concludes with the following recommendation:

> How about we stop lavishing our home-and-native assets on newborns unless their mothers have spent a few years in the country, preferably as landed immigrants or citizens themselves; instead, let's issue one-way, exit-only, good-for-travel-back-to-the-motherland documents for the infants. Canadian citizenship shouldn't be a freebie to anyone whose mother waddles through the airport arrivals lounge. I expect Grandfather Chong would approve.[103]

As Foucault reminds us, discourse is productive. Thus, Wong's story of national attachment offers a helpful corrective to invocations of Juno Beach and associations of "true" Canadian-ness with the country's engagement in solidaristic military adventures with Britain. Yet Wong is relying on the dissonance of her racialized story in relation to the white European norm of Canadian national identity narratives in order to make her argument: that Canadian settlers – white or Asian – are equally disgusted with queue-jumpers. As such, her vociferous condemnation of maternity tourism further amplifies the hostility that has long marked the incorporation of new citizens, especially racialized citizens, into the Canadian nation.[104]

More broadly, the objection to *jus soli* citizenship for the children of foreign mothers disregards the lottery dimensions of birthright. Wong notes her good fortune. She got lucky because her grandfather made an extraordinary sacrifice. It was not *her* bravery or careful decision-making that produced her citizenship, nor that of *any other* birthright Canadian. If we think that citizenship should be a function of connection and commitment, it would make more sense to focus on the substantive requirements for political belonging of currently resident or engaged Canadians, rather than the circumstances of an infant's birth and the morality of that infant's mother. Yet the birth criteria that define national inclusion enable an end run around these broader considerations of inclusion and exclusion. Rather than focusing on what political membership should mean for contemporary Canadians, we use proxies, like maternity tourists, to express the possibilities, limits, and inherent biases of national belonging.

The contestation around foreign women giving birth in Canada mobilizes babies as the stalking horse for broader articulations of national identity and who is worthy to be a member of the political community. It is not, after all, the mothers who are gaining citizenship, or at least not in the first instance. Yet the argument infers that parents have to earn the right to pass on national citizenship to their children – that their integration must be demonstrated.[105] More menacingly, the "maternity tourism" argument is subtended by assumptions that these mothers are immoral (engaged in misrepresentation and fraud) and, since families are important sites for citizen integration, that this immorality might be passed along to their children. Somehow, babies who are lucky enough to be born in Canada to parents with a more extended residence in the country are seen to have a greater claim to political membership than babies born to mothers who consciously seek out Canadian political membership for the long-term benefit of their families. In truth, we do not know anything about these women. They may be refugees, international students, visitors to Canada who gave birth unexpectedly due to medical complications, or indeed, women intent on ensuring a citizenship option for their newborns and possibly themselves.[106] Yet the "maternity tourism" label collapses this breadth of human experience, flattening these varied relationships to the Canadian state – and a very small proportion of births in Canada – into a singular category of undeserved membership. Rather than being understood as selfless mothers willing to seek out a brighter future for their children, these new mothers are read as selfish takers

who abuse Canadian generosity and eschew a meaningful connection and commitment to the Canadian nation.

Conclusion

The examination of contestations over *jus sanguinis* and *jus soli* citizenship in
the context of actual babies reveals the degree to which birth criteria disguise
much more substantive beliefs about the nation, identity, and belonging, as well
as the ways in which these concepts both order and are ordered through race,
gender, sexuality, and class. In short, whether we are talking about babies or
the adults they become, the contours of citizenship debates largely remain the
same. Of course, in the case of babies, the energy of the debate shifts from the
(contested) citizens themselves to their parents. This displacement puts kinship
in hyper-focus. Political membership is a function of one's family, a fact that is
true even in a *jus soli* context, as the furor surrounding the children of foreign
mothers clearly indicates. To the extent that liberal-democratic evocations of
consent are present, that consent lies with existing citizens and their feelings
about the acceptability of new members, rather than the willingness of prospective members to accede to the authority of the state. The club determines the
rules of belonging, a task its members undertake by forgetting about their own
paths to national inclusion and asserting their privileged role as gatekeepers.

The Federal Court of Appeal's insistence, in *Kandola,* that biological/genetic
relationship is essential to establishing *jus sanguinis* citizenship, despite the
long-standing principle of paternal (now parental) presumption, asserts a
conception of national belonging that can be found in the blood. Connection
to the nation is biological rather than a function of conscious articulation or
physical presence. The Quebec Superior Court's decision in *Caron* is definitely
an improvement over *Kandola* in its recognition of the capacity of Canadian
parents to confer citizenship on their children in the absence of a biological
relationship, but it continues to rely on birth criteria, that is, on kinship rules.
National belonging tracks through the Canadian parent whose child is born in
the context of a relationship that is recognized by the Canadian state. Thus, the
emphasis shifts from *sanguinis* to *jus* – from blood to law – while simultaneously underscoring the degree to which blood *is* law.

The dog whistle of "maternity tourism" reveals related anxieties about met-
rics of connection in the context of birth in the territory. Here the argument
is not about shifting conceptions of territory or shifting borders, but about
the adequacy of birth in the territory as a proxy for national attachment. The
original motivation of *jus soli* – to incorporate conquered peoples and new settlers within the ambit of the freshly extended empire – falls from view. *Jus soli*
relies on the likelihood of connection, or future connection, emerging from
physical presence. Yet it is precisely this possibility of a (future) connection that

invigorates its opponents. Instead, *jus soli's* broadly inclusive logic, and its colonizing evil twin, is replaced by an originary claim to belonging and a legitimacy to determine who may be included in the national family.

The social and technological innovations that gave rise first to *Kandola* and then to *Caron,* and the lively debate around reforming *jus soli*, demonstrate that it is possible to change the criteria of blood and soil, although it is not certain whether the direction of change is necessarily toward greater inclusion. More fundamentally, the contestation surrounding the citizenship of babies underscores how the global context of inequality and the birthright lottery together make broader reconsiderations of citizenship acquisition both necessary and highly challenging. The citizenship of babies is no less immune from nationalist projection than the citizenship of adults. So perhaps the time has come to dispense with the ruse of birthright and seriously consider the terms on which we form political communities that will ensure security, certainty, and dignity for all who would make a claim to belonging.

8
Alternatives

My central concern in this book has been to examine the diverse processes that have created lost Canadians, analysing these complex situations as limit cases for birthright citizenship. I have suggested throughout these pages that birthright citizenship is a very peculiar, if ubiquitous, method of membership selection for a democratic polity. This is because birthright citizenship enables people to claim entitlement to political membership based on lineage rather than a substantive engagement or encounter with the state. Membership via birthright does not ensure representation of the governed, since some who are governed are not entitled to access the mechanisms of representation, while others can claim membership despite very infrequent exposure to the effects of a particular state's governance. And perhaps most perniciously, birthright citizenship creates and reproduces legal categories of belonging – including gender, race, and nation – that incite division and undergird structures of oppression.

Drawing from the experiences of the lost Canadians and others outlined in the previous chapters, my aim in this conclusion is to expound on the paradox of the rule-governed character of birthright citizenship, to rehearse a sampling of the significant scholarly contributions to the birthright citizenship debate, and to advance the outlines of two alternative visions for political membership. One alternative is a reformist set of policy proposals, arising from ongoing and newly emerging difficulties with Canada's birthright citizenship provisions as outlined in the previous chapters. My interest in advancing a set of modest reforms is motivated by a recognition that Canada will not be instituting a wholesale rethinking of birthright citizenship criteria anytime soon. There is no powerful mobilization for its demise, the status quo is easier, and, as we have seen, people regard the nation as a key site for the articulation of belonging. Yet given the obvious inadequacies of birthright citizenship, it seems necessary to offer a second alternative: a more radical, consent-based vision for political membership. Informed as I am by progressive values and a deep commitment to equality and social justice, and attentive as I am to the intensification of exclusivity and suspicion with regard to citizenship and migration in the international community, it strikes me as particularly risky to engage in a debate that offers the prospect of undermining access to political membership. In this global context, birthright citizenship may appear to offer a sense of stability, certainty, and even equality (in the sense, for example, that all children born in the territory, regardless of the citizenship status of their parents, are citizens). My central argument, however, is that all of this is a chimera – that birthright citizenship offers no moral bulwark against a political agenda of exclusion and that the integrity of our democracy would be better served by a consent-based, constitutionally protected model of political membership in which the desired conditions for our shared fate were regularly developed through conscious deliberation.

Liberal democracies maintain their dubious support of birthright citizenship as a result of an intuitive connection between birth and nature rather than birth and politics. Birth is a biological process, runs the argument. Since one has no control over the circumstances of one's birth, no legal disability should result. This is the same logic used to undermine the legal status of illegitimacy. Put simply, it is a fundamental injustice to mark an innocent child with a lifelong, deleterious status designation. Yet as the existence of a status of il/legitimacy shows us, and as the distinction between deleterious and advantageous status (*qua* citizenship) indicates, the natural process of birth is also always happening in a political context. The law defines relationships between parent and child, between the political community and the family, between the individual and the state. This is true whether or not a particular state grants citizenship to a child born in its domain, whether any other state claims the child, or whether birth produces statelessness. In cleaving to an association of birth with nature rather than politics, we are blinded to the ways in which the delineation of territory, the naming of parents, and the legitimating of children are choices, decisions, and expressions of power that constitute our political communities. We decide, as a political community, that these rules will determine who can be a member of the polity. And we could decide otherwise, in ways that uphold principles of consent, inclusion, the protection of human rights, and aversion to statelessness. Of course, there is no guarantee that we would make citizenship laws that upheld these principles, but it is very clear that birthright citizenship provides no assurance of such an outcome either. Indeed, I would argue that birthright makes it *less* likely that we can realize such aspirations. Our adherence to birthright citizenship may well be an instance of what Lauren Berlant terms "cruel optimism" – an attachment to a mode of inclusion that is, in fact, an obstacle to our collective flourishing.[1] Perhaps if we consider what some of those alternatives are, and the risks we can identify in them, we can begin to consider whether they might offer a better way to establish membership while also coming to a fuller understanding of the contingency of birthright itself. Without the vision of a better future, we cannot begin the adventure of realizing it.

In preparation for offering the broad outlines of two proposals to address Canada's current birthright citizenship practices, I review of some of the significant themes, stakes, and concerns that animate the scholarly debate surrounding birthright citizenship, drawing most heavily on the contributions of Jacqueline Stevens, Ayelet Shachar, Peter Schuck and Rogers Smith, and Joseph Carens. I have limited myself to scholars working in the liberal-democratic tradition, since this is primarily where the contemporary conversation regarding birthright citizenship has been conducted. Of course, membership has also been a very hot topic for Indigenous scholars theorizing and envisioning the conditions of belonging in Indigenous nations. Grappling with the colonial experience of dispossession through loss of land and the imposition of externally imposed membership criteria, among other factors, has generated compelling analyses of membership struggles and constraints.[2] Notably, many critical Indigenous scholars advance conceptions of membership that emphasize inclusion and connection and that challenge strict conceptions of blood-based descent in the interests of countering the settler state's logic of elimination and the racialization of Indigenous nations.

Liberalism and the Contradictions of Kinship

As has been evident throughout these chapters, my thinking on birthright citizenship owes an enormous debt to the work of Jacqueline Stevens. Readers who have been interested in the theoretical architecture supporting my analysis have likely already gleaned a number of Stevens's central points – or at least those points that help us make sense of the paradoxes of birthright citizenship that have been endemic to the lost Canadians. Here though, I want to engage Stevens's work in *States without Nations: Citizenship for Mortals,* in which she lays out a series of proposals for rethinking legal structures that offend the equality and fairness principles of the liberal-democratic state. In this work, Stevens takes on inheritance, marriage, private property, and religion, in addition to birthright citizenship. For Stevens, each of these state-sanctioned institutions offends against liberalism's commitment to self-rule, autonomy, and equality because they rely on lineage and a passive notion of citizenship.[3] One's state-sanctioned heritage of attachments, rather than ensuring that every individual faces the conditions of her existence from a level playing field, establishes highly differentiated life paths. To envision what a world built on rigorous liberal principles would entail, Stevens sets out a series of broad-stroke proposals for institutional reforms and considers the various objections those proposals are likely to incite. For my purposes, however, I will limit my reflections to her proposals surrounding birthright citizenship.

Stevens methodically demonstrates how rules, rather than nature, are fundamental to the construction of families, and in turn how the kinship rules that produce families define membership in the state. She does this by observing the inter-workings of legal and political structures with invocations of nature, biology, and blood. Because birthright citizenship is directly connected to notions of lineage, it also conveys a sense of one's connection to the past and the future, invoking a sense of immortality, or at least continuity, through familial and political affiliation. This conflation of hereditary and political identities gives rise, in turn, to the concept of ethnicity, *qua* French, English, Chinese, and even Canadian, and also to race when those birthright membership rules rely on "an observed or imagined physical characteristic associated with a political territory of origin."[4] It is not nature or biology that makes us Ukrainian or white, but political structures that mobilize kinship to define who we are as political subjects, as citizens.

As long as the state relies on birth criteria for membership, Stevens argues, the laws of family and the kinship basis of nation and state provide a means to live beyond one's own singular mortality and thus address a deep-seated fear of death. The consequence of this fear of one's own mortality, and the elaborate state structures designed to mitigate it, is to turn us "into the sort of people who design and are designed for affinities and hatreds of kinship ... [and maintain] 'us' and 'them' in a world riven by blood vengeance, family violence, and enduring, pervasive inequality."[5] The form of the adversarial nation-state, and in particular its birthright criteria for membership, are in Stevens's view "the root cause of systemic violence and inequality within and among political societies."[6] The way out, she argues, is to come to terms with our mortality and stop relying on criteria of birth as the basis for political belonging. Families and notions of lineage might persist, but their political force, once divested of their role in defining state membership, would be weakened, enabling an end "to organized violence and freeing resources for more creative purposes, for sustaining rather than suffocating impulses of empathy."[7] It should be noted that Stevens's proposal is not directed at reforms to a single nation-state, but rather would require an international system of states without nations, "where people belong because of choice, residence, and commitment."[8] In the absence of a wholesale restructuring of the nation-state system, divisions based on national difference would persist, as would the violence those divisions incite. To the charge of utopianism that such a project surely invites, Stevens replies that "naysayers in the sphere of social change, those who extrapolate the future from the present, are the ones whom history has repeatedly defeated."[9]

Birthright, Nationalism, and Belonging

Having set out her own case regarding the pernicious effects of the nation's use of intergenerational forms of identity and belonging, Stevens takes on a number of liberal citizenship theorists, observing the various *il*liberal dimensions of their interventions. Given liberalism's origins in the refutation of hereditary privilege and its embrace of free market principles, Stevens notes that "one might expect those claiming liberal credentials [would] call for open borders."[10] Instead they have largely endorsed birthright citizenship.[11] She then demonstrates this tendency in the work of Isaiah Berlin, John Rawls, Michael Walzer, and James Tully, noting shared tendencies in Charles Taylor and Will Kymlicka. In each of them she finds an appeal to the human need for belonging, which they, in turn, locate in the nation. In the case of Berlin, for example, who draws on the eighteenth-century German philosopher Gottfried Herder for his inspiration, connections among belonging, the nation, and birth are located in the idea of a "national spirit." Although Berlin was a staunch critic of totalitarianism and fascism, he did not regard nationalism as inherently dangerous. Rather, following Herder, he advocated for an idea of nation that is deeply non-aggressive. Belonging to the nation gave people a sense of comfortable familiarity, of "being at home," of kith and kin, as well as a sense of feeling closer to some people than others; yet there was nothing in this formulation that inherently led to violence.[12] He noted, for example, that nationalism in "sated nations," that is, the nations of North America, Western Europe, Australia, New Zealand, and Japan, was benign.[13] In these countries, he asserted, distinct cultural identities were "unwounded or healed."[14] The assertion that a shared national culture addresses a "profound natural need" has been sufficiently persuasive, Stevens notes, so as "to adduce an enclosed hereditary community's self-determination as an individual right," as in the inclusion of the "right to a nationality" in the UN Declaration of Human Rights.[15]

Rawls's conception of national belonging rests on the belief that "'liberal peoples' [are] those whose membership is determined in the first instance by heredity, not shared liberal values."[16] Drawing inspiration from J.S. Mill, Rawls asserts that only a political society based on the common sympathies of shared race and descent enable a "community of recollections; collective pride and humiliation, pleasure and regret, connected with the same incidents in the past."[17] Yet as Stevens points out, Rawls does not explain how it is that heredity per se leads to a "community of recollections," or how it is that racial identities come to be known and shared.[18] The creation of a sense of shared identity and the associated recollections – triumphs and humiliations – are after all a function not of genetics but of social interaction, cultural and material consumption and production, school curriculum, and, generally, the work entailed in imagining the political community. Rawls's elision of lineage with collective identity reveals both his inattention to the rule-governed character of kinship (i.e., his assumption that kinship is natural) and the various processes, from storybooks to national historic celebrations, that are mobilized in the service of creating a sense of national belonging.

Rita Dhamoon levels a similar critique regarding the association of national culture with birth and a blindness to power in the work of Will Kymlicka.

Kymlicka rejects the notion that culture is primordial, or at least pre-social, yet that very assumption animates his theory. Dhamoon notes his claim that adopting a "new" societal culture is extremely challenging, and thus that it is reasonable for people to want to access their native, that is, natural culture.[19] He rejects blood-based definitions of ethnocultures but nonetheless regards nationality as especially significant to cultural identity because it begins early in life – earlier, he contends, than sexual identity.[20] Despite his protestations to the contrary, Kymlicka eventually succumbs to a biological basis for culture – intriguingly, in the context of a discussion of whether Deaf culture would fit within his definition of multiculturalism. Ultimately, Kymlicka concludes, the Deaf do not meet his criterion of having a full societal culture because they are unable to guarantee the *reproduction* of Deaf children and thus "can never become a genuinely 'national' minority."[21] A full societal culture – a culture worthy of the name – is thus national and structured through birth. For Dhamoon as for Stevens, this insistence on the inter-generationality of culture via nation obscures many meaningful cultural forms that emerge from human creativity and interaction and that can also give meaning to life, even if they cannot also offer the illusive promise of immortality.[22] Moreover, the failure to recognize culture and nation as products of, and productive for, power, obscures the political character of national identity and belonging.

In their critiques of these liberal theorists, Stevens and Dhamoon are at pains to show us how even liberalism's most renowned representatives are seduced by the explanatory force of reproduction, familial attachment, and thus a pre- or a-political conception of human interaction. One implication to be drawn from their critical interventions is that these internal inconsistencies ultimately undermine the integrity of these liberal-nationalist theories, and that either liberalism should live up to its own principles (Stevens) or we should be attentive to the will-to-power that exists within liberal accounts of social phenomena (Dhamoon). Taking a different tack, Rogers M. Smith, an avowed liberal himself, fully acknowledges that liberalism and nationalism are incompatible but argues for a sense of peoplehood as an unavoidable dimension of large-P Politics.[23] He describes the great strains that a vigorous liberalism (and republicanism) places on people to be inclusive, if not fully cosmopolitan. Sharing Stevens's assessment of the contradictions of birthright citizenship for liberal-democratic polities, Smith observes, for instance, that "the logic of Enlightenment liberalism points away from particular national memberships and toward more inclusive, if not cosmopolitan political arrangements."[24] He also notes that neither liberalism nor democratic republicanism "offers much reassurance that even most hardworking individuals will ultimately avoid being eclipsed by their own mortality."[25] Yet the game of politics will always make a pitch to national identity a compelling option, since it provides a means to provoke emotion and identification. The political advantages of channelling those strong feelings toward a particular political party may result in significant electoral advantage.

Moreover, without a sense of national distinctiveness, Smith argues, there would be no basis on which to prefer one liberal-democratic polity over another, or to appreciate the intrinsic worth of one's own political community, and thus no basis on which a political authority might demand loyalty and mount a collective defence.[26]

Unlike other liberal citizenship theorists, then, Smith engages the political calculus of the connection between birthright and belonging. He, like Stevens, is wary of the xenophobia that may result from a "strong concept of peoplehood," preferring morally defensible expressions of peoplehood "in which leaders ... praise their own people and traditions while pledging respect and esteem for others." But he also recognizes that "policies advanced simply in the name of positive visions of one community may work in very harsh ways against the interests of many outsiders, even if they are not specifically denigrated."[27] Still, while Smith may worry about the harshness of exclusivity and recognizes the demands of a rigorous liberalism, it is in his concern with the *necessity* of fealty to the nation-state that he and Stevens part company. In Stevens's view, citizenship based on birth enables the state to mobilize populations to fight and die on its behalf. National difference is used to obscure the shared mortal condition of people, and nations provide an illusion of certainty in a human condition riddled with doubts.[28] The magic of the nation-state is to imbue the accident of birth – an everyday event, after all – with a political meaning, with citizenship. In turn, citizenship divides people born according to one set of rules or in one bordered territory, from those born under different rules, potentially only metres away. And the mythologizing, story-telling, and history-making that go along with division and difference promote a common sense of injury and/or entitlement against which other injured and entitled groups are arrayed and must be called to account.

More playfully, Stevens invites us to consider the inconsistencies between principle and practice in liberal membership arguments for political belonging. With regard to membership and merit, for example, she notes that "just as sports teams do not allow uncoordinated children of sports stars to join their teams, those not up to a country's standards would have to leave, regardless of their place of birth or ancestry."[29] Noting that opposition to immigration is often framed as a risk to the national standard of living, the implication is, of course, that those with a birthright claim to belonging do not pose a similar risk. And if they did, Stevens wryly posits, then it would make sense to expatriate the poor and unskilled who already inhabit the ranks of its nationals.[30] The power of nationalist affinity is evident in our rejection of these satirical proposals, but the fact that we might react negatively to calls to expatriate "our" poor and vulnerable, is, I think, a compelling example of how powerful nationalism is in creating a sense of common obligation, of fellow feeling. Of course, Canadian courts and border officials did what they could to limit access to the nation for undesirable characters with criminal records, as we saw in chapter 6, but it is also true that the sense of national, even familial responsibility "to our own" carried the day – at least in the parliamentary debate. It seems to me that in the absence of such an appeal, a central worry for progressive people confronting the proposal to abandon birthright citizenship is that they cannot know what would happen if we did not at least have birth as a national leveller. What would prevent an ideologically motivated government from denying or casting out people who offended against the preferred national identity – be that identity defined in terms of ability, wealth, race, health, criminality, sexuality or something else? But because, in the end, who is in and who is out is really just about the rules, we might well ask, what prevents it now?

Stevens does not offer a fully worked out alternative to a birthright membership regime – or a system of states without nations – but she does recommend some first principles. The basis of belonging within the political community would be grounded in choice, residence, and commitment.[31] It is clear that she values an active citizenship – which she describes as "the prerogatives of citizens to shape law" – over the passivity of birth.[32] She also notes that the exercise of active citizenship requires certain competencies – "the age of reason ... local knowledge, good judgment, and a dedication to a state's well-being."[33] She indicates an affinity for a stakeholder model of decision-making in which one's claim to participate is based in being affected by the outcome.[34] This would enable a conception of citizenship as a relationship of governance rather than affinity of birth, in which direct action was combined with "the space for creative self-governance, an open-source means for government to benefit from those most qualified and interested in offering guidance for rules affecting public order, the public committed to that organization and affected by its rules."[35] Residence would provide a basis for the necessary expertise to govern, since it provides a familiarity with a place and an understanding of its practices.[36] Finally, Stevens's alternative citizenship regime would require free movement among existing states, the capacity to expatriate and acquire membership in another state after learning its particularities (she suggests a residency requirement of three to five years) and to hold multiple memberships, and "the abolition of state-sanctioned marriage, to abolish official lineages transcending mortal lifespans and thereby making families synchronic and not diachronic."[37]

In sum, Stevens sees the primary harms of birthright criteria for political belonging as leading to mass violence, the degradation of liberal values, and the construction of hierarchical identity structures formed around gender, race, ethnicity, and nation. Her alternative is to refigure the global system of states through open borders, active, participatory membership, and a clear-eyed embrace of human mortality. Since our current arrangements are supported by rules, not nature, it should be entirely possible to change them and thus create a world more conducive to liberal-democratic values.

As will be clear from the proposal I advance at the end of the chapter, there is much that I find compelling in Stevens's first principles. Yet when one considers the particular circumstances of the Canadian state and its treatment of Indigenous peoples, Stevens's proposal to sever the tie between lineage and the nation is precipitous. In the colonial project of eradicating Indigenous political societies and establishing a white settler society, the experience of violence, injury, and entitlement plays out precisely as Stevens predicts. Yet while her diagnosis may be accurate, what of her remedy? I worry that were we to adopt her proposal without attending to the travesties of colonial dispossession, and physical and cultural genocide, without respecting the integrity of Indigenous nations and self-determination, the prescription for Canada's Indigenous peoples might simply read "get over it" – that an assimilative logic would continue to prevail.

Indigenous peoples are working diligently to assert their claims to nation, identity, and distinctive political and cultural practices, often expressed with reference to the knowledge of ancestors and a responsibility to future generations. This work of reclamation is an important counter to the Canadian state's project of both naming Indigenous peoples and limiting their claims to rights and self-government to what the Canadian state designates as legitimate. This same work necessarily involves the articulation of a political identity, one that we may recognize as racialized. Yet the work of race in this context is complicated. It is an instrument of oppression, but it also forms identities around which people mobilize to challenge oppression. Indeed, it is precisely the racial basis of Indigenous national belonging that many Indigenous scholars have refused, noting the ways in which the *Indian Act* has instituted blood-based criteria for "Indianness" and replaced historical forms of nation-making that incorporated non-kin members.[38] Moreover, Horn-Miller, Napoleon, and Simpson, among many others, note the importance of meeting one's obligations to the political community as a basis for membership.[39]

Unsurprisingly, blood-based belonging has presented a significant conundrum for the decolonization efforts of Indigenous communities in Canada. In recent years, many communities have struggled to devise membership rules apart from the *Indian Act*'s status rules.[40] Sometimes these membership criteria repeat the racist logic of blood quantum; other times, they emphasize cultural knowledge and acceptance by the community.[41] It may well be that these more innovative, participatory membership criteria could provide some guidance to the rest of the Canadian polity regarding how to formulate a conception of political belonging based on connection to the community rather than birth. In any event, the abandonment of birthright citizenship and the demise of intergenerational political membership would require measures of redress to right past wrongs, as well as a willingness to respect the autonomy of Indigenous nations, including their right to determine their own membership rules and launch a comprehensive strategy of decolonization.

Birthright and the Distribution of Opportunity and Income

Like Stevens, Ayelet Shachar in *The Birthright Lottery: Citizenship and Global Inequality* identifies the profound contradictions of birthright citizenship for liberal values, but she regards their primary harm as promoting a massively skewed global distribution of income and opportunity. Drawing an extended analogy from inheritance law, which recognizes, unlike birthright citizenship, the injustice of enriching people who had no hand in creating their wealth, Shachar proposes that the inequities of birthright be redressed through a global, redistributive levy. This levy would tax the transmission mechanism of birthright citizenship, would be calculated at the time of a child's birth, and would be transferred from rich countries to fund infrastructure programs for children's development in recipient countries.[42] Shachar also addresses the over- and under-inclusive tendencies of *jus soli* and *jus sanguinis* citizenship rules through the addition of the principle of genuine connection (*jus nexi*). As part of this effort, she draws another analogy from property law, the doctrine of adverse possession (of which squatters' rights are a subset), to argue in favour of granting citizenship to people who have resided in a state for a requisite period and have built up social connections within that state, but who entered the state illegally.[43] Ironically, such a claim would seem to form the basis of settler colonialism.

Shachar's work reminds us of the inherent tension in the association of citizenship with equality. Since the field of citizenship theory, as distinct from migration studies, has tended to be nationally bounded and focused,[44] citizenship in this context is understood as a condition for equality, what Shachar calls its enabling function.[45] The fact that citizenship also defines the borders of that equality, and thus names who shall *not* be entitled – those outside the national community (even if they reside inside its territorial boundaries) – means that inequality is also a central constituent of citizenship. Shachar terms this citizenship's gatekeeping function. Like Stevens's observation that national borders form the boundaries of our non-emergency expressions of compassion, Shachar's insistence on the unfairness of the distribution of birthright privilege demands that we consider the transnational effects of membership based on birth.[46] This insistence on how citizenship works to further inequities then forms the basis of her levy proposal.

In many respects, Shachar's proposals are daring and provocative, but, as Linda Bosniak argues, their radicalism is attenuated.[47] Shachar argues that birthright citizenship reinforces the worst effects of global inequality, which in turn establishes a legal obligation to ameliorate that inequality through a redistributive tax on birthright citizenship.[48] The current organization of states and privilege remains intact in this vision, even if the disparities between rich and poor are lessened through a much more substantial, effective, and rational transfer of wealth and resources from rich countries to improve the life prospects of children in poor countries. Yet she also envisions that rich countries might meet their obligations by increasing the number of migrants they admit and by sending their privileged youth to do good works in poor countries.[49] There is a strong taint of "noblesse oblige" in these proposals, since they do not envision a role for receiving states in determining priorities and thus demonstrate little concern for their sovereign authority. And while proponents of global justice might regard such attention to sovereignty as misplaced given the magnitude of human need, it bears noting that the distribution of attentiveness to and respect for sovereignty and self-determination corresponds pretty well with the distribution of the winners and losers in the birthright lottery. To be clear, I am not opposed to a wholesale, equitable redistribution of the world's wealth, nor would I support a conception of sovereignty as unbridled state autonomy; however, I am not persuaded that a birthright levy is any more effective or persuasive a way to address global inequality than a robust commitment to human rights, the reform of global capital, or a perversely motivated development strategy to reduce "unwanted migration" by investing in the development of poor countries so as to reduce the compulsion to leave.[50]

While Shachar's proposed levy continues to rely on birthright itself as the basis for membership in the polity, the latter part of her book advances an alternative to, or at least a modification of, the birthright basis of citizenship. This alternative, again, is based on a principle of genuine connection, *jus nexi*, and it emerges from Shachar's analysis of the tendency of both *jus sanguinis* and *jus soli* to over- and under-include people within the bounded membership of the political community. Shachar usefully reminds us that the appeal of birthright citizenship as a membership criterion is that birth in the territory or citizenship by blood serve as proxies for future involvement in the political community.[51] Furthermore, as Carens helpfully points out, "children born to parents who are citizens of the state where their children are born, and who live in that state as well, are citizens automatically, in all democratic states."[52] The problem, however, is that birth is *only* a proxy. Under both *jus soli* and *jus sanguinis* membership principles, some children will inherit citizenship in a state in which neither they nor their parents have lived and about which they know little. Under a strict *jus sanguinis* regime, children may be born in a country where they will live out their lives yet have no opportunity to be recognized as full members of the community. And under a strict *jus soli* regime, a child may take up long-term residence but be unable to claim membership as of right, since she was absent at the magic moment of birth.

To address these over- and under-inclusive effects, Shachar's *jus nexi* membership criteria work on ascending and descending membership entitlement scales. Analogizing again from the laws of inheritance, Shachar advances a generationally descending entitlement to citizenship, following the logic that the greater one's distance from the actual moment of wealth creation – or, in this case, the originary moment of citizenship acquisition – the weaker one's claim to entitlement.[53] This is a more principled way of expressing the sentiment that Canadians, for example, should not be able "to pass on their citizenship to endless generations born outside Canada."[54] Intriguingly, Shachar suggests that this declining entitlement scale offers a means to curb the "re-ethnicization of membership," since it would limit blood-based claims to belonging external to the territory. At the same time, however, and as the 2008 and 2014 reforms to Canada's *Citizenship Act* amply demonstrate, an appeal to nationalist sympathies and related ethnic identities can be heightened when the curbing of *jus sanguinis* entitlement is framed in a broader context of limiting citizenship entitlement and "strengthening the value" of national membership.

Shachar also proposes an ascending entitlement to citizenship, through which the moral weight of a claim to connection grows the longer a person has resided in the state.[55] As Shachar explains, "connections may develop out of experiences of social interaction that take place under the normative umbrella of a given political community and with a particular geographical location. In this way, *jus nexi* reflects the idea of democratic inclusion, according to which those who are habitually subject to the coercive powers of the state must gain a hand in shaping its laws, if they so choose."[56] Shachar is also concerned, however, that establishing such a connection does not *compel* citizenship, or ascribe citizenship status, as would be the case under an *ex lege* system of automatic naturalization after some period of residence.[57] In her formulation, then, *jus nexi* creates the conditions for eligibility to consent but does not impose membership if a person, despite long residence, is not interested in claiming it.[58]

The principle of genuine connection has a lot of democratic appeal as a membership criterion, of course, but it also raises practical concerns with regard to determining connection itself and the measure of genuineness. And most worrying, particularly in relation to what are widely (though wrongly) perceived to be the straightforward criteria of birthright membership, is the opportunity that an assessment of genuine connection opens up for discretionary interpretation.[59] The solution is a retreat to proxies – time instead of birth, for example. And while this is less than ideal as a robust basis for political membership, it does offer a possible limit on the exercise of majoritarian power.[60]

We can certainly see all of the shortcomings Shachar identifies with the over- and under-inclusion of *jus sanguinis* and *jus soli* citizenship in the stories of the lost Canadians. Furthermore, Shachar's *jus nexi* alternative offers a useful foundation for the more pragmatic of my alternatives to Canada's current citizenship laws that I outline below. That said, though, I find it curious that, having asserted her fierce criticism of the birthright transfer mechanism of citizenship, she does not argue more vigorously for *jus nexi* as a "complete alternative."[61] Instead, she is willing to accept birthright citizenship as long as its worst effects (global inequality) are mitigated by her proposed levy, as well as the adoption of at least some *jus nexi* elements. Unlike Stevens, Shachar does not regard the kinship basis of political membership as sufficiently egregious to advocate for the complete delinking of birth from citizenship. She notes that "treating family relations as the constitutive basis for our legal ties with the rest of the political community is likely to lead to a situation in which state officials regularly scrutinize intimate relationships,"[62] yet the harms of nationalism, the distinctions of ethnicity and race, and the gendered logic of citizenship transmission largely evade her critical interrogation. In short, Shachar offers some extremely useful suggestions for modifying the exclusive consequences of birthright citizenship. Her focus on birthright as a citizenship transmission system, however, fails to interrogate the actual mechanics of parentage determination, the political meaning of blood, and the particular consequences of those kinship mechanisms for reinforcing borders. As a result, and despite her clear intentions, the affinity of birth and citizenship remains largely intact in her birthright levy and *jus nexi* proposals.

While I read Shachar's contribution to the birthright citizenship debate as broadening the scope for inclusion in the bounded community, much of the contemporary debate focuses on narrowing the circle of citizenship. The UK, Australia, and New Zealand have all modified their strong *jus soli* citizenship regimes by limiting territorial birthright claims to the children of citizens and legal residents.[63] The debate about whether to adopt similar modifications crops up with predictable regularity and viciousness in the US as well, and, as we saw in the previous chapter, has also made recurring appearances in the Canadian context. And while some proponents of these limitations argue that they are motivated by a concern to enhance the integrity of a consent-based citizenship regime, the consent that concerns them is that of the sovereign state – the host country and its settler-colonial members – rather than that of recent arrivals and their children.

Consent and the American Birthright Citizenship Debate

Perhaps the best-known articulation of the argument to limit *jus soli* citizenship to the children of citizens and legal residents is *Citizenship Without Consent* by Peter Schuck and Rogers M. Smith.[64] Although both authors have now distanced themselves from this work, or at least the anti-immigration stance it has been used to justify, the position they advanced continues to animate – indeed, define – the birthright citizenship debate in the US.[65] Their argument revolves around the proper interpretation of the Fourteenth Amendment and its robust grant of *jus soli* citizenship. Section 1 of the amendment reads: "All persons born or naturalized in the United States, and subject to the jurisdiction thereof, are citizens of the United States and of the state wherein they reside."[66] Schuck and Smith then focus on the phrase "subject to the jurisdiction thereof" and the Supreme Court's interpretation of those words in *Elk v. Wilkins* (1884) to deny birthright citizenship to Indigenous Americans while granting it to African Americans.[67] In the Reconstruction Era, with the issue of post-Independence British loyalists long resolved, the citizenship entitlement of white Americans was taken as given.[68]

According to Smith, the task that confronted America's jurists and legislators was to devise a logic for a post–Civil War citizenship regime in which Blacks were to be included while Indigenous peoples were excluded, a consensual basis for the liberal polity could be expressed, and the *jus soli* tradition from the British common law could be maintained.[69] This tall order was met by drawing on the philosophical guidance of international law theorists Emmerich de Vattel and Jean-Jacques Burlamaqui, who had informed the thinking of America's Founding Fathers.[70] These thinkers managed to finesse the relationship between consent and *jus soli* belonging through their contention "that parents should be understood to demand the offer of citizenship to their children as a condition of their own consent to membership."[71] Enter the kinship basis of political membership in a liberal-democratic polity. Vattel then provided the argument for excluding Indigenous peoples from this polity-making scene, by designating Indigenous peoples as members of dependent nations (a handy evasion of the fact of their colonization) who wished to maintain their limited autonomy. Thus, neither they nor their children could be understood to have expressed their consent to the jurisdiction of the United States.[72] This precedent for denying citizenship to people who were, very clearly, born in the territory of the United States, and, as Smith later conceded, very clearly were subject to the ultimate jurisdiction of the United States, forms the basis for Schuck and Smith's claim that the same rationale could be used to deny birthright citizenship to the US-born children of aliens.[73] In this highly politicized rendition of the origins of America's citizenship law we see an outstanding example of the rule-governed character of birthright citizenship and its uses in pursuit of both historical and contemporary political agendas.

Shifting from the citizenship status of people already in the polity to the status of the children of migrants, Schuck and Smith draw on the principle that sovereign states have the ultimate authority to determine their own membership criteria and that migrants who enter the state without adhering to those criteria have not been accepted by "the people." As Schuck and Smith explain, "it is difficult to defend a practice that extends birthright citizenship to the native-born children of illegal aliens. The parents of such children are, by definition, individuals whose presence within the jurisdiction of the United States is prohibited by law. Society has explicitly denied them membership."[74] To make this argument, though, Schuck and Smith have to shift the emphasis in the consensual dynamic they have established in their birthright origin story, so as to refocus on the will of the polity rather than the demands of parents on behalf of themselves and their children. Because the parents lack legal migration status, the polity cannot have consented to their inclusion, and by extension, neither could it have consented to the inclusion of their children.[75] The parents' migration status (i.e., legal or not) is what determines the children's entitlement to citizenship, not the children's (or parents') likely future connection to the polity or a basic commitment to equal citizenship for everyone born on the territory. And while Schuck and Smith are particularly concerned about the rewarding of illegal behaviour that they contend *jus soli* citizenship provides, a broader concern about unwarranted citizenship acquisition may also be extended to children born to parents who are in the country legally, but only temporarily – as visitors, in transit, or as students. Anecdotal evidence of pregnant women entering the US to give birth to "anchor babies" – or "maternity tourists" – receives a mention in this regard.[76]

The seventeenth-century Swiss philosophers provided the magical incantation that fused the consent of parents (by which they meant fathers, of course) with the birthright entitlement of children. Even so, Schuck and Smith evidently recognized that they needed more than bold statements to address the democratic conundrum posed by the absence of consent regarding children who had reached the age of majority. Their proposal sought to address this problem through provisional citizenship and an opt-out or expatriation option by the age of majority, to the US-born children of citizens and legal residents, but no such provisional citizenship guarantee to "the native born child of illegal aliens and 'non-immigrant' aliens who have never received the nation's consent to their residence."[77] Furthermore, prospective citizen children were to be protected from "any denial of consent to their membership on the part of the state."[78] It is also important to note that, notwithstanding Schuck and Smith's relentless insistence that illegal immigration constituted a violation of consent, and that migrants were at fault, they recognized that the polity itself could be the abuser. Notably, with regard to the issue of unjust exclusion, they worried about the possibility of denying opportunities for the inclusion of newcomers on discriminatory grounds, the risks of denationalization, and the prospect of statelessness that such action might engender.[79] In such cases, they note, "adherence to consent may well violate liberalism's other deep commitment to insuring that the basic human rights of all be secured as fully as possible."[80]

As already noted, both Schuck and Smith have clarified and moderated their arguments in the wake of the embrace of *Citizenship without Consent* by immigration restrictionists. In 1996, for example, Smith insisted that their book did not endorse the denial of birthright citizenship to the children of illegal aliens, but rather argued that the Constitution was "most coherently read as permitting Congress to decide that question."[81] In 2008, he concluded that the recurring failure of Congress to pass any legislation curtailing birthright citizenship, despite very protracted debate, is sufficient evidence that the American populace has now tacitly consented to a robust *jus soli* entitlement, regardless of the citizenship status of a child's parents.[82] Schuck is not prepared to cede that much ground. In a 2010 *New York Times* opinion column and again with Smith in 2018, he argued for a *jus nexi* citizenship reform, proposing that citizenship for children born in the US to non-citizen, non-resident parents be granted after some years of American schooling, after which these children would receive their citizenship retroactively, regardless of their parents' immigration status.[83]

Schuck and Smith's efforts to contend with the contradictions of birthright citizenship in a supposedly consensual democratic polity are highly instructive, if also problematic. In drawing our attention to the "we" of political membership, and its power to include and exclude, they make their own citizen privilege abundantly clear. While the legal position of Indigenous peoples is obviously important to their argument, Schuck and Smith largely evade the complication of the sovereign authority of Indigenous peoples to assert a "we," and their legal/ moral basis on which to refuse to consent to the inclusion of migrants in *their* bounded communities. As Peter Nyers observes, "claims to origins are always political because they shape what is to follow and, more crucially, disavow other points of departure and modes of being."[84] Thus, in ignoring the ethical foil that Indigenous peoples present to their argument, Schuck and Smith remind us again of the inherently political character of birthright citizenship.

In addition to the issue of who constitutes the "we" and the power that inheres in the designation of a political beginning, Schuck and Smith also draw our attention to the issues of denationalization and expatriation as the corollaries of consent. And while an individual's right to choose among polities, or at least to leave one and join another, is a human right – more aspirational than real in many cases – the state's ability to take away citizenship is a rather more problematic power with which to contend in a liberal-democratic scenario.[85] Schuck and Smith's plan explicitly protects birthright and legal resident children from denationalization. As noted earlier, this limit on the state's ability to withdraw its consent is justified on the grounds of the need to protect human rights. "Although a thoroughgoing commitment to pure consensual membership might seem to imply a national power to denationalize citizens at will, the existence of such a power might threaten the vigorous exercise of basic constitutional freedoms, such as First Amendment political rights, or might create a condition of involuntary statelessness and thus of acute human vulnerability."[86] That said, it is also Schuck's contention – and an expression of his privilege – that respect for human rights does not in fact require citizenship. A more modified package of rights and obligations might be offered to long-term residents or the innocent children of law-evading parents without having to grant full membership.[87] Presumptive citizens can refuse to sign on to the polity, and the polity can create a modified form of inclusion, establishing gradations of membership that can be activated by both individuals and the state. None-theless, some people – those children of citizen parents born in the territory – receive extra protection from denationalization, and in the end, it is only the circumstances of their birth – the fact that they won the birthright lottery – that ensures their access to this privilege.

Placing Schuck and Smith in conversation with Jacqueline Stevens highlights the extent to which *Citizenship without Consent* remains deeply attached to kin-ship as the legitimate basis of the polity. For Schuck and Smith, the idea that the citizenship of children should derive from the citizenship of their parents is unproblematized even in a context of democratic consent. They assume, with the Swiss philosophers who inspired the Founding Fathers, that parents want citizenship for their children and that privileged access to citizenship should follow. But parents want a lot of things for their children that the state does not agree to provide. Indeed, as Joseph Carens points out, there are many social situations in which we feel it is improper to favour family members over others, particularly when the stakes are high.[88] Moreover, if we think of citizenship not simply as a status but also as a set of skills, as a practice of political engagement, then the capacity to exercise those skills falls on the individual, independent of his or her familial connections. Dad may have a driver's licence and want his daughter to drive, but she still has to learn how before she can be granted her own licence. Why shouldn't citizenship work the same way? Or at the very least, why shouldn't it rely on the child's own relationship to the polity, established over time, to provide the basis of membership? The family, however, is a black box for Schuck and Smith. For them, the ties that bind parents to children, bind, or fail to bind, families to the polity.

Finally, and as a valid rejoinder to Stevens's argument that the demise of birthright citizenship will lessen nationalist attachments and the violence to which they can be harnessed, Schuck asserts that a strongly consensual polity offers the prospect of reinforcing political fealty. With great rhetorical gusto, he argues that the benefit of a consensually based polity is to

> more truthfully proclaim to citizens, resident aliens, and illegal aliens alike that American citizenship stands on a firm foundation of freely willed membership. It could more credibly claim the contemporaneous allegiance and, if necessary, the personal sacrifice of its citizens than it was able to do during the Vietnam War and other corrosive national conflicts. It could more persuasively invoke what it now can only baldly assert – a legitimacy grounded in a fresh, vital, and always revocable consent.[89]

Schuck is making an important point here: citizens who feel strongly commit-ted to a political community to which they have actively consented and which they have worked hard to govern may well feel willing to defend it, were its foundational principles to come under threat. Importantly, though, this would not be the "consensual" polity that Schuck and Smith advanced, given their continued commitment to the special access to citizenship that comes from blood and territory. Schuck's political community retains the vestiges of nation that Stevens is so centrally concerned to undermine.

In short, Schuck and Smith, in *Citizenship without Consent* and in their subsequent modifications to that argument, provide us with an informative origin story regarding consent and birthright. They offer a modest if still birth-based proposal for enhancing the consensual basis of membership. And, finally, they provide a very important discussion of the need to limit the state's power to denationalize citizens – or withdraw the consent of the "we." Their retreat from an unmodified refusal of *jus soli* citizenship to the children of aliens underscores the ethical and humanitarian failings of a rigid adherence to status-based claims, and their advocacy of a strongly consensual polity and its people-making capacity forces some consideration as to whether the affinities of political membership could be incited to violent ends, even without an appeal to the immortality of the nation.

Joseph Carens – Birthright in the Midst of Social Membership and Open Borders

The final interlocutor in this discussion of birthright citizenship and its alternatives is Joseph Carens, who is well-known for his elaboration of an open borders position and for his strong advocacy of principles of inclusive belonging through his theory of social membership. Carens's 2013 effort to develop a "theory from the ground up" concerning a democratic ethics of immigration provides outstanding guidance for reimagining the polity on the basis of social membership and the ethical claim that people subject to the exercise of state power should be entitled to participate in their governance.[90] He invites readers to weigh the principle of a state's sovereign right to self-determination against the values of equality, liberty, and justice.[91] In doing so, he asks us, again, to consider the making of the "we" of liberal consent, challenges the view that illegal entry constitutes an especially egregious offence, and makes a strong argument against deportation (and denationalization) when people have established substantive social ties to and within the state. He also provides a persuasive argument for dual or multiple citizenships. Yet in developing his theoretical argument, and in testing current practice against an ethics of democratic inclusion, he is prepared to defend birthright citizenship despite its obvious inconsistency with democratic principles.

The focus of Carens's work is the scene of immigration, and he makes his first sortie into a discussion of birthright citizenship by way of the status of the children of settled migrants. Acknowledging that states clearly have a right in international law to determine their own membership criteria, he nonetheless wants to draw our attention to the normative dimension of membership to ask whether states have a moral obligation to extend birthright citizenship to these children.[92] Carens reasons that since birthright citizenship is how the vast majority of people obtain their citizenship in the world as we currently find it, and because citizenship is a means of conferring moral worth on people, the children of settled immigrants should be entitled to birthright citizenship, just as the children of citizens are.[93] This is a fairly straightforward statement against a form of *jus sanguinis* membership entitlement that maintains the children of migrants as perpetual outsiders – the situation that pertained in Germany, for example, until its citizenship reforms came into effect in 2000.[94] As one might then surmise, Carens also fully supports birthright citizenship in the more usual context of citizenship acquisition, arguing that a state would act wrongly, from a democratic perspective, and would eschew the requirements of justice, by failing to grant birthright citizenship to the children of resident citizens.[95] Under contemporary conditions, babies need citizenship. Since they have no past, they have no experience through which to justify a more consensually derived form of citizenship.[96] Moreover, Carens is advancing an argument for membership entitlement on the basis of social connection. Babies are unavoidably socially connected both to their families and to the political community.[97] In making this latter observation, Carens acknowledges that the political community structures the family itself, as well as other important social relationships and access to social goods.[98]

While Carens explicitly recognizes that birthright citizenship is a political choice rather than "a natural outcome of being born," he has a great deal of difficulty sustaining that awareness as he develops his moral justification for birthright citizenship.[99] A central challenge for him in this regard is to disconnect a blood-based logic of membership and its ethnic associations from democratic citizenship. He asserts that the use of *jus sanguinis* in settler societies like Canada and the United States (in addition to *jus soli*, of course) cannot be regarded as a means to extend an ethnic conception of nationality, since "American" and "Canadian" do not constitute ethnic identities in the normal sense of the term.[100] As the lost Canadians' impassioned appeals to blood-based claims of identity make clear, and as the testimony of both racialized Canadians and newcomers to these settler colonies would undoubtedly indicate, Carens's assertion here is, at the very least, arguable. More critically though, by appealing to a "normal sense of the term" for an understanding of ethnicity, Carens sacrifices his analytical insight regarding the inherently *political* processes that give meaning to birth, to "the common sense" that draws organic connections among kinship, culture, and political membership. My point here is that the "ethnic identities" of the countries that form the implicit contrast to Carens's reading of Canada and the United States are every bit as politically contingent as the national identities of settler societies. What merits explanation here is the fact that our common sense tells us there is a distinction between what birthright citizenship does in "ethnic" nations that is different from what it does in "civic" or settler nations.

In any event, Carens continues, the availability of *jus sanguinis* citizenship claims in these polities is "simply a way to meet the legitimate moral claims that children of emigrants have to be recognized as members of their parents' political community of origin."[101] Why do children have a legitimate claim to be regarded as members of their parents' political community of origin? Carens has already told us that babies have no past, so what is the nature of this connection to the parents' polity, if not an ancestral or "ethnic" one? Children clearly have a legitimate claim to be members of families and to expect the support of the people who have legal and social responsibility for their care. But Carens does not explain why this familial connection forms the basis of a political connection, particularly when that political connection is not to the country in which the family is currently residing. Perhaps if the family planned to return to the country of parental citizenship, it would make sense for a child to have some kind of interim status in order to ensure that the family could move together. Yet this is really a rationale for maintaining the integrity of the family in a context of international mobility, rather than an argument for birthright citizenship. Carens concedes this point later in his book when he argues that the moral claim of the children of emigrants to their parents' citizenship is not, in fact, compelling.[102] Nonetheless, the availability of *jus sanguinis* citizenship does, he insists, address a number of practical problems.[103] At least in the case of *jus soli*, one can see the direct effects of governance on the child, so a claim to some kind of status makes sense under his social connection logic. Yet because Carens wants to insist on "the family" as the necessary transmission point and locus of connection between the individual and the polity in the birthright scenario, he inevitably falls back on a blood-based rationale for political belonging regardless of whether children gain their citizenship by virtue of their social connection to their families in the state in which they live – a modification of *jus soli*, or a *jus sanguinis* claim.

Carens's attachment to birthright citizenship is instructive, even if, or perhaps *because*, it does not stand up to close scrutiny. The challenges of maintaining one's grasp on the insight that families are political, not natural, is well-demonstrated in his analysis, and he has a great deal of company among most citizenship theorists, as well as policy makers, legislators, and jurists. That said, his development of a theory of membership based on social connection and his bold pitch for open borders offer a more provocative and compelling set of considerations from which to construct an alternative basis for citizenship, or, he suggests, perhaps an alternative to citizenship altogether. In providing a foundation for moral claims to legal rights, the theory of social membership is in fact, in Carens's estimation, more fundamental than citizenship.[104]

Building from the social membership rationale that justified the birthright entitlement of the children of immigrant parents, Carens makes a related case for the citizenship of children who spend their formative years in the polity, and for the citizenship of adults who have similarly developed social connections that tie them to a particular state. Even if the social formation of adult immigrants has happened elsewhere, people should still have the opportunity to become members of the society in which they live.[105] "They acquire interests and identities that are tied up with other members of the society. Their choices and life chances, like those of their children, become shaped by the state's laws and policies."[106] Furthermore, because people who reside in a country for a period of time are necessarily subject to its laws, their substantive residence leads to a legitimate democratic claim to participate in their own governance and thus gives rise to a claim to citizenship.[107] With regard to the question of how much time is required for such a membership to develop, he suggests that a year or two is probably insufficient but that five years without criminal convictions should be adequate.[108]

Carens's argument is a clear, principled rejection of the position advanced by Schuck and Smith in the mid-1980s and still mobilized by immigration restrictionists. For Carens, it is the fact that a person forms ties to the community – through work, friendships, family – as well as more formal expectations around paying taxes and otherwise upholding the law, that make the case for political membership. Carens maintains this principle regardless of whether people gained access to the polity through legal or illegal means. Unlike those who insist that the harm of illegal entry is so grave as to prohibit any prospect of membership – that illegality underscores the lack of consent by the "we" – Carens argues that the fact that people make their lives within a society, and do so over several years, is proof enough of inclusion and, in effect, consent. Furthermore, he rejects the insistence that membership determination should be regarded simply as a matter of discretionary choice, noting that "it is a sad truth of our history that popular majorities, political authorities, and even our courts of law have said at various times that Americans of African or Asian or indigenous descent could not be full legal members of our society because the self-governing people refused to consent to their belonging."[109] Because Carens is so wary of the nefarious motivations that can undergird arguments for discretionary selection, he is at pains to limit their use. Despite his strong advocacy for social connection, he insists that time and residence serve as the bases from which to assess the existence of a social membership, rather than some more substantive set of evaluative measures.[110] The restriction on discretion limits the prospects for abuse, he asserts, besides being administratively more efficient.[111]

Elizabeth Cohen's work on the political value of time puts a sharper point on Carens's argument here. Cohen is at pains to point out that time is more than a proxy for connection. Rather, because people may associate a range of meanings to time (for example, a residency requirement may establish knowledge of the polity for some; loyalty to the polity for others), time can serve to "gloss over ... differences and come to agreements about how to transact over power."[112] Commensuration processes thus "make it possible to obtain agreement where agreement is necessary, and to make it unnecessary to obtain agreement where agreement is impossible."[113] Ideally, perhaps, it would be preferable to have a full airing of perspectives and an assessment of belonging based on shared principles. Yet in the interests of a functioning political community, time, in both its precision and its ambiguity, may be the optimal norm for inclusive membership.

In response to the high-mindedness that attends restrictionists' assessments of the moral worth of people who violate migration law in order to seek out a better life, Carens downplays the harms of migration violations. He observes that they find their sanctions in the domain of administrative violations rather than criminality.[114] Moreover, after a lengthy period of residence, it seems only fair that the gravity of the initial violation should diminish. Citing Mae Ngai, he advocates for a statute of limitations on the deportation of long-settled migrants.[115] That said, Carens does find it morally defensible for a democratic polity to refuse entry to adults who have been convicted of serious crimes and to expel such people if they have not resided in the polity for an extensive period. Children of immigrants who commit such crimes should not, in his view, be subject to deportation. Even in the case of adults, though, after a certain period of residence, people who commit criminal acts should be understood to be the responsibility of the polity in which they reside and should face their prosecution without fear of expulsion.[116]

The final innovation Carens offers with regard to an alternative citizenship structure departs quite dramatically, as he fully acknowledges, from his stated desire to build his theory of social membership from the world as he sees it. His advocacy of open borders is well-known and has been both roundly celebrated and summarily dismissed.[117] And while he is under no illusions regarding the likelihood of its adoption, stating that "'from a political perspective, the idea of open borders is a nonstarter,'" he makes a persuasive case for undertaking the thought experiment nonetheless.[118] "Even if we must take deeply rooted social arrangements as givens for purposes of immediate action in a particular context," he asserts, "we should never forget about our assessment of their fundamental character. Otherwise we wind up legitimating what should only be endured."[119]

Like Shachar and Stevens, Carens reminds us that we are living in a world in which the logic of feudal class privilege or caste continues to animate the organization of political membership.[120] Clearly this arrangement is antithetical to democratic principles and should be redressed by a broad commitment to free movement. Carens then sets out three reasons supporting his *prima facie* case for open borders. First, freedom of movement is an essential prerequisite for the enjoyment of other freedoms and for the exercise of autonomy.[121] Second, freedom of movement is essential for equality of opportunity. People have to be able to move to where the opportunities are.[122] Third, given that all people should be accredited equal moral worth, it is also incumbent upon people committed to democratic values to promote economic, social, and political equality.[123] Freedom of movement helps in this regard, although as he notes later, it is not by any means a complete solution. Having set out the case, he then considers a series of objections and notes the necessity for some limited constraints around open borders stemming from national security concerns, public order (controlling the flow of migration), the welfare state (ensuring the capacity to meet people's needs), and culture (but only for especially fragile polities).[124] As one might surmise, Carens has little truck with the view that migrants are inherently dangerous or at least worthy of suspicion. Rather, the overwhelming majority of people who move to a new state are simply seeking to improve their life chances or those of their children. For people and polities that are committed to democratic values, he finds no basis to deny that opportunity. I am fully in agreement.

Carens's theory of social membership, his commitment to democratic freedom and equality, and his open borders proposal are extremely compelling, provocative, and brave. In the face of this radical view, however, I am stymied by his conventional perspective on birthright citizenship. In this I suggest that Carens succumbs to the conservative end of his own caution – legitimating what should only be endured.

What Is to Be Done?

At base, citizenship – birthright or otherwise – *is* exclusive. The fundamental logic underpinning the formal rules of membership delineates the included from the excluded. One could, of course, launch a critique of citizenship itself, as Carens suggests, or reject the "status" basis of citizenship in favour of acts of citizenship, as Peter Nyers argues, but since my imagination is more limited, or at least more constrained by the fact situations of the lost Canadians, I will maintain a commitment to formal citizenship.[125] Short of world government, then, limits on who is in and who is out of a particular political society are unavoidable. Of course, conservatives, and, as it turns out, many liberals too, would argue that this exclusiveness is a good thing. Exclusions, they assert, enable the maintenance of communities of shared values, and they provide security and permit the stewardship of limited resources – jobs, housing, potable water, clean air, and so on. Articulations of the nation are particularly instrumental in this process, since they reinforce a sense of belonging and togetherness for those inside the charmed circle while simultaneously establishing justifications for gatekeeping. Moreover, as Rogers S. Smith argues, the exclusiveness of the nation provides a rationale for preferring one liberal-democratic state over another. In the absence of such national specificity, Smith argues, people will not feel that their political society is "worthy in itself" and will be unlikely to undertake the sacrifices and support the political projects advanced by their political leaders.[126]

But at the same time, exclusions limit people's life chances, foment division and violence, and inure us to our responsibilities for human suffering outside the borders of "our own" political communities.[127] These latter considerations are sufficiently grave that, in my view anyway, they compel the development of a membership process in which the consequences of exclusion are mitigated. And while I appreciate the political power of blood-based claims to national virtue, even when these are couched in the language of liberal consent, it should be possible to devise a political community that takes its contingency and heterogeneity seriously and without fear. To do so would provide a basis for living together that is democratically accountable, responsive to changing circumstances, and worthy of support, not because of its promise to fulfil our fantasies of immortality, but because of its intrinsic integrity. To the extent that a sense of "fellow feeling" is a necessity when collective sacrifice is required – say, in response to a pandemic – it will emerge from the high degree of engagement that such a polity requires. We may well agree that membership should be limited to people who are primarily resident in a particular territory and who are thus subject to the laws of a particular government. But it should also be possible for people who want to live within that territory to do so, and to become members after acquiring sufficient knowledge of and connections within the political community and experience of its policies.

In that spirit, I offer two alternatives for addressing the citizenship conundrums raised by the lost Canadians. The first simply offers some revisions to current practice, drawing from Shachar and Carens to advance a *jus nexi* citizenship rationale to address the underinclusiveness of the current blanket restriction on citizenship faced by the foreign-born children of (non-governmentally employed) Canadians who were born abroad. I also advance a social membership argument to address the unnecessarily restrictive requirement of (pseudo-)genetic relationship as the basis for derivative, birthright citizenship. The second alternative citizenship proposal is, as Carens would say, a political non-starter, in that it would dispatch with birthright citizenship and advance a regime of political membership based on subjection to governance, time, and residence. Yet the fact that such a proposal is so impractical offers an important provocation – and an invitation – to explore the many facets of our collective refusal to consider alternatives to birthright citizenship.

Alternative I – The Realm of Possibilities

In the wake of the Conservative government's 2008 reforms to the *Citizenship Act* – reforms, it should be noted, that were unanimously approved in the House of Commons – it quickly became clear that the price for restoring citizenship to the thousands of Canadians who had fallen victim to the idiosyncracies of the 1947 and 1977 *Citizenship Acts* would be the creation of a new category of loss. The government's public service video "Waking up Canadian" put a positive spin on the expansion of citizenship entitlement: a doughy white man of ambiguous age counts down the days on his calendar, awaking on 17 April 2009 to the National Anthem, a Black, red-serged, smiling Mountie at his door, poutine to eat, hockey to play, and not a woman in sight. But the fact that the government was also keen to limit access to citizenship cast the sovereign's dark shadow over the obligation to bring the *Citizenship Act* into fuller conformity with the *Charter*.[128] News stories began to appear profiling beautiful babies who were no longer entitled to Canadian citizenship as a result of the limitation of derivative citizenship to one generation born abroad.[129]

While I strongly object to the punitive tone of the justification for this limitation – to the presumption that having children abroad necessarily triggers a negative assessment of one's commitment and attachment to Canada – the broader principle of limiting membership to people with a genuine connection to the polity is undeniably valid. The blanket denial of citizenship to children of Canadian parents also born abroad, however, is an unnecessarily blunt (albeit administratively simple) means to realize the objective. In this regard, Canada might take a lesson from the US provisions and require the citizen parent to have resided in Canada or worked abroad for the Canadian government for some required period. For example, Canada's *Citizenship Act* could be amended to provide that the Canadian citizen parent must have been physically present in Canada before the child's birth for a minimum of three years after the parent's fourteenth birthday. A child born abroad to a Canadian parent who was born abroad, but who had resided in Canada for some time and sought citizenship for her child, might be assumed to have an intention to return to Canada. Under Carens's logic of social connection, and given the need for babies to have citizenship, a child in this situation should be granted that citizenship. Alternatively, or additionally, the child could be required to affirm her citizenship by the age of majority and/or spend some minimum period of residency in the country in order to secure her citizenship, as indeed, was the case under the terms of the 1977 Act. Obviously, these requirements would have to work in such a way as to avoid creating a situation of statelessness. It should be a straightforward matter to convey those requirements to the parent at the time of the child's citizenship registration.

The second challenge faced by Canada's existing birthright citizenship provisions is to clarify the definition or appropriate interpretation of parent and child in the *Citizenship Act* and regulations, as well as change the guidance provided in Citizenship and Immigration's Operational Bulletin. Even with the recognition of the parentage, and thus the Canadian citizenship, of a child of same-sex parents who is born with the assistance of reproductive technologies, there may well be additional need for interpretation. It seems likely that the legal rationale for recognizing the parentage, and thus the citizenship, of children born to same-sex couples is simply an extension of the long-standing paternal – now parental – presumption that attributes parentage to the partner of a woman who gives birth. Yet reproductive technologies – and domestic parental status legislation – complicate parental status designation well beyond the two-parent model. Would Canadian parents who undertake a parental project abroad, with the assistance of a surrogate, be able to convey their Canadian citizenship to that child? And what about the recognition of citizenship in a multiple-parent project – such as the situations envisioned in the provincial parentage statutes in British Columbia, Ontario, and Saskatchewan? The government has legitimate concerns regarding child abduction and trafficking and may even feel a moral responsibility to prevent the exploitation of foreign women who act as surrogates or egg donors, but it is not clear that holding fast to a two-parent model for citizenship attribution will be sustainable given the rate of technological and social change. Thus, in addressing the various weaknesses in the definition or interpretation of parent and child, the federal government would be well advised to make special provisions for children born abroad with the assistance of reproductive technologies, perhaps requiring prospective parent(s) in this situation to declare a "parental project" in advance of travel or, if living abroad, in advance of accessing reproductive services. The downside of these provisions is that they require unfortunate invasions of people's privacy and attentiveness to the provisions of citizenship law, but these harms must be weighed against the complicated moral economy of seeking out reproductive assistance abroad, particularly in less wealthy countries.

Alternative II – The Utopian Vision

Reflecting on this rich body of theoretical work and the empirical case of the lost Canadians, my own proposal for a reformed citizenship regime would be based on a combination of consent, time (*jus temporis*), residence, and, most importantly, engagement with or subjection to governance.[130] It would also operate in a context of open borders, the resolution of outstanding land claims, and a state of decolonization. I would argue that when a person falls under the purview of a polity's legal regime for an extended time, they acquire a moral right to have a say in how that governance is conducted. As Robert Goodin notes, "the principle that 'all those who will be bound by a rule should have a say in making the rule' ... looks pretty attractive as a principle in its own right, with a robustly democratic pedigree traceable to the notion of what it is to 'give laws to ourselves.'"[131] Beyond the level of principle, the experience of living in the polity itself has important effects on how we live and aspire to live. And in turn, on behalf of everyone who is affected by the state's governing force, there is a strong case to be made for a right of participation. In this regard, Rogers Smith trenchantly observes:

> It seems undeniable that when governments impose educational systems, religious practices, economic systems, marital and familial structures, forms of expression, and systems of government on people, rewarding those who live as the governments wish and punishing those who do not, they necessarily shape (if they do not indeed constitute) the core values, affiliations and senses of self of many of those people.[132]

Connection and substantive contribution (or commitment) are also relevant to my membership scheme, but, with Carens, I worry that requiring explicit evidence of these criteria may invite oppressive applications of discretion on behalf of the admitting community and, in any event, are likely to be realized through time and residence rather than produced independently from those elements. There are exceptions of course. Joe Taylor would assert a connection to Canada, yet his only encounter with its governance has been in the specific context of his claim for citizenship. In such a situation, my proposed consent-based regime would require that connection be shored up with a requisite period of residence, and thus a stake in the collective project of the polity itself, rather than a more ephemeral identity claim. Of course, Taylor would be welcome to feel attachment to Canada on the basis of his lineage. It is just that lineage would not make him a citizen.

Critics might also make the valid point that people who are on the outside of borders against their wishes, as Joe Taylor was, are also subject to state governance and in ways that are less conducive to democratic principles since they lack the membership status to seek reform. A regime of open borders would largely address this situation by creating the conditions in which a person could become a member through fulfilment of the residency period and a more direct experience of governance.

Peter Nyers cautions against reliance on residency as a basis of membership, querying why presence in the polity is so fundamental with regard to the distribution of rights, and noting that diasporic groups often have "real and genuine ties" to a political community without the need to be territorially present.[133] This observation is keenly accurate with regard to people who work abroad and send remittances to their families, for example, or who have fled from civil unrest. In such cases, it seems likely that a past period of residency would do the work of establishing a claim to membership. But again, in situations in which people are claiming a national attachment based on ethnic or lineage connections, without otherwise encountering the juridical power of the state, my model of membership would not include them.

In terms of a requisite time period for residence, I would suggest three years. Such a pronouncement is arbitrary of course, but three years would provide a person with sufficient time to become acquainted with the community and to decide whether membership is, in fact, what they want. For people who decided that they did not want to become members of the polity, my assumption of open borders would enable them to seek opportunities elsewhere, if their present circumstances were deemed unsuitable. Alternatively, if a person wanted to stay but opted not to be a member, then, as now, there could be access to a more limited set of rights and entitlements.

The issue of active versus passive consent to membership is also central to this proposal. If the desire is to create the conditions for a polity in which people are active participants, or at least understand their inclusion as a matter of conscious choice rather than the good (or bad) fortune of birth, it makes most sense to advocate for active consent. There is a risk that people might neglect to undertake the necessary processes to ensure their status, or that requirements of active consent might invite mendacious efforts by ideologically motivated politicians to thwart consent. These objections strike me as cautions meriting appropriate process and constitutional safeguards rather than strong arguments against consent altogether or active consent in particular. Having consented to membership, a citizen's entitlements would consist of a right to unconditional residence and return, as well as the right to political representation.[134] Citizens who chose not to consent would not hold a right to political representation. Since my scheme envisions a relatively straightforward process of becoming a citizen and the prospect of multiple memberships, this distinction between citizens and denizens is justifiable. Other rights, entitlements, and obligations of citizens and residents would be determined by the polity itself.

The capacity of citizens to decline membership or expatriate themselves raises the question of whether the community should have grounds to refuse membership and what those grounds should be. These questions are also provoked by the cases we explored in the chapter on security. On this score it seems to me that if a polity produces bad actors, it must attend to their punishment and rehabilitation without resorting to denationalization and deportation. Someone who has met the criteria regarding minimum time, residency, and subjection to governance and has done so without engaging in serious criminal behaviour (treason, terrorist acts), but who does engage in criminality after becoming a member, would be subject to the polity's criminal proceedings without fear of expulsion. Where someone has not met those criteria, age would be a factor. I would argue that if the person was youthful, and had been raised in the polity, then the polity has to take responsibility for their bad behaviour and cannot expel them. If the person is seeking to enter the political community from else-where and she is an adult, however, I am less inclined to see an obligation to accept her. Bearing in mind the UN Convention on the Reduction of Stateless-ness,[135] the cost of criminal behaviour within a state and prior to membership could be some modified package of rights – such as those that might be granted to people who rejected membership but wanted to remain. Serving time and a period of good behaviour, along with meeting the other membership require-ments, could then bring such a person within the ambit of citizenship.

In a membership regime that abandons birthright citizenship, perhaps the most obvious considerations circulate around the status of children. Clearly, some status needs to be provided until children reach an age at which they can choose political membership for themselves. In this pre-citizenship period, parents could determine whether a child should enjoy interim status in the state in which they reside, or in some other state in which a parent has citizen-ship, if that would facilitate family mobility. At the age of majority, though, an individual would be required to meet (or have met) the residency requirement. I acknowledge that such a provision would do little to disturb the logic of the birthright lottery, since most people will become citizens in the state in which they were born. It is not so simple, after all, to decamp from one's family and from familiar surroundings. But at least this alternative vision offers the oppor-tunity to explore a wider range of locations for making a life.

The disconnection of legal definitions of family, parentage, and children from determinations of citizenship closes down at least one site of potential objections to the pluralization of family forms and the recognition of fami-lies based on the caring relationships among adults and children rather than conjugal status. Once lineage no longer provided a means to acquire citizen-ship, the state would lose the basis for an argument for retaining biological/genetic definitions of family. Some of this cleaving to lineage might be retained in the interim status determinations of children, but a polity that is committed to delinking lineage from membership should be amenable to avoiding such residual vestiges of birthright.

My schema would also provide for multiple memberships. If a person has acquired knowledge of a place through meeting the minimum residence requirements, is willing to accede to the governance of two or more jurisdic-tions, and has some connection or contribution to make to two or more poli-ties, this prospect is fully reasonable. One could imagine some requirement of affirmation after a certain length of time away, as well as ongoing contri-bution requirements as a way of maintaining the reciprocity of the relation-ship between the citizen and the community. Objections to dual or multiple membership tend to focus on the disloyalty that could arise from split allegiances, issues of state responsibility in situations of diplomatic or security crisis abroad, and the unfairness of being able to vote in two or more states.[136] With the demise of mandatory military service as a citizenship obligation in many countries, the allegiance issue is less salient than it once was.[137] The prospect of a need for diplomatic intervention, though, as we saw with the evacuation of Canadians from Lebanon and in other heavily publicized cases, does seem worthy of some consideration. A principle that the last country of residence should normally take responsibility for the individual may offer a possible resolution. Finally, with regard to the unfairness of enjoying the right to vote in multiple jurisdictions, a state could suspend voting rights after some period of absence (and reinstate them upon a period of residence). Generally, though, if we accept that people have a right to participate in their own governance, and a person is living subject to the governance of two states, the issue of fairness would seem best resolved by enabling that person to exercise his democratic right of participation.

As we have seen, a predictable feature in any discussion of citizenship is the assumption of a self-governing community with the requisite sovereign right to determine who belongs. The "we" of that community are the people who are already there – the hosts, if you like, the people understood to be, or who assert themselves as, the autochthonous subjects. But of course, there is magical thinking in that assertion, especially obvious in a place like Canada, where the First Peoples have been colonized. In order to claim the power to decide who is in and who is out, the settler-colonizers have to forget or reimagine the circumstances by which they came to be in the territory in the first place, in terms of both Indigenous peoples and subsequent migrant entrants. We can see this phenomenon at work in familiar arguments about "every Tom, Dick, and Harry" wanting to get in and in the related presumption that we should be deeply suspicious of Tom, Dick, and Harry.[138] But the fact is that in Canada, unless you are Indigenous, everyone is Tom, Dick, or Harry. For much of the population, the immigration experience is not so distant. The rest, if asked, would likely tell a family history that included a migration narrative. It may even be that this situation of settler colonialism creates the conditions of possibility to challenge the hold of claims to blood and lineage as the basis for political membership and (mortal) belonging. Yet as with the political character of birthright citizenship, the recognition that most Canadians are settlers has a tendency to come in and out of consciousness. Unless, of course, you are Indigenous.

Ultimately, my critical engagement with the birthright citizenship difficulties that pervade the stories of the lost Canadians has led me to advocate for a citizenship regime founded on residence, time, consent, and subjection to governance. This alternative vision of political membership appeals to me because it offers a way to live together that upends historical claims to political belonging and their related gendered, heteronormative, and racial hierarchies. It includes an expectation that political membership is a lively, ongoing process of negotiation in which everyone has a stake. As a member of the Canadian polity, I think it is critically important to be attentive to the state's political origins in colonization and settlement as well as to the creative and destructive processes that the making of a settler society has entailed. Some critics might argue that abandoning birthright citizenship and its intergenerational character will create the conditions for decision-making in which we are no longer future-oriented, or indeed, that we will neglect the lessons and obligations of our past, including the consequences of colonization. If our children do not have a stake in the polity to come, why should we commit ourselves to making it better? This kind of argument is morally bereft. We can continue to care about the future and attend to the damages we and our ancestors have wrought, even if, or precisely because, our political membership is limited by our mortality. It was, of course, ever thus.

Appendix:
Canadian Citizenship through the Acts

Prior to the Citizenship Act 1947

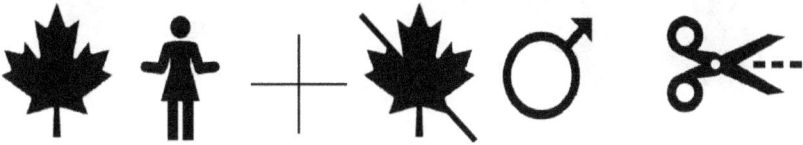

If a Canadian woman marries a foreign (non-Canadian) man, it results in loss of Canadian citizenship for her.

Child born abroad to (formerly) Canadian woman married to a foreign (non-Canadian) man does not acquire Canadian citizenship.

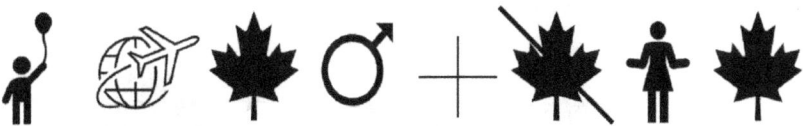

Child born abroad to a Canadian man married to a foreign (non-Canadian) woman is a Canadian citizen.

Prior to the Citizenship Act 1947 (*cont.*)

Child born abroad to an unwed Canadian woman is a Canadian citizen.

Child born abroad to an unwed Canadian man is NOT a Canadian citizen.

Citizenship Act 1947–1977

If a Canadian woman marries a foreign (non-Canadian) man, she retains her Canadian citizenship. All the citizenship outcomes for a child born abroad remain the same.

Citizenship Act 1977–

Child born abroad on or after 15 February 1977 to a Canadian woman, whether she is married or not, is a Canadian.

Child born abroad on or after 15 February 1977 to a Canadian man, whether he is married or not, is a Canadian.

Notes

1 Introduction

1 When Pierre Elliott Trudeau was justice minister in 1967, he famously stated that "there is no place for the state in the bedrooms of the nation" as his justification for advancing legislation that, among many other provisions, decriminalized homosexual acts performed in private and legalized abortion if the procedure was approved by a committee of three doctors. See https://www.cbc.ca/archives/entry/omnibus-bill-theres-no-place-for-the-state-in-the-bedrooms-of-the-nation. Despite Trudeau's claim, however, the Canadian state has continued to be highly engaged in people's intimate lives – as this book demonstrates.

2 Until amendments were made to the *Citizenship Act* in 2008 and 2014, the citizenship of children born before 15 February 1977 was tied to the citizenship of their "responsible parent." If a child was born in the context of a marriage, her responsible parent was her father. If she was born out of wedlock, her responsible parent was her mother.

3 Canada, Standing Committee on Citizenship and Immigration, 39th Parliament, 2nd Session. *Reclaiming Citizenship for Canadians: A Report on the Loss of Canadian Citizenship* (Ottawa: Standing Committee on Citizenship and Immigration, December 2007), 2–4.

  A note on the dates of the Citizenship Acts – throughout the book I adopt the common practice of referring to the 1947 *Citizenship Act* and the 1977 *Citizenship Act* – but the formal, legal reference to these acts locates them in 1946 and 1976 respectively. I use the years in which these Acts came into force, as distinct from when they were passed in Parliament.

4 *Ibid.*, 9. As Dr Edmonston pointed out, there was also a question of how many people may have been aware that their citizenship was in doubt but were fearful that if they brought their situations to the attention of the Department of Citizenship and Immigration, they might find themselves rendered stateless.

5 See *Canada (Citizenship and Immigration) v. Taylor* 2007 FCA 349 (CanLII)
   2007–11–02.
6 *Benner v. Canada (Secretary of State)* (1997) 1 S.C.R. 358.
7 See chapter 6 for a more detailed discussion of the Benner case.
8 Rates of migration increased significantly in the second decade of the 2000s due
   to the severe displacements brought about by wars in Syria and northern Africa.
   Even so, in 2019 the number of international migrants globally constituted 3.5 per
   cent of the world's population. Thus, the vast majority of people reside in their
   countries of birth. Sadly, though, that situation does not necessarily entitle
   them to citizenship. See United Nations, International Organization for Migration,
   2019, *World Migration Report 2020*, https://www.un.org/sites/un2.un.org
   /files/wmr_2020.pdf; and United Nations High Commission for Refugees, n.d.,
   "Statelessness around the World," https://www.unhcr.org/statelessness-around-the
   -world.html.
9 Stevens, *Reproducing the State*. See also Stevens, *States without Nations*.
10 Siobhan Somerville notes the connection between the naturalization of plants and
   the naturalization of people. The process of naturalization, she observes, is one in
   which the difference between the indigenous and the imported becomes effaced.
   Most significantly, the process of naturalization automatically entitles the children
   of naturalized citizens to citizenship by birth. See Somerville, "Notes toward a
   Queer History of Naturalization," 667, 669.
11 Gaudry and Leroux, "White Settler Revisionism," 116. See also Tuck and Yang,
   "Decolonization Is Not a Metaphor," 8–9.
12 Gaudry and Leroux, "White Settler Revisionism," citing Reuben Gold Thwaites,
   ed., *The Jesuit Relations and Allied Documents: Travels and Explorations of the
   Jesuit Missionaries in New France, 1610–1791*, vol. 5, 209.
13 Gaudry and Leroux, "White Settler Revisionism," 117. Gaudry and Leroux are
   primarily interested in the increasing prevalence of people claiming a Métis
   identity without attachment to or knowledge of (or hostility to) the political
   origins of the Métis Nation as a distinct political community originating in the Red
   River. Chris Andersen offers a fascinating book length treatment of this political
   phenomenon in "*Métis*."
14 Henderson, "*Sui Generis* and Treaty Citizenship," 418.
15 Simpson, *Mohawk Interruptus*, 25.
16 Stevens, *Reproducing the State*.
17 Stevens, *Reproducing the State*, 56.
18 Stevens, *Reproducing the State*, 107.
19 Stevens, *Reproducing the State*, 226–7.
20 Bala and Ashbourne, "The Widening Concept of 'Parent' in Canada," 529–30.
21 Mykitiuk, "Beyond Conception," 782.
22 The reality was more complicated. In the US, the Cable Act of 1922 declared that
   marriage had no effect on a woman's citizenship. Thus, Canadian women who

married American men simultaneously lost their Canadian citizenship (or rather, British subject status) but did not gain US citizenship. This effectively rendered them stateless. See Girard, "'If two ride a horse,'" 40.

23 See Stasiulis and Ross, "Security."
24 Canada, *Debates* 30 April 2007 at 16:45 (Andrew Telegdi).
25 *Canada (Citizenship and Immigration)* v. *Kandola* 2014 FCA 85 (CanLII).
26 *Caron c. Attorney General of Canada* (2020) QCCS 2700 (CanLII) [*Caron*].
27 Shachar, *The Birthright Lottery*.
28 Borrows, "'Landed' Citizenship."
29 Many thanks to Isabel Altamirano for her engagement on these questions with me and for sharing a number of models – including the Citizenship Code of the Fort William First Nation. I have also benefited from the insights of John Borrows (2002), James (Sa'ke'j) Youngblood Henderson (2002), Kahente Horn-Miller (2018), Val Napoleon (2005, 2013), Pamela Palmater (2011), and Audra Simpson (2014).
30 Mulgrew, "Canadians who aren't," A6.
31 Standing Committee on Citizenship and Immigration, 39-1, No. 38 (26 February 2007) at 11:45 (Sheila Walshe).
32 Anderson, *Imagined Communities*.
33 See, for example, Borrows, "'Landed' Citizenship."
34 For fascinating analyses of dispossession, property, and Indigenous conceptions of land and political community, see Coulthard, *Red Skin White Masks*; Bhandar, *Colonial Lives of Property*; and Nichols, *Theft Is Property!*.
35 Stevens, *Reproducing the State*, 61. My emphasis.
36 Shachar, *The Birthright Lottery*.
37 Duffy, "Baby born in midair," A5.
38 See, for example, Dhamoon et al., eds. *Unmooring the Komagata Maru*; Dua, "Exclusion through Inclusion"; and Satzewich, "Racism and Canadian Immigration Policy."
39 Razack, *Race, Space, and the Law*; Sharma, *Home Economics*; Thobani, *Exalted Subjects*.
40 Sharma, *Home Economics*, 27. See also Stasiulis, "The Political Economy of Race, Ethnicity and Migration," 141–66.
41 Honig, *Democracy and the Foreigner*, 84.
42 Honig, *Democracy and the Foreigner*, 93.
43 Chapman, *The Lost Canadians*, 24.
44 Ahmed, "Embodying Diversity," 42.
45 Stevens, *States without Nations*, 10.
46 Elizabeth Cohen, *The Political Value of Time: Citizenship, Duration, and Democratic Justice*, (Cambridge: Cambridge University Press, 2018).
47 Cohen, *The Political Value of Time*, 10.
48 Cohen, *The Political Value of Time*, 38.

49 Cohen, *The Political Value of Time*, 54.
50 Cohen, *The Political Value of Time*, 56.
51 Cohen, *The Political Value of Time*.
52 That said, it must be acknowledged that positive responses from the Canadian state were not likely to gain attention.
53 Canada, *Citizenship Act* S.C. 1946, c. 15, s 21(c).

2 Operation Daddy, War Brides, and the Making of Canadians: Canadian Citizenship Law, or the Canadian National Family

1 Canada, House of Commons Debates, 41–2, No. 53 (27 February 2014) at 15:25 (Chris Alexander), http://www.parl.gc.ca/HousePublications/Publication.aspx?Pub=Hansard&Doc=53&Parl=41&Ses=2&Language=E&Mode=1.
2 As with note 1. Unfortunately, most Canadians are wholly unfamiliar with Mathieu da Costa's contributions to Canada's formation as a nation-state.
3 *Supra* note 1.
4 *Supra* note 1.
5 *Supra* note 1.
6 Although the 2008 reforms were designed to reinstate citizenship for most categories of lost Canadians, the Conservative government's concern was that people lacking substantive ties to Canada (evidenced through their residence outside of Canada) would be able to pass their citizenship on through successive generations. As a result, children born abroad after 17 April 2009 to a Canadian citizen who was born abroad are unable to claim Canadian citizenship. Canada, *Citizenship Act* R.S. 1985 c.C-29, s. 3.3. As a result of the 2014 amendments, people born abroad prior to 1 January 1947 to a Canadian parent became eligible for Canadian citizenship as of 11 June 2015.
7 Shachar, *The Birthright Lottery*, 112.
8 Bothwell, "Something of Value?"
9 Heidi Bohaker and Franca Iacovetta observe a similar rendering of Indigenous people as immigrants in the post–Second World War period. As they note, from 1950 to 1966, Indian Affairs was a branch of the Department of Citizenship and Immigration, and both Indigenous people and immigrants were targeted for similar "Canadianization" programs. See Bohaker and Iacovetta, "Making Aboriginal People 'Immigrants Too.'" They also note that Métis and non-Status Indians were understood as "regular" Canadians, while Inuit remained a distinct citizenship/racial category, as did Status Indians.
10 Johnson, "First Nations and Canadian Citizenship."
11 Stasiulis, "The Political Economy of Race, Ethnicity, and Migration," 146.
12 McLaren, "Stemming the Flood of Defective Aliens," 190.
13 Whitaker, *Canadian Immigration Policy since Confederation*, 9–10.
14 Knowles, *Forging Our Legacy*, 38.

15 Dua, "Exclusion through Inclusion."

16 Hoerder, "'Of Habits Subversive.'"

17 Blackstone, *Commentaries*, 442.

18 Martin, "Citizenship and the People's World," 68.

19 Canada, House of Commons Debates, 20–1, Vol. 2 (2 April 1946) at 503 (Paul Martin).

20 *Supra* note 19, at 502.

21 Martin, "Citizenship and the People's World," 71.

22 *Supra* note 19, at 502 (Paul Martin).

23 *Supra* note 19, at 505 (Paul Martin).

24 *Supra* note 19, at 510 (John Diefenbaker).

25 *Supra* note 19, at 512 (John Diefenbaker).

26 *Supra* note 19, at 512 (John Diefenbaker).

27 *Supra* note 19, at 513 (John Deifenbaker). The issue of race and ethnic diversity was very present in this debate.

28 Canada, House of Commons Debates, 20–2, Vol 2 (5 April 1946) at 598 (T.L. Church).

29 *Supra* note 28, at 623 (Maxime Raymond).

30 Ferguson, *All in the Family*, 15.

31 Ferguson, *All in the Family*, 23.

32 Ferguson, *All in the Family*.

33 *Supra* note 19, at 505 (Paul Martin).

34 Canada, *Citizenship Act* S.C. 1946, c. 15.

35 *Martin*, as with note 19 at 74.

36 Martin, "Citizenship and the People's World," 72.

37 Martin, "Citizenship and the People's World," 76.

38 Martin, "Citizenship and the People's World."

39 Martin, "Citizenship and the People's World," 78.

40 Billig, *Banal Nationalism*; Anthony Smith, *The Antiquity of Nations*; Hobsbawm, *Nations and Nationalism since 1780*.

41 Stevens, *States without Nations*, 6.

42 The complexities of the war brides' experiences are also well articulated in a number of collections of their first-hand accounts. See, for example, Joyce Hibbert ed., *The War Brides* (Toronto: PMA Books, 1978); Linda Granfield, ed. *Brass Buttons and Silver Horseshoes: Stories from Canada's British War Brides* (Toronto: McClelland and Stewart, 2002); Melynda Jarratt, *War Brides: The Stories of the Women Who Left Everything behind to Follow the Men They Loved* (Stroud: Tempus, 2007).

43 Stacey and Wilson, *The Half-Million*, 136.

44 Stacey and Wilson, *The Half-Million*, 140. Stacey and Wilson note that some of these marriages might have occurred between Canadians or between a Canadian and another foreign national on British soil, but that the overwhelming majority of them were between Canadian men and British women.

45 Stacey and Wilson, *The Half-Million*, x.
46 Costello, *Love, Sex and War 1939–1945*, 317. Costello recounts the case of Charles Eugene Gautier, who was hanged at Wandsworth prison after he was convicted of murdering a British woman when she began dating another Canadian, and Victor Eric Gill, who murdered his pregnant British girlfriend because she had dated another Canadian sergeant. Gill was tried and convicted of manslaughter.
47 Gallant, "Introduction," xii.
48 Stacey and Wilson, *The Half-Million*, 136.
49 Stacey and Wilson, *The Half-Million*.
50 In parliamentary speeches responding to questions about the costs of repatriating soldiers and their dependents, government ministers indicated that these costs were borne by the Canadian government. See, for example Canada, House of Commons Debates, 20–1, Vol. 1 (15 October 1945), at 1070–1 (G.K. Fraser).
51 Stacey and Wilson, *The Half-Million*.
52 Stacey and Wilson, *The Half-Million*, 138.
53 Ctd in Wolgin and Bloemraad, "'Our Gratitude to Our Soldiers,'" 56.
54 Rains, Rains, and Jarratt, *Voices of the Left Behind*, 2; Stacey and Wilson, *The Half-Million*, at 148.
55 Ctd in Nadja Durbach, "Private Lives, Public Records," 322.
56 Stacey and Wilson, *The Half-Million*, 148–9; Paul Cornes, *No More Damned Secrets: An Anglo-Canadian War Child's Quest for Roots and Identity* (Sussex: Book Guild, 2013), 168.
57 Stacey and Wilson, *The Half-Million*, 148–9.
58 Keshen, *Saints, Sinners, and Soldiers*, 234.
59 *Order in Council re entry into Canada of dependents of members of the Canadian Armed Forces*, PC 1946–858 C Gaz, 308.
60 See *Canada (Citizenship and Immigration) v. Taylor* 2007 FCA 349 at para 52; Canada, Standing Committee on Citizenship and Immigration, 39–1, No. 36 (19 February 2007).
61 Jarratt, *War Brides*, 25; Wolgin and Bloemraad, "'Our Gratitude to Our Soldiers,'" 55.
62 Canada, House of Commons Debates, 19–5, Vol. 1 (6 June 1944) at 3572 (John Ritchie MacNicol and Thomas Crerar); Canada, House of Commons Debates, 20–1, Vol. 1 (4 October 1945) at 761 (G.K. Fraser); Canada, House of Commons Debates, 20–1, Vol 1. (12 October 1945) at 976 (D.S. Harkness); Jarratt, *War Brides*, 16–17; Cornes, *No More Damned Secrets*, 168–9; Wolgin and Bloemraad, "'Our Gratitude to Our Soldiers,'"55.
63 Jarratt, *War Brides*, 32.
64 Matrix, "Mediated Citizenship and Contested Belongings," 79.
65 Honig, *Democracy and the Foreigner*, 76.
66 Peterson. "Political identities"; Yuval-Davis, *The Politics of Belonging*, 95.
67 "Survey shows Canadian war brides contented," 1, ctd in Jarratt *War Brides*, 28.

68　Hammerton, "The Quest for Family," 271.

69　Thobani, *Exalted Subjects.*

3 Feminine Virtues and Lost Canadians

1　Stevens, *Reproducing the State,* 56.

2　Canada, *Citizenship Act 1946.* s. 9.1(c) and s. 9.2(c).

3　*Ibid.,* s.6(a).

4　*Ibid.,* s. 20.

5　*Ibid.,* s. 18.

6　Bramham, "Loss of Citizenship."

7　Bramham, "War bride, 87."

8　Bramham, "Citizenship battle ends."

9　Bramham, "War bride, 87."

10　Bramham, "War bride, 87."

11　Bramham, "War bride, 87."

12　Much of my analysis of Taylor's case was previously published in Lois Harder, "'In Canada of All Places': National Belonging and the Lost Canadians," *Citizenship Studies* 14, no. 2 (2010): 203–20.

13　*Canada (Citizenship and Immigration) v. Taylor* 2007 FCA 349 (CanLII) 2007–11–02, at para 6.

14　*Ibid.,* at para 16.

15　*Ibid.,* at paras 8–9.

16　Revisions to the *Citizenship Act* had extended the age by which one had to affirm citizenship to twenty-four from twenty-two.

17　*Canada (Citizenship and Immigration) v. Taylor* 2007, at para 61.

18　*Taylor v. Canada (Citizenship and Immigration)* (2006) FC 1053 (CanLII) 2006–09–01, at para 245, 277.

19　*Canada v. Taylor* 2007, at para 71.

20　*Ibid.,* at paras 105–7 and at 91–8.

21　Seamus O'Regan, "Child of WWII couple finally wins citizenship." In her first appearance as minister before the Standing Committee on Citizenship and Immigration, Diane Finley stated that while the Government of Canada was appealing the Taylor case, "she was not unsympathetic to his plight" Canada, Standing Committee on Citizenship and Immigration, 39–1, no. 36 (19 February 2007) at 11:15 (Diane Finley).

22　*Windsor Star,* "A war story."

23　Canada, House of Commons Debates, 39–1, Vol. 143 (30 April 2007) at 16:45 (Andrew Telegdi).

24　*Ibid.*

25　Canada, Standing Committee on Citizenship and Immigration, 39–2, No. 10 (6 February 2008) at 15:55 (Melynda Jarratt).

26 Canada, Standing Committee on Citizenship and Immigration, 39–1, No. 38
    (26 February 2007) at 11:50 (Joe Taylor).
27 *Ibid.*
28 *Ibid.*
29 *Supra* note 18, at para 273; Daphne Bramham, "It's official: Joe Taylor is finally a
    Canadian citizen; Son of soldier and war bride had been denied his Canadian-ness
    until now," *Vancouver Sun*, 25 January 2008; Seamus O'Regan, "Child of WWII
    couple finally wins citizenship."
30 Canada, Standing Committee on Citizenship and Immigration, 39–1, No 60
    (29 May 2007) at 11:15 (Lisa Cochrane), at 12:05 (Melynda Jarratt); Canada,
    Standing Committee on Citizenship and Immigration, *Reclaiming Citizenship for
    Canadians: A Report on the Loss of Canadian Citizenship*, 39–2 (December 2007) at 6–7.
31 Canada, Standing Committee on Citizenship and Immigration, 39–1, No. 60
    (29 May 2007) at 12:05 (Melynda Jarratt).
32 Canada, House of Commons Debates, 39–1, No. 143 (30 April 2007) at 16:45
    (Andrew Telegdi).
33 Foot, "'Lost' citizen regains status."
34 CBC "Committee report urges citizenship for 'Lost Canadians.'"
35 O'Regan, "Child of WWII couple finally wins citizenship."
36 Bramham, "It's official."
37 The facts of Scott's case are presented in *Scott v. Canada (Minister of Citizenship
    and Immigration)* Application for Judicial Review, Applicant's Memorandum of
    Fact and Law, Court File No. T-418-12, 25 March 2013.
38 Stella Holiday, Citizenship Analyst to Jackie Scott, 26 January 2012. Included as
    Exhibit A in *Scott v. Canada*, as at note 37.
39 *Scott v. Canada*, as at note 37.
40 Canada, House of Commons Standing Committee on Broadcasting, Films and
    Assistance to the Arts, "Bill C-20, an Act respecting citizenship," Minutes of
    Proceedings and Evidence, No. 36 (27 February 1976) at 6.
41 *Scott v Canada*, as at note 37, at paras 118–20.
42 Day, *Multiculturalism and the History of Canadian Diversity*, 131.
43 Honig, *Democracy and the Foreigner*.
44 Scott was not subject to the loss provisions because she was still in Canada when
    she reached the age of twenty-four.
45 Holiday to Scott, as at note 38.
46 Rains, Rains, and Jarratt, *Voices of the Left Behind*, 137.
47 Rains, Rains, and Jarratt, *Voices of the Left Behind*.
48 The social construction of identity is alive and well in this symbol of ethnic
    belonging. In fact, totem poles are a phenomenon of West Coast Indigenous
    cultures and were not part of traditional Ojibwa villages. See Aldona Jonaitis and
    Aaron Glass, *The Totem Pole: An Intercultural History* (Vancouver: Douglas and
    McIntyre, 2010).

49 Gazze, "60 years later." The *Indian Act* requires that the father's name be included
    on a child's birth certificate. In the hypothetical situation described here, whether
    the woman named or failed to name the father, the presumption would be that
    the father lacked status, and thus status would not be granted to the child. See
    Palmater, *Beyond Blood*, 106.
50 Palmater, *Beyond Blood*.
51 The revelations concerning Eric Clapton's Canadian paternity were first publicized
    in 1998. See, for example, "Guitarist Clapton finds lost family here."
52 Paul Cornes, *No More Damned Secrets: An Anglo-Canadian War Child's Quest for
    Roots and Identity* (Sussex: Book Guild, 2013).
53 Cornes, *No More Damned Secrets*, 4–5.
54 Cornes, *No More Damned Secrets*, 183.
55 Mary Pipher, *Reviving Ophelia: Saving the Selves of Adolescent Girls* (2019) ctd in
    Cornes, *No More Damned Secrets*, 152.
56 Marilyn Strathern, "Enabling Identity? Biology, Choice, and the New Reproductive
    Technologies" (1996), ctd in Yuval-Davis, *Gender and Nation*, 28.
57 Strathern, *Kinship, Law and the Unexpected*, 9.
58 *Citizenship Act* R.S.C. 1985, c. C-29 s. 5(a).

4 The Veranda of Citizenship: The 1977 *Citizenship Act* and After

1   Canada, House of Commons Debates, 30–1, Vol. 6 (21 May 1975) at 5984 (James
    Faulkner).
2   *Ibid.*, at 5986 (James Faulkner) (on character); Canada, Standing Committee
    on Broadcasting, Films and Assistance to the Arts, 30–1, No. 34 (24 February
    1976), at 18.
3   Canada, *Citizenship Act* 1974–75–76, c. 108, s. 5 (3 year residency), s. 31
    (Commonwealth citizen).
4   Elizabeth Cohen, *The Political Value of Time: Citizenship, Duration, and
    Democratic Justice,* (Cambridge: Cambridge University Press, 2018), 5.
5   Canada, Royal Commission on the Status of Women. Ottawa: Royal Commission
    on the Status of Women, Ottawa: 1970, 364.
6   *Ibid.*, at 363.
7   *Ibid.*
8   *Ibid.*, at 364.
9   Canada, *Citizenship Act* 1974–75–76, c. 108, s. 10(2).
10 Canada, Standing Committee on Broadcasting, Films and Assistance to the Arts,
    30–1, No. 36 (27 February 1976) at 5.
11 *Ibid.*, at 6.
12 *Ibid.*, at 5–6.
13 Canada, Standing Committee on Broadcasting, Films and Assistance to the Arts,
    30–1, No. 39 (9 March 1976,) at 8–9.

14 Given the magical powers attributed to 1 January 1947 with regard to the existence of Canadian citizenship, the fact that women could have first lost and then regained a status that apparently did not exist is a particularly interesting claim.

15 Canada, *supra* note 13 at 9.

16 *Ibid.*, at 11.

17 *Ibid.*, at 14.

18 *Citizenship Act* 1974–75–76, c.108, s. 5(2)(b).

19 *Ibid.*, s. 18(1).

20 Canada, *supra* note 1 at 5983.

21 Honig, *Democracy and the Foreigner*, 76.

22 Honig, *Democracy and the Foreigner*.

23 Honig, *Democracy and the Foreigner*.

24 Canada, House of Commons Debates, 30–1, Vol. 9 (8 December 1975) at 9808 (Bill Jarvis).

25 Canada, House of Commons Debates, 30–1, Vol. 6 (21 May 1975) at 5987 (Gordon Fairweather).

26 Canada, House of Commons Debates, 29–2, Vol. 2 (26 April 1974) at 1813 (Roderick Blaker).

27 *Ibid.*

28 Canada, Standing Committee on Broadcasting, Films and Assistance to the Arts, 30–1, No. 34 (24 February 1976) at 29.

29 Stevens, *States without Nations*, 10.

30 Canada, House of Commons Debates, 30–1, Vol. 10 (10 December 1975) at 9908 (J.A. Maclean).

31 *Ibid.*, at 9912 (W.C. Scott).

32 *Ibid.*

33 Canada, Standing Committee on Broadcasting, Films and Assistance to the Arts, 30–1, No. 41 (12 March 1976) at 9.

34 See, for example the remarks of Howard Johnston, Canada, House of Commons Debates, 30–1, Vol. 9 (8 December 1975) at 9814 (Howard Johnston).

35 See, for example the remarks of Benno Friesen, Canada, House of Commons Debates, 30–1, Vol. 12 (13 April 1976) at 12793 (Benno Friesen).

36 Pammett and LeDuc, *Explaining the Turnout*, http://www.elections.ca/res/rec/part/tud/TurnoutDecline.pdf.

37 Canada, House of Commons Debates, 30–1, Vol. 12 (13 April 1976) at 12793 (Benno Friesen).

38 Canada, House of Commons Debates, 30–1, Vol. 9 (8 December 1975) at 9814 (Howard Johnston).

39 Canada, House of Commons Debates, 30–1, Vol. 6 (21 May 1975) at 5986 (James Faulkner).

40 Canada, House of Commons Debates, 30–1, Vol. 10 (10 December 1975) at 9905 (Len Marchand).

41 Many years later, in 2005, the Assembly of First Nations passed a resolution calling
    for a halt to all immigration until "the federal government addresses, commits,
    and delivers resources to First Nations to improve the housing conditions,
    education, health and employment in First Nations communities and that the
    federal government acknowledge and agree they are bringing immigrants into
    our lands and using our resources without our consent." Cited in Harald Bauder,
    "Re-Imagining the Nation: Lessons from the Debates of Immigration in a Settler
    Society and an Ethnic Nation" *Comparative Migration Studies* 2, no. 1 (2014): 20.
42 Canada, House of Commons Debates, 30–1, Vol. 6 (21 May 1975) at 5986-7
    (James Faulkner).
43 As with note 42, at 5987 (Gordon Fairweather).
44 Canada, Standing Committee on Broadcasting, Films and Assistance to the Arts,
    30–1, No. 39 (9 March 1976) at 10.
45 Canada, Standing Committee on Broadcasting, Films and Assistance to the Arts,
    30–1, No. 34 (24 February 1976) at 25.
46 Canada, House of Commons Debates, 30–1, Vol. 6 (21 May 1975) at 5986 (James
    Faulkner).
47 Canada, *Citizenship Act* 1974–75–76, c. 108, ss. 20, 28.
48 Canada, House of Commons Debates, 30–1, Vol. 12 (13 April 1976) at 12792
    (Benno Friesen).
49 Canada, House of Commons Debates, 30–1, Vol. 9 (8 December 1975) at 9826,
    9827 (Gordon Towers).
50 Weil, *How to Be French*, 188.
51 Weil, *How to Be French*, 190-2.
52 Weil, *How to Be French*, 192.
53 Canada, *Citizenship Act* 1974–75–76, c.108, s. 6.
54 *Ibid.*, at s. 20.
55 *An Act to Amend the Canadian Citizenship Act* S.C. 1952–53, c. 23.
56 Canada, *Citizenship Act* 1974–75–76, c. 108, s. 7.
57 Canada, House of Commons Debates, 29–2, Vol. 2 (26 April 1974) at 1815
    (Donald Munro).
58 Canada, Standing Committee on Broadcasting, Films and Assistance to the Arts,
    30–1, No. 34 (24 February 1976) at 24-5.
59 *Ulin v. Canada* [1973] F.C. 319, at para 16.
60 *Ibid.*
61 There were situations, for example when a Canadian married a foreigner after
    1 January 1947, in which a Canadian woman might gain a second citizenship
    by virtue of marriage, without being required to renounce her Canadian
    citizenship. See *Ulin v. Canada* at para. 8.
62 Canada, Standing Committee on Broadcasting, Films and Assistance to the Arts,
    30–1, No. 41 (12 March 1976) at 9.
63 Schuck, *Citizens, Strangers, and In-Betweens,* 218.

64 Abu-Laban and Gabriel, *Selling Diversity*; Bloemraad, "Who Claims Dual Citizenship?," 393.
65 Canada, Standing Committee on Broadcasting, Films and Assistance to the Arts, 30–1, No. 41 (12 March 1976) at 8.
66 *Ibid.*, at 5.
67 *Ibid.*, at 3, 12.

5 Lost to Canada by Ordinary Means

1 Canada, Department of the Secretary of State, *Citizenship '87: Proud to be Canadian.* (Ottawa: Supply and Services Canada, 1987). In the interests of space and focus I will refrain from a discussion of this remarkable document. For readers interested in the power of Canada's national rhetoric to whitewash the country's history, though, I would highly recommend reading it. The following quote, with its failure to recognize policies of colonialism and land-grabbing applied against Indigenous peoples, and the grave mistreatment and racism visited upon Eastern European immigrants, and especially on Asian railway workers, provides a sense of the discourse:

> Drawn by the prospect of farmland and prosperity in the New World, thousands streamed into Canada from the Ukraine, Poland, Germany, and other parts of Europe. They were welcomed eagerly by a country which had an abundance of land and a shortage of people to develop it. Thousands more from China, Japan, and the Indian sub-continent were drawn to the developing Pacific coast. The Chinese, who came to help build the transcontinental railroad, referred to Canada as Gam San, the "Golden Mountain", and so it must have seemed to many who arrived. (6)

2 *Re Chute* [1981] F.C.J. No. 67 (Quicklaw).
3 *Ibid.*, at paras 1–2.
4 *Ibid.*, paras 2.
5 Interview with Douglas Chute (23 October 2015).
6 Interview with Douglas Chute (23 October 2015).
7 Canada, *Citizenship Act* 1974–75–76, c.108, s. 5(2)(a).
8 *Re Chute* [1981], *supra* note 2 at para 4.
9 *Ibid.*
10 *Ibid.*
11 *Ibid.*, at para 11.
12 *Ibid.*
13 Email from Douglas Chute to Lois Harder (21 August 2015).
14 *Glynos v. Canada* (C.A.) [1992] F.C.J. No. 875. (Quicklaw).
15 *Ibid.*
16 *Ibid.*, at para 2.

17 In this case, Anita was deemed to be authorized to make the application, although the judgment notes that the issue of her eligibility was uncertain. Because the government did not raise the issue in the legal proceedings, the court chose to assume that she was deemed authorized. See *Ibid.*, paras 4 and 5.

18 *Ibid.*, at para 5.

19 *Glynos v. Canada* [1991] F.C.J. No. 168. (Quicklaw).

20 *Glynos v. Canada [1992], supra* note 14 at paras 8–9.

21 *Glynos v. Canada [1991], supra* note 19.

22 *Ibid.*

23 *Ibid.*

24 *Glynos v. Canada [1992], supra* note 14 at paras 13–15.

25 *Ibid.*, at para 15.

26 *Ibid.*, at para 16.

27 *Ibid.*, at paras 18–21.

28 *Ibid.*, at para 22.

29 *Crease v. Canada* [1994] 3 FCR 480 (CanLII).

30 *Wilson v. Canada (Citizenship and Immigration)* 2003 FC 1475 (CanLII).

31 See Chapman, *The Lost Canadians*; www.blog.lostcanadian.com.

32 See, for example his testimony at Canada, House of Commons Standing Committee on Citizenship and Immigration, hearings on C-18, 37-2, No 14 (28 January 2003) (Don Chapman).

33 *Ibid.*

34 *Ibid.*

35 Canada, *Citizenship Act* 1946 s. 18.

36 In his 2015 book, Chapman states that he visited the Citizenship and Immigration Canada office in Vancouver when he was eighteen to inquire as to Canadian citizenship. According to his account, he was told that he was ineligible and he was not informed of the reinstatement provision (Chapman, *The Lost Canadians* 10).

37 This discussion of Don Chapman's citizenship claim and advocacy for lost Canadians is a slightly revised version of material first published in Lois Harder, "'In Canada of All Places.'"

38 Foot, "Bill to restore citizenship for 'lost Canadians.'"

39 Canada, Standing Committee on Citizenship and Immigration, hearings on C-18, 37-2, No 19 (10 February 2003).

40 Canada, Standing Committee on Citizenship and Immigration, *Reclaiming Citizenship for Canadians: A Report on the Loss of Canadian Citizenship*, 39-2 (December 2007), 13.

41 *Ibid.*

42 Mennonites are members of a Protestant denomination in which adult baptism, pacifism, and a commitment to a simple life are fundamental theological tenets. A substantial population of Mennonites settled in Russia in the 1700s but emigrated or fled between the late 1800s and 1924 and again in the late 1940s. They dispersed

to Canada, the US, Paraguay, Belize, and Bolivia. Subsequently, a group of these people who landed in Canada chose to relocate to Mexico in order to escape Canadian efforts to regulate the education of their children (see below).

43 Mulgrew, "Canadians who aren't."

44 Canada, Standing Committee on Citizenship and Immigration, *Reclaiming Citizenship for Canadians: A Report on the Loss of Canadian Citizenship*, 39–2 (December 2007), 13.

45 Canada, Standing Committee on Citizenship and Immigration, 39–2, No. 10 (6 February 2008) at 16:10 (Don Chapman).

46 Peggy Becklumb, "Bill C-37: An Act to Amend the Citizenship Act," Legislative Summary (Ottawa: Parliamentary Information and Research Service, 2008), 5.

47 If a person is rendered stateless by the 2008 amendments to the *Citizenship Act*, they can receive a mandatory grant of citizenship if they are under twenty-three, have lived in Canada for three of the last four years prior to application, have always been stateless, and have not been convicted of various offences, primarily related to terrorism (Section 5.4 *Citizenship Act* R.S., 1985 c.C-29). As Peggy Becklumb explains, Canada, as a signatory to the UN Convention to Reduce Statelessness, is required to grant its nationality to a person not born on Canadian territory who would otherwise be stateless, if the nationality of one or both of the person's parents at the time of the person's birth was Canadian. Such a grant of nationality may be subject to certain stipulated conditions, however. In Becklumb's assessment, the provision included in the amended citizenship act is compliant with the Convention, but only minimally so (2008, 14). The statelessness of the lost Canadians attracted the UN's attention and found its way into a special issue of the Commission on Refugees' monthly publication. This development was reported in an Ontario local newspaper as follows: "tucked in the centerfold of the glossy-paged magazine, behind images of developing countries and bare-bottomed children living in destitute poverty, is a colour photo of a straight-backed Mountie dressed in red serge." ("Citizenship loophole sinks Canada's Record: UN report singles out country's policies as near the bottom of a worldwide list" *Kitchener-Waterloo Record,* 23 October 2007). As this evocative description makes clear, the newspaper felt that it was a national embarrassment for Canada, a country of wealth, order, and tradition, to have its citizenship laws included alongside countries so far beneath Canada's ranking in the global hierarchy. This embarrassment underscores Canada's investment in its national image. Sunera Thobani observes that "Canadians routinely describe their citizenship, immigration and refugee policies as the most humanitarian and compassionate in the world. These claims shape their sense of collective pride and national identity" (Thobani, *Exalted Subjects*, 69).

48 Royden Loewen, *Village among Nations: "Canadian" Mennonites in a Transnational World, 1916-2006* (Toronto: University of Toronto Press, 2013), 40. Another 2,000 people went to Paraguay at the same time.

49 Regehr, *Mennonites in Canada*, 134–5.

50 Loewen, *Village among Nations*, 177–8.
51 *Veleta v. Canada* (Minister of Citizenship and Immigration), 2005 FC 572.
52 *Veleta v. Canada* (M.C.I.), 2006 FCA 138 at para 3.
53 *Ibid.*, at para 4.
54 *Ibid.*, at para 5.
55 *Ibid.*
56 *Ibid.*, at para 13.
57 *Veleta v Canada [2005], supra* note 51 at para 30.
58 *Ibid.*, at para 22–24, 28, 31–33
59 *Veleta v Canada [2006], supra* note 52 at para 15.
60 *Ibid.*
61 *Ibid.*, at para 16.
62 *Ibid.*, at para 25.
63 My thanks to William Janzen, an advocate for Mennonites facing citizenship difficulties, and Nelson Martell (now a retired officer with Citizenship and Immigration), for providing me with this information.
64 CBC News, "Second-generation Canadians get into the act" (March 2007), https://www.cbc.ca/news2/background/lostcanadians/born-abroad-babies.html.
65 *Ibid.*
66 Canada, Standing Committee on Citizenship and Immigration, *Reclaiming Citizenship for Canadians: A Report on the Loss of Canadian Citizenship*, 39–2 (December 2007), 12.
67 *Ibid.*
68 O'Neill, "Arcane law strips Canadians of their citizenship."
69 Canada, Standing Committee on Citizenship and Immigration, 39–1, No 61 (29 May 2007) at 15:50 (Rose Anne Poirier).
70 Canada, Standing Committee on Citizenship and Immigration, 39–1, No 41 (19 March 2007) at 11:15 (Johan Teichroeb).
71 The resistance of conservative Mennonites to COVID vaccines and public health mandates may have weakened this reputation.
72 Canada, Standing Committee on Citizenship and Immigration, *Reclaiming Citizenship for Canadians: A Report on the Loss of Canadian Citizenship*, 39–2 (December 2007), 13.
73 Letter from William Janzen to Jason Kenney (20 September 2010), letter on file with author.
74 William Janzen, "Two Problem Areas For Some Born-Abroad Canadians: The Loss/Retention Provision and the Legacy of the Born-in-Wedlock Requirement," submission to the Parliamentary Committee on Citizenship and Immigration by Mennonite Central Committee Canada (MCCC), 26 February 2007, Ottawa. On file with author.
75 Again, I have William Janzen to thank for bringing this issue to my attention and explaining its technicalities; *Ibid.*

76 It must be said that Canada's current *Citizenship Act* is a remarkably challenging document to decipher. Nonetheless, see *Citizenship Act* ss. 3(g) and 3(k) (reinstating citizenship to people who had been born or naturalized in Canada prior to 1977 and 1947, but had subsequently lost their citizenship); ss. 8 and 3(1) (f)(iii) (repeal of age 28 affirmation requirement and reinstatement of citizenship); and s. 3(4) (second generation cut off as of 17 April 2009).

77 Birthright citizenship finds particular argumentative purchase when it is cast in the context of children's legal status. Crudely framed, the argument runs that consensual models of citizenship determination leave children's national status unaddressed. Some alternative and temporary status might presumably be crafted to attend to the citizenship and mobility requirements of children. For a rehearsal of some elements of this debate, see Costica Dumbrava and Rainer Bauböck, eds. *Bloodlines and Belonging: Time to Abandon Jus Sanguinis?*, European University Institute Working Papers, 2015. http://cadmus.eui.eu/bitstream /handle/1814/37578/RSCAS_2015_80.pdf?sequence=1&isAllowed=y.

78 Canada's *Citizenship Act* R.S., 1985 c.C-29, s. 5.4. The 2014 amendments to the *Citizenship Act* included the possibility of citizenship revocation for dual citizens convicted of terrorism-related offences (s. 10). This provision could be read as an instance of citizenship loss through a deemed absence of, or negative, connection. The J. Trudeau Liberals subsequently repealed this provision.

79 Stevens, *Reproducing the State*, 267.

80 Stevens, *Reproducing the State*.

6 Security and Birthright Citizenship Determination

1 See, for example, *Galati v. Canada (Governor General)* 2015 FC 91 (CanLII) at paras 66–7, 72–5, in which, among other claims, the plaintiff argued that s. 8 of the *Strengthening Citizenship Act* (Bill C-24) was beyond the legislative capacity of Parliament under the *Constitution Act 1867,* on the grounds that citizenship is an inalienable and immutable right. Unsurprisingly, the Federal Court disagreed.

2 See Macklin, "Citizenship Revocation," 53, on the distinction between citizenship as a right, citizenship as a privilege, and the privilege to be a citizen.

3 Hansen, "A Case for Seduction?," 369; Daiva Stasiulis and Darryl Ross, "Security, Flexible Sovereignty," 335.

4 Macklin, "Citizenship Revocation," 9.

5 Dhamoon and Abu-Laban, "Dangerous (Internal) Foreigners and Nation-Building," 163–83.

6 Brodie, "From Social Security to Public Safety," 692.

7 Honig, "The Foreigner as Citizen," 7; italics in the original.

8 For Arar this process involved a public inquiry, a public apology, compensation, and the firing of high-ranking public officials (Commission of Inquiry, 2006). In March 2017 the federal government offered an apology, and in November 2017

it paid out a settlement to Abdullah Almalki, Ahmad El Matti, and Muayyed Nureddin, who were also falsely accused of terrorism, imprisoned in Syria, and tortured, and whose treatment was the subject of a 2008 federal commission of inquiry that found that Canadian government agencies had indirectly contributed to their imprisonment and torture. See Pillay, "Pillay." On the contradictions surrounding Arar see Abu-Laban and Nath, "From Deportation to Apology."

9 Cowen and Gilbert, "Citizenship in the 'Homeland'"; Kaplan, "Homeland Insecurities."

10 See Nath, *Far from Belonging*.

11 Harder and Zhyznomirska, "Claims of Belonging." This concern regarding "abuse" of Canadian citizenship was manifest in a 2014 amendment to the *Citizenship Act* that allows the minister to revoke citizenship from a naturalized Canadian deemed to lack the intention to permanently reside in Canada. See *Citizenship Act* s. 5(1) (c.1)(i) and discussion in Macklin, "Citizenship Revocation," 24.

12 Note the forgetting of the immigrant history of all non-Indigenous Canadians that is required in order for such a statement to make sense.

13 Macklin, "Citizenship Revocation," 30.

14 *Drinnan* (Re) 1982 F.C.J. No. 709 (Quicklaw) [Drinnan].

15 *Ibid.*

16 *Ibid.*

17 *Bell v. Canada (Minister of Employment and Immigration)* [1994] F.C.J. No. 372 (*Bell 1994*); *Canada (Minister of Employment and Immigration) v. Bell* [1996] F.C.J No. 641 (*Bell* 1996).

18 *Bell [1994]*, at para 11.

19 *Ibid.*, at para 7.

20 *Ibid.*, at para 14.

21 *Ibid.*, at para 15.

22 *Ibid*, at para 11. In Bell's case, of course, his adoptive father was also his biological father, but in more typical circumstances, the adoption process transforms non-biological parents into "natural" parents.

23 *Bell [1996]*, *supra* note 17.

24 *Ibid.*, at 5.

25 I certainly do not mean to imply that security, citizenship, and precarity are things of the past. As the 2014 reforms to the *Citizenship Act* regarding the revocation of Canadian citizenship from dual citizens convicted of terrorism-related offences, the continuing use of security certificates, and the indefinite detention of deportees and refugee claimants all make clear, the intersection of citizenship law, immigration law, and the Criminal Code can be a very dangerous place – an "exceptional place" in the language of Schmitt and Agamben.

26 *Benner v. Canada* (Secretary of State) [1994] 1 FC 250, para 17. QL [*Benner* FC].

27 *Ibid.*, at para 20.

28 *Citizenship Act* 1976, ss. 18 and 20.

29 *Canadian Charter of Rights and Freedoms*, Part I of the *Constitution Act, 1982*, being Schedule B to the *Canada Act 1982* (U.K.), 1982, c. 11. s. 1.; *Benner* FC para 47, 50.
30 *Benner* FC, para 2–3.
31 *Ibid.*, at para 3.
32 *Ibid.*, at para 72.
33 *Ibid.*, at para 40.
34 *Ibid.*, at para 44
35 *Ibid.*, at para 46
36 *Ibid.*, at para 69
37 *Ibid.*, at para 69
38 *Ibid.*, at para 70
39 *Benner v. Canada (Secretary of State)*, [1997] 1 S.C.R. 358 QL, at para 44.
40 *Ibid.*, at para 56
41 *Ibid.*, at para 77.
42 *Ibid.*, at para 89–90.
43 *Ibid.*, at para 95.
44 *Ibid.*, at para 96–97.
45 *Ibid.*, at para 104.
46 *Augier v. Canada (Minister of Citizenship and Immigration)* [2004] 4 F.C.R. 150.
47 *Ibid.*
48 Helfend, "Asian Organized Crime," http://www.loc.gov/rr/frd/pdf-files /AsianOrgCrime_Canada.pdf.; Off, "Dream merchants," http://www.cbc.ca/news /background/merchants.
49 W-Five, "Citizens of Canada."
50 *Canada (Citizenship and Immigration) v. Taylor* 2007 FCA 349 at paras 57, 71.
51 Canada, House of Commons Debates, 38–1, Vol. 140, No. 35 (30 November 2004) at 13:01 (John Reynolds).
52 Canada, House of Commons Debates, 38–1, Vol. 140, No. 54 (10 February 2005) at 17:47 (John Reynolds).
53 Canada, House of Commons Debates, 38–1 Vol. 140, No. 35 (30 November 2004) at 13:20 (Hedy Fry)
54 Canada, House of Commons, Standing Committee on Citizenship and Immigration, *Reclaiming Citizenship for Canadians: A Report on the Loss of Canadian Citizenship* (December 2007), 24.
55 *Clark v Canada (Minister of Public Safety and Emergency Preparedness)* 2006 FC 1512 CanLII.
56 *Clark v Canada (Minister of Public Safety and Emergency Preparedness)* 2009 FC 311 CanLII.
57 Canada, *Reclaiming Citizenship*, 23.
58 *Ibid.*, 23–4.
59 Currently, and also preceding the Conservative government's reforms to the *Citizenship Act's* revocation provisions, the only ground for revocation is having fraudulently obtained citizenship.

60 See CBC Radio, "John McCallum on rolling back controversial Citizenship Act," *The House*, 27 February 2016. McCallum (Liberal Minister of Immigration, Citizenship and Refugees from 2015 to 2017) noted that revoking Canadian citizenship from someone who obtained it fraudulently is a "different thing" from taking it away from a legitimate citizen. "If you tell lies or give wrong information in the process of obtaining your citizenship, then you shouldn't have that citizenship in the first place. So that's when it should be taken away."

61 Bechard, Becklumb, and Elgersma, "Legislative Summary of Bill C-24," https://lop .parl.ca/About/Parliament/LegislativeSummaries/bills_ls.asp?ls=c24&Parl=41&Ses =2&Language=E#a39.

62 Forcese, "A Tale of Two Citizenships," 569.

63 Bechard, Becklumb, and Elgersma, "Legislative Summary of Bill C-24."

64 Bechard, Becklumb, and Elgersma, "Legislative Summary of Bill C-24."

65 Forcese, "A Tale of Two Citizenships," 569.

66 Forcese, "A Tale of Two Citizenships," 579.

67 Wells, "Not for turning."

68 *Ibid.*

69 *Ibid.*

70 *Ibid.*

71 *Ibid.*

72 *R. v. Amara* 2010 ONSC 441 (CanLII) at para 40.

73 Michael Friscolanti, 'Still-present dangers: very little movement has been made on a range of promises – from better equipping spies to jet purchases" *Maclean's* 24 October 2016.

74 *R. v. Amara, supra* note 72.

75 Forcese, "A Tale of Two Citizenships," 571.

76 Forcese, "A Tale of Two Citizenships," 573.

7 Reproductive Technologies and "Maternity Tourism": *Jus sanguinis* and *Jus soli* Redux

1 Material in this chapter has been previously published in *Canadian Journal of Law and Society; Revue europeenne des migrations internationals.*

2 Canada, House of Commons Debates, 39–1, Vol. 141 (13 June 2006) at 12:58 (Monte Solberg).

3 The ineligibility of children of foreign diplomats to Canadian birthright citizenship is outlined in *Citizenship Act* R.S.C. 1985, c. C-29, s. 2.

4 Canadian law also allows for the adoption of adults, often in circumstances in which the child has been fostered by a Canadian for an extended period. This situation is not considered in this chapter.

5 Freeman and Richards, ""DNA Testing and Kinship," 72; Mykitiuk, "Beyond Conception," 779.

6 The legal recognition of same-sex common law relationships and marriage in Canada did not extend the paternal presumption to the same-sex partner of a

birth parent, since parentage is a provincial responsibility. After many years of slow legal reform, that presumption does now pertain in most provinces and territories in the context of birth registration, though not as widely in parental status law.

7 British Columbia, *Family Law Act* S.B.C. 2011, c.25 [BC FLA]; Ontario *Children's Law Reform Act* R.S.O. 1990, c. C. 12 [ON CLRA]; Saskatchewan, *Children's Law Act* SS 2020, c.2. [Saskatchewan CLA]. In BC, these multiple parent arrangements – outside the surrogacy context – require that the gestational mother be a parent (BC FLA s. 30). The provisions regarding surrogacy do not specify the number of people who can be parents and does not require that intended parents be genetically related to the child (BC FLA s. 29). In Ontario and Saskatchewan, multiple parentage provisions apply if a preconception parentage agreement exists among the parties. In Ontario, such an arrangement may involve a surrogate (who waives her rights to parentage) and does not require a genetic relationship between the child and any of the parents ON CLRA s. 10. In Saskatchewan, such an arrangement requires that the birth parent be a party to the parentage agreement SK CLA, s. 61.

8 *Alberta Family Law Act* S.A. 2003, c. F-4.5 [AB FLA]; *Manitoba Family Maintenance Amendment Act* S.M. 2021, c.63 [MB FMA].

9 Quebec, Comité consultative sur le droit de la famille, *Pour un droit de la famille adapté aux nouvelles réalités conjugales et familiales,* https://www.justice.gouv .qc.ca/fileadmin/user_upload/contenu/documents/Fr__francais_/cen tredoc /rapports/couple-famille/droit_fam7juin2015.pdf.

10 Alberta, *supra* note 8 at s. 8.2; British Columbia, *supra* note 7 at s. 29, 31; Manitoba, *supra* note 8 at s. 24; Ontario, *supra* note 7 at s. 10 (7); *Nova Scotia, Birth Registration Regulations,* NS Reg 390/2007, s. 3; Saskatchewan, *supra* note 7 at s. 62. Quebec forbids surrogacy but has recognized the practice through special consent adoptions (Adoption – 09184, 2009 QCCQ 9058, [2009] RJQ 2694 – and see discussion in Angela Campbell, "Law's Suppositions about Surrogacy," esp. 53–6. In provinces and territories that do not make explicit provisions for surrogacy (Newfoundland and Labrador, New Brunswick, Northwest Territories, Nunavut, PEI), parents are required to adopt the child.

11 Alberta, *supra* note 8; British Columbia, *supra* note 7 at ss. 27 and 29; Nova Scotia, *supra* note 10 at s.5(2)(e); *Ontario, supra* note 7 at s. 10; Saskatchewan, *supra* note 7 at s. 62.

12 *Citizenship Regulations,* SOR/93/246, s. 2.

13 *Citizenship Act* R.S.C., 1985, c. C-29, s. 2(1).

14 Marco Mendicino, Minister of Immigration, Refugees and Citizenship, cited in Burns, "Ottawa changes law."

15 Citizenship and Immigration Canada, "Operational Bulletin 381."

16 *Ibid.*

17 *Ibid.*

18 Burns, "Ottawa changes law."
19 *Canada (Citizenship and Immigration)* v. *Kandola* 2014 FCA 85 (CanLII).
20 *Kandola v Canada (Minister of Citizenship and Immigration)* 2013 FCJ No 374 (Quicklaw), at para 8.
21 *Ibid.*
22 *Ibid.*, at para 32.
23 *Ibid.*, at para 24.
24 *Canada v. Kandola* (2014), *supra* note 19 at para 54. It seems unlikely that the judge considered the implications of this claim very carefully. In effect, if a child can become a Canadian citizen through legitimation, unmarried single-parent foreigners should be marrying Canadians as quickly as they can to ensure a fast track to citizenship.
25 *Ibid.*, at para 22.
26 *Ibid.*, at para 59.
27 Mainville J.A. dismissed the relevance of the distinctions drawn between the French and English texts, regarding them as a function of administrative redrafting rather than legislative amendment and finding that such changes were not intended to change the law. Ibid., paras 89 and 91. From there he offered an analysis of the meaning of "parent" in the law, including an extensive analysis of the paternal presumption (indeed, it forms the primary focus of his dissent). Parliament, in his estimation, would have been well aware of the paternal presumption when it drafted the derivative citizenship provisions of the *Citizenship Act*. Since those provisions did not explicitly exclude non-genetic fathers, as they did adoptive parents, the federal government's argument for a rigidly genetic definition of "parent" in the case at bar was, in his view, unpersuasive (at para 108).
28 *Ibid.*, at 72.
29 *Ibid.*, at 75. As well, a marital status argument could be advanced by same-sex couples with regard to the recognition of their parentage.
30 The derivative citizenship clause of the *Citizenship Act* reads: "Subject to this Act, a person is a citizen if the person was born outside Canada after February 14, 1977 and at the time of his birth one of his parents, other than a parent who adopted him, was a citizen."
31 *Ibid.*, at 66.
32 *Ibid.*, at 76.
33 The Federal Court of Appeal's decision was handed down on 31 March 2014. Second reading and the committee stage for consideration of Bill C-24 – where such an amendment might have been introduced – occurred between 29 May and 4 June 2014. No amendments to the Act were adopted. See Canada, Standing Committee on Citizenship and Immigration, "Report 3," http://www.parl.gc.ca /HousePublications/Publication.aspx?DocId=6634456&Language=E&Mode=1 &Parl=41&Ses=2.

34 *Caron c. Attorney General of Canada* (2020) QCCS 2700 (CanLII) [*Caron*]. The jurisdictional issue is notable here. The Quebec Superior Court agreed that it was the appropriate venue for the case since Caron's argument concerned the constitutionality of s. 3(1b) of the *Citizenship Act* and/or the minister's interpretation of that section (the definition of parent). Caron had not undertaken a court action seeking to quash the Ministry of Citizenship and Immigration's decision regarding Benjamin's citizenship – an action that would have properly been heard before the Federal Court (at para 7).

35 Interview of Laurence Caron (15 July 2020.)

36 *Caron, supra* note 34 at para 23.

37 Interview of Laurence Caron, 15 July 2020.

38 Interview of Laurence Caron, 15 July 2020.

39 Interview of Laurence Caron, 15 July 2020.

40 *Caron, supra* note 34 at para 6.

41 Burns, "Ottawa changes law."

42 Stevens, *Reproducing the State*, 173–208.

43 CTVNews.ca, 2016. "Is 'birth tourism' a problem in Canada? Doctors on frontline of debate," https://www.ctvnews.ca/health/health-headlines/is-birth -tourism-a-problem-in-canada-doctors-on-frontline-of-debate-1.3023973.

44 *Ibid.*

45 Griffith, "What the previous government learned."

46 Favaro and Flanagan, "'Birth tourism' rising fast in Canada."

47 The Canadian Institute for Health Information relies on hospital financial data to derive these figures, since people without health care coverage must pay the hospital bill themselves. Thus, the existing data may include Canadian citizens as well as visitors, international students, and non-Canadians working in Canada under various employment visas. Refugee claimants and permanent residents who have not completed the three-month waiting period for health care coverage are not included in these numbers, as they fall into a separate coding category (Griffith, "What the previous government learned"; Gaucher and Larios, "Birth Tourism."

48 Gold, "Growth coalition"; David Ley, *Millionaire Migrants*.

49 Ley, "Global China," 19.

50 Ley, "Growth coalition," 9.

51 Ley, "Global China," 20.

52 David Ley's research found that the funds that Asian investors are using to purchase Canadian real estate are not derived from successful business ventures in Canada. He notes that "despite their high levels of human capital at landing, tax filer data show that their declared incomes have been lower than any other visa category, *including refugees*"(Ley, "Global China," 25) Instead, these real estate purchases are financed by wealth acquired outside of Canada.

53 Ley, *Millionaire Migrants,*" 9.

54 Ley, "Global China," 20.

55 Gold, "Growth coalition," 47.
56 Asia Pacific Foundation of Canada, "Vancouver's Foreign-Owned Real Estate."
57 Canada, *Canadian Citizenship: A Sense of Belonging*, 17.
58 Canada, Standing Committee on Citizenship and Immigration, 35–1 (5 May 1994) at 10:31 (Richard Nolan).
59 Dolan and Young. *Legislative History of Bill C-18*, http://publications.gc.ca /Collection/YM32-3-442-2002-11-01E.pdf.
60 Minister of Immigration, Jason Kenney, ctd in Yelaja, "Birth tourism," https://www.cbc.ca/news/canada/birth-tourism-may-change-citizenship -rules-1.1164914.
61 See, for example, Carlaw, "Authoritarian Populism."
62 Griffith, "What the previous government learned"; Yeates, "Government of Canada briefing," 1, https://multiculturalmeanderings.files.wordpress. com/2013/06/citizenship-reform-proposal-19-birth-on-soil.pdf.
63 Yeates, "Government of Canada briefing," 11–12.
64 Griffith, "What the previous government learned."
65 Yeates, "Government of Canada briefing,"1.
66 For a fascinating discussion of this phenomenon in the German context see Castañeda, "Paternity for Sale."
67 Mouritsen, Kriegbaum Jensen, and Larin, "Introduction," 601.
68 Yeates, "Government of Canada briefing."
69 Yeates, "Government of Canada briefing," 4.
70 Griffith, "What the previous government learned."
71 Ctd in Griffith, Griffith, "What the previous government learned."
72 Black, "Ottawa to consult with provinces."
73 Raj and Maloney, "Federal Tory Delegates Vote." Party resolutions are not binding on an elected government. In this case, however, Conservative Party leader Andrew Scheer endorsed the resolution as it applied to "birth tourism." Dickson, "Scheer defends birthright policy."
74 Bourgon, "Why women are coming to Canada"; Humphrey, "Tory motion to end birthright citizenship." By contrast, a petition to reinstate popular hockey personality Don Cherry, after he was fired by Sportsnet for making anti-immigrant comments on air, amassed more than 200,000 signatures in two days. See Lau, "'Bring back Don Cherry' petition."
75 Wood, "Birth tourism rates."
76 Conservative Party of Canada, *National Policy Committee Convention Package*, 10, https://cpcassets.conservative.ca/wp-content/uploads/2019/04/03155332 /DUCw9_byfAlGSAE.pdf.
77 Bronskill, "'Not consistent and uniform.'" It should be noted, though, that at least one member of the Liberal caucus disagreed. Joe Peschisolido, whose riding is also in Richmond, presented a petition to Parliament in 2018 opposing maternity tourism. That petition collected approximately 11,000 signatures. See Campbell, "Richmond MP."

78 Gaucher and Larios, "Birth Tourism."
79 Llana, "When does birthright citizenship."
80 Llana, "When does birthright citizenship."
81 Llana, "When does birthright citizenship."
82 Llana, "When does birthright citizenship."
83 Thobani, *Exalted Subjects*, 79.
84 Llana, "When does birthright citizenship."; Bourgon, "Why women are coming to Canada."
85 Bourgon, "Why women are coming to Canada."
86 Ctd in Tasker, "'It's fraudulent.'"
87 Tasker, "'It's fraudulent.'"
88 Angus Reid Institute, *Birthright Citizenship*.
89 Angus Reid Institute, *Birthright Citizenship*.
90 Canadian Press, "Feds studying birth tourism."
91 Meloni et al., "Children of Exception:"
92 Canada, *Regulations Amending the Immigration and Refugee Protection Regulations*.
93 Forcier and Dufour, "Immigration, Neoconservatism, and Neoliberalism," 5.
94 Griffith, "What the previous government learned."
95 Ley, *Millionaire Migrants*, 4.
96 Ngai, "Birthright Citizenship," 2521.
97 Ngai, "Birthright Citizenship,"
98 Sean Wang, "'Fetal citizens'? Birthright Citizenship, Reproductive Futurism, and the 'Panic' over Chinese Birth Tourism in Southern California," *Environment and Planning D: Society and Space* 35, no. 2 (2017): 269–70.
99 Wong, "Canada's birthright citizenship policy."
100 This would have been an extraordinary sum of money and a very uncommon circumstance, given the lengths to which the Canadian government went to prevent Asian migration to Canada. Li. "Reconciling with History."
101 Wong, "Canada's birthright citizenship policy."
102 Wong, "Canada's birthright citizenship policy."
103 Wong, "Canada's birthright citizenship policy."
104 This insight is adapted from Sean Wang's work on responses to Asian maternity tourism in the US. See Wang, "Fetal Citizens?," esp. 270.
105 Van Houdt, Suvarierol and Shinkel. "Neoliberal Communitarian Citizenship," 419.
106 Gaucher and Larios, "Birth Tourism."

8 Alternatives

1 Berlant, *Cruel Optimism*, 1.
2 Audra Simpson, "Consent's Revenge," *Cultural Anthropology* 31, no. 3 (2016): 328. In fact, Simpson's project refuses to analyse the internal membership struggle

of the people of Kahnawà:ke, but here and in *Mohawk Interruptus,* she offers a compelling look at the constraints around the membership conversation.

3 Stevens, *States without Nations,* 56.
4 Stevens, *States without Nations,* 50. Although the idea of a Canadian ethnicity may seem ephemeral, the Federal Court of Appeal's ruling in *Kandola,* discussed in the previous chapter, offers a vivid example of the use of law to construct ethnicity/national identity.
5 Stevens, *States without Nations,* 96.
6 Stevens, *States without Nations,* 75.
7 Stevens, *States without Nations,* 102.
8 Stevens, *States without Nations,* 77.
9 Stevens, *States without Nations,* 26.
10 Stevens, *States without Nations,* 32.
11 Stevens, *States without Nations.*
12 Gardels, "Two Concepts of Nationalism."
13 Gardels, "Two Concepts of Nationalism."
14 Gardels, "Two Concepts of Nationalism."
15 Stevens, *States without Nations,* 32.
16 Stevens, *States without Nations,* 33.
17 Stevens, *States without Nations,* 33–4.
18 Stevens, *States without Nations,* 34.
19 Dhamoon, *Identity/Difference,* 25.
20 Dhamoon, *Identity/Difference,* citing Kymlicka, *Finding Our Way,* 97–8.
21 Kymlicka, *Finding Our Way,* 102.
22 Stevens, *States without Nations,* 85–92.
23 Stevens, *States without Nations,* 38. See also Smith, *Stories of Peoplehood.*
24 Smith, *Stories of Peoplehood,* 37.
25 Smith, *Stories of Peoplehood.*
26 Smith, *Stories of Peoplehood,* 53–4.
27 Smith, *Stories of Peoplehood,* 70.
28 Stevens, *States without Nations,* 76.
29 Stevens, *States without Nations,* 30.
30 Stevens, *States without Nations.*
31 Stevens, *States without Nations,* 77.
32 Stevens, *States without Nations,* 56
33 Stevens, *States without Nations.*
34 Stevens, *States without Nations,* 78.
35 Stevens, *States without Nations,* 79.
36 Stevens, *States without Nations,* 79–80.
37 Stevens, *States without Nations,* 80.
38 Andersen, *"Métis,"* 2014; Horn Miller, "How Did Adoption Become a Dirty Word?"; Palmater, *Beyond Blood*; Simpson, *Mohawk Interruptus,* 2014.

39   Horn Miller, "How Did Adoption Become a Dirty Word?"; Napoleon "Aboriginal
     Self Determination"; Simpson, *Mohawk Interruptus*.
40   Amendments to the *Indian Act* in 1985 recognized the rights of Indigenous
     communities (or bands) to make their own membership determinations. As a
     result, someone may be a Status Indian but lack membership in a community,
     and vice versa.
41   See, for example, *Club Native*, dir. Tracey Deer; Kolopenuk, *Canada's Indians
     [sic]*; and Lawrence, "Regulating Native Identity by Gender," 59–79.
42   Shachar, *The Birthright Lottery*, 102.
43   Shachar, *The Birthright Lottery*, 184–8.
44   Bosniak, *The Citizen and the Alien*, 1–2.
45   Shachar, *The Birthright Lottery*, 35.
46   Stevens, *States without Nations*, 10.
47   Bosniak, "Citizenship in an Unequal World," esp. 622.
48   Shachar, *The Birthright Lottery*, 101.
49   Shachar, *The Birthright Lottery*, 98–9. For a more elaborate critique of Shachar's
     global volunteer corps, see Nyers, "Alien Equality," 6.
50   Both the "resurrect-the-border crowd," as Shachar describes them in *The
     Birthright Lottery* at 188, and progressives might find themselves advocating this
     policy goal, though for completely different reasons.
51   Shachar, *The Birthright Lottery*, 112.
52   Carens, *The Ethics of Immigration*, 23.
53   Shachar, *The Birthright Lottery*, 171.
54   Citizenship and Immigration Canada, *Frequently Asked Questions*, http://www
     .cic.gc.ca/english/citizenship/rules_2009.asp.
55   Shachar, *The Birthright Lottery*, 171.
56   Shachar, *The Birthright Lottery*, 178–9.
57   Shachar, *The Birthright Lottery*, 179.
58   Shachar, *The Birthright Lottery*.
59   Jane Junn makes this argument, though she argues in favour of birthright
     citizenship over Shachar's *jus nexi* principle. See Junn, "Citizenship in an Unequal
     World," 635.
60   See Elizabeth Cohen, *The Political Value of Time: Citizenship, Duration,
     and Democratic Justice* (Cambridge: Cambridge University Press, 2018), for
     a full elaboration of time's usefulness as a salve to contentious normative
     disagreements.
61   Shachar, *The Birthright Lottery*, 16, 179.
62   Shachar, *The Birthright Lottery*, 156.
63   *British Nationality Act* 1981 c. 61; *Australian Citizenship Act* 1987, s. 12; *New
     Zealand Citizenship Act* 1977 No 61., as amended in 2005.
64   Schuck and Smith, *Citizenship without Consent*.
65   Smith, "Birthright Citizenship." Schuck's retreat is more equivocal, as I outline.
     They have also used the Trump administration's xenophobia to re-rehearse their

argument. See Schuck and Smith, "The Question of Birthright Citizenship,"
https://www.nationalaffairs.com/publications/detail/the-question-of-birthright
-citizenship.

66 US Constitution, Fourteenth Amendment, §14.

67 *Elk v. Wilkins* 112 U.S. 94 (1884).

68 Elizabeth Cohen offers a fascinating discussion of the citizenship challenges
    posed by those British loyalists after the War of Independence. See Cohen,
    "Reconsidering US Immigration Reform," 577–8.

69 Smith, "Birthright Citizenship," 1329–30.

70 Smith, "Birthright Citizenship."

71 Smith, "Birthright Citizenship," 1330.

72 Smith, "Birthright Citizenship."

73 Schuck and Smith, *Citizenship without Consent*, ch. 4.

74 Schuck and Smith, *Citizenship without Consent*, 94.

75 Schuck and Smith, *Citizenship without Consent*.

76 Schuck and Smith, *Citizenship without Consent*, 95.

77 Peter Schuck, *Citizens, Strangers and In-Betweens: Essays on Immigration
    and Citizenship* (Boulder: Westview Press, 1998) 214–15; Schuck and Smith,
    Citizenship without Consent, 60.

78 Schuck and Smith, *Citizenship without Consent*, 72.

79 Schuck and Smith, *Citizenship without Consent*, 37.

80 Schuck and Smith, *Citizenship without Consent*.

81 Schuck and Smith, "Citizenship without Consent," 25, https://www
    .thesocialcontract.com/pdf/seven-one/consent.pdf

82 Smith, "Birthright Citizenship," 60.

83 Schuck, "Birthright of a Nation," A19. Schuck and Smith, "The Question of
    Birthright Citizenship," 66.

84 Nyers, "Alien Equality," 1.

85 The UN Declaration of Human Rights, Articles 13–15, addresses issues of
    migration, asylum, and nationality.

86 Schuck, *Citizens, Strangers and In-Betweens*, 215.

87 *Ibid.*, 216.

88 Carens, *The Ethics of Immigration*, 274.

89 Schuck, *Citizens, Strangers and In-Betweens*, 198, 216.

90 Carens, *The Ethics of Immigration*.

91 Carens, *The Ethics of Immigration*, 19–20, 233.

92 Carens, *The Ethics of Immigration*, 19–20.

93 Carens, *The Ethics of Immigration*, 21–2.

94 Carens, *The Ethics of Immigration*, 19.

95 Carens, *The Ethics of Immigration*, 23.

96 Carens, *The Ethics of Immigration*, 21.

97 Carens, *The Ethics of Immigration*, 23.

98 Carens, *The Ethics of Immigration*.

99 Carens, *The Ethics of Immigration*, 21.

100 Carens, *The Ethics of Immigration*, 33.

101 Carens, *The Ethics of Immigration*.

102 Carens, *The Ethics of Immigration*, 163.

103 Carens, *The Ethics of Immigration*.

104 Carens, *The Ethics of Immigration*, 160–1.

105 Carens, *The Ethics of Immigration*, 50.

106 Carens, *The Ethics of Immigration*.

107 Carens, *The Ethics of Immigration*.

108 Carens, *Immigrants and the Right to Stay*, 18.

109 Carens, *Immigrants and the Right to Stay*, 40.

110 Carens, *The Ethics of Immigration*, 55.

111 Carens, *The Ethics of Immigration*, 166–7.

112 Cohen 2018, 13.

113 Cass Sunstein, "Incompletely Theorized Agreements in Constitutional Law," ctd in Cohen (2018), 14.

114 Carens, *The Ethics of Immigration*, 42.

115 Carens, *The Ethics of Immigration*, 44. Ayelet Shachar too, in her analogizing of the claims to membership of "illegal" migrants with the doctrine of adverse possession, notes that legal breaches are forgiven in a range of contexts, "including the semisacred realm of private property." Shachar, *The Birthright Lottery*, 188.

116 Carens, *The Ethics of Immigration*, 55.

117 On celebration, see, for example, Linda Bosniak's contribution to the Forum section of Carens, *Immigrants and the Right to Stay*. For dismissal, Carens himself cites John Isbister's assessment that the case for open borders "defies common sense." Isbister, "A Liberal Argument for Border Controls: Reply to Carens," *International Migration Review* 34, no. 2 (2000): 629–35, ctd in Carens, *The Ethics of Immigration*, 231.

118 Carens, *The Ethics of Immigration*, 229.

119 Carens, *The Ethics of Immigration*.

120 Carens, *The Ethics of Immigration*, 226.

121 Carens, *The Ethics of Immigration*, 227.

122 Carens, *The Ethics of Immigration*, 227–8.

123 Carens, *The Ethics of Immigration*, 228.

124 Carens, *The Ethics of Immigration*, 276–86.

125 Nyers, "Alien Equality," 10–11.

126 Smith, *Civic Ideals*, 38.

127 Jacqueline Stevens observes that in non-emergency situations, "the nation-state comprises the limits for empathy, regardless of the location where the most suffering occurs. As long as problems lie outside one's intergenerational group – for example, of family, ethnicity, nation, race – or one's religion, then they may be

ignored, and equitable, pragmatic solutions can be dismissed as utopian." Stevens, *States without Nations*, 10.

128 See https://www.youtube.com/watch?v=eDeDQpIQFD0.

129 MacInnis, "Having children abroad?," https://www.reuters.com/article/us-expats -children-citizenship-idUSTRE6AO22120101125,

130 Cohen, "Reconsidering US Immigration Reform," 576–7.

131 Goodin, "Enfranchising All Affected Interests," 49.

132 Smith, "'Living in a Promiseland?,'" 548.

133 Nyers, "Alien Equality," 9.

134 Rainer Bauböck identifies these as two of the most important citizenship rights. Bauböck, "Boundaries and Birthright," 1, DOI 10.2202/1539–8323.1123.

135 UN General Assembly, *Convention on the Reduction of Statelessness*, 30 August 1961, United Nations, Treaty Series, vol. 989, 175, http://www.refworld.org /docid/3ae6b39620.html.

136 Carens, *The Ethics of Immigration*, 39–43.

137 Carens, *The Ethics of Immigration*, 42.

138 Razack, "'Simple Logic,'" 182.

Bibliography

Government Documents

Legislation

An Act to Amend the Canadian Citizenship Act S.C. 1952–53, c. 23.
Alberta Family Law Act S.A. 2003, c. F-4.5 [AB FLA].
Australian Citizenship Act 1987, s. 12.
British Columbia Family Law Act S.B.C. 2011, c. 25
British Nationality Act 1981 c. 61.
Children's Law Act SS 2020, c. 2.
Children's Law Reform Act R.S.O. 1990, c. C. 12.
Citizenship Act R.S. 1985 c.C-29, s. 3.3.
Citizenship Act 1974–75-76, c. 108.
Citizenship Act S.C. 1946, c. 15.
Citizenship Regulations, SOR/93/246, s. 2.
Manitoba Family Maintenance Amendment Act S.M. 2021, c. 63.
New Zealand Citizenship Act 1977 No 61.
Nova Scotia, Birth Registration Regulations, NS Reg 390/2007, s. 3.
Ontario Children's Law Reform Act R.S.O. 1990, c. C. 12.
Order in Council re-entry into Canada of dependents of members of the Canadian Armed Forces, PC 1946–858 C Gaz, 308.
Regulations Amending the Immigration and Refugee Protection Regulations, Vol 147, No 20 (18 May 2013).
Saskatchewan, Children's Law Act SS 2020, c. 2.
US Constitution, Fourteenth Amendment §14.

Jurisprudence

Augier v. Canada (Minister of Citizenship and Immigration) [2004] 4 F.C.R. 150.
Bell v. Canada (Minister of Employment and Immigration) [1994] F.C.J. No. 372.

Benner v. Canada (Secretary of State) [1994] 1 FC 250.

Canada (Citizenship and Immigration) v. Kandola 2014 FCA 85 (CanLII).

Canada (Citizenship and Immigration) v. Taylor 2007 FCA 349.

Canada (Minister of Employment and Immigration) v. Bell [1996] F.C.J.

Caron c. Attorney General of Canada (2020) QCCS 2700 (CanLII).

Clark v Canada (Minister of Public Safety and Emergency Preparedness) 2006 FC 1512.

Crease v. Canada [1994] 3 FCR 480.

Drinnan (Re) 1982 F.C.J. No. 709.

Elk v. Wilkins 112 U.S. 94 (1884).

Galati v. Canada (Governor General) 2015 FC 91.

Glynos v. Canada (C.A.) [1992] F.C.J. No. 875.

Kandola v Canada (Minister of Citizenship and Immigration) 2013 FCJ No 374 (Quicklaw).

Re Chute [1981] F.C.J. No. 67.

R. v. Amara 2010 ONSC 441.

Scott v. Canada (Minister of Employment and Immigration), [1986] F.C.J. No. 500, 5F.T.R. 227 (Application for Judicial Review, Applicant's Memorandum of Fact and Law).

Taylor v. Canada (Citizenship and Immigration) (2006) FC 1053 (CanLII).

Ulin v. Canada [1973] F.C. 319.

Veleta v. Canada (M.C.I.), 2006 FCA 138.

Veleta v. Canada (Minister of Citizenship and Immigration), 2005 FC 572.

Wilson v. Canada (Citizenship and Immigration) 2003 FC 1475.

Debates

Canada, House of Commons Debates, 19–5, Vol. 1 (6 June 1944).

Canada, House of Commons Debates, 20–1, Vol. 1 (17 June 1945).

Canada, House of Commons Debates, 20–1, Vol. 1 (4 October 1945).

Canada, House of Commons Debates, 20–1, Vol. 1 (12 October 1945).

Canada, House of Commons Debates, 20–2, Vol. 2 (2 April 1946).

Canada, House of Commons Debates, 20–2, Vol. 2 (5 April 1946).

Canada, House of Commons Debates, 29–22, Vol. 2 (26 April 1974).

Canada, House of Commons Debates, 30–1, Vol. 6 (21 May 1975).

Canada, House of Commons Debates, 30–1, Vol. 9 (8 December 1975).

Canada, House of Commons Debates, 30–1, Vol. 10 (10 December 1975).

Canada, House of Commons Debates, 30–1, Vol. 12 (13 April 1976).

Canada, House of Commons Debates, 38–1, Vol. 140 (30 November 2004).

Canada, House of Commons Debates, 38–1, Vol. 140 (10 February 2005)

Canada, House of Commons Debates, 39–1, Vol. 141 (13 June 2006).

Canada, House of Commons Debates, 39–1, Vol. 143 (30 April 2007).

Canada, House of Commons Debates, 41–2, Vol. 147 (27 February 2014).

Standing Committees

Canada. *Canadian Citizenship: A Sense of Belonging. Report of the Standing Committee on Citizenship and Immigration.* Ottawa: Queen's Printer, 1994.

Canada, Parliament, House of Commons, Standing Committee on Broadcasting, Films and Assistance to the Arts, 30–1, No. 34 (24 February 1976).

Canada, Parliament, House of Commons, Standing Committee on Broadcasting, Films and Assistance to the Arts, 30–1, No. 36 (27 February 1976).

Canada, Parliament, House of Commons, Standing Committee on Broadcasting, Films and Assistance to the Arts, 30–1, No. 39 (9 March 1976).

Canada, Parliament, House of Commons, Standing Committee on Broadcasting, Films and Assistance to the Arts, 30–1, No. 41 (12 March 1976).

Canada, Parliament, House of Commons, Standing Committee on Citizenship and Immigration, 37–2, No. 14 (28 January 2003).

Canada, Parliament, House of Commons, Standing Committee on Citizenship and Immigration, 37–2, No. 19 (10 February 2003).

Canada, Parliament, House of Commons, Standing Committee on Citizenship and Immigration, 39–1, No. 36 (19 February 2007).

Canada, Parliament, Standing Committee on Citizenship and Immigration, *Reclaiming Citizenship for Canadians: A Report on the Loss of Canadian Citizenship*, 39–2 (December 2007).

Canada, Parliament, House of Commons, Standing Committee on Citizenship and Immigration, 39–1, No. 38 (26 February 2007).

Canada, Parliament, House of Commons, Standing Committee on Citizenship and Immigration, 39–1, No. 41 (19 March 2007).

Canada, Parliament, House of Commons, Standing Committee on Citizenship and Immigration, 39–1, No. 61 (29 May 2007).

Canada, Parliament, House of Commons, Standing Committee on Citizenship and Immigration, 39–6, No. 10 (6 February 2008).

Canada, Parliament, House of Commons, Standing Committee on Citizenship and Immigration, "Report 3: Bill C-24, An Act to Amend the *Canadian Citizenship Act*", 41–2 (4 June 2014).

Secondary Material

Abu-Laban, Yasmeen, and Christina Gabriel. *Selling Diversity: Immigration, Multiculturalism, Employment Equity, and Globalization.* Toronto: University of Toronto Press, 2002.

Abu-Laban, Yasmeen, and Nisha Nath, "From Deportation to Apology: The Case of Maher Arar and the Canadian State." *Canadian Ethnic Studies* 39, no. 3 (2009): 71–98.

Ahmed, Sara. "Embodying Diversity: Problems and Paradoxes of Black Feminists." *Race, Ethnicity, and Education* 12, no. 1 (2009): 41–52.

Andersen, Chris. *"Metis": Race, Recognition, and the Struggle for Indigenous Peoplehood.* Vancouver: UBC Press, 2014.

Anderson, Benedict. *Imagined Communities: Reflections on the Origin and Spread of Nationalism,* rev. ed. London: Verso, 1991.

Angus Reid Institute, *Birthright Citizenship: Plurality of Canadians See It as Good Policy, but Also Say Some Changes Are Needed* (14 March 2019).

Asia Pacific Foundation of Canada. 2015. "Vancouver's Foreign-Owned Real Estate: Perceptions, Facts, Comparisons." 25 November 2015.

Bala, Nicholas, and Christine Ashbourne. "The Widening Concept of 'Parent' in Canada: Step-Parents, Same Sex Partners, and Parents by ART." *Journal of Gender, Social Policy, and the Law* 20, no. 3 (2012): 525–60.

Bauböck, Rainer. "Boundaries and Birthright: Bosniak's and Shachar's Critiques of Liberal Citizenship." *Issues in Legal Scholarship* 9, no. 1 (2011). https://doi-org .ezproxy.library.uvic.ca/10.2202/1539-8323.1123.

Bauder, Harald. "Re-Imagining the Nation: Lessons from the Debates of Immigration in a Settler Society and an Ethnic Nation." *Comparative Migration Studies* 2, no. 1 (2014): 9–27.

Bechard, Julie, Peggy Becklumb, and Sandra Elgersma, "Legislative Summary of Bill C-24, "An Act to amend the Citizenship Act and to make consequential amendments to other acts," 41–2 (8 July 2014).

Becklumb, Peggy. "Bill C-37: An Act to Amend the Citizenship Act," Legislative Summary. Ottawa: Parliamentary Information and Research Service, 2008.

Berlant, Lauren. *Cruel Optimism.* Durham: Duke University Press, 2011.

Bhandar, Brenna. *Colonial Lives of Property: Law, Land, and Racial Regimes of Ownership.* Durham: Duke University Press, 2018.

Billig, Michael. *Banal Nationalism.* Los Angeles: Sage, 1995.

Black, Debra. "Ottawa to consult with provinces on dealing with 'birth tourism.'" *The Star* (Toronto), 6 February 2014.

Blackstone, William. *Commentaries on the Laws of England: 1765–1769.* London: Dawsons, 1966.

Bloemraad, Irene. "Who Claims Dual Citizenship? The Limits of Postnationalism, the Possibilities of Transnationalism, and the Persistence of Traditional Citizenship." *International Migration Review* 38, no. 2 (2004): 389–426.

Bohaker, Heidi, and Franca Iacovetta. "Making Aboriginal People 'Immigrants Too': A Comparison of Citizenship Programs for Newcomers and Indigenous Peoples in Postwar Canada, 1940s–1960s." *Canadian Historical Review* 90, no. 3 (2009): 427–61.

Borrows, John. "'Landed' Citizenship: An Indigenous Declaration of Interdependence." In *Recovering Canada: The Resurgence of Indigenous Law.* Toronto: University of Toronto Press, 2002.

Bosniak, Linda. *The Citizen and the Alien: Dilemmas of Contemporary Membership.* Princeton: Princeton University Press, 2006.

– "Citizenship in an Unequal World: A Discussion of *The Birthright Lottery: Citizenship and Global Inequality.*" *Political Perspectives* 9, no. 3 (2011): 621–4.

Bothwell, Robert. "Something of Value? Subjects and Citizens in Canadian History." In *Belonging: The Meaning and Future of Canadian Citizenship,* edited by William Kaplan, 30–1. Montreal and Kingston: McGill-Queen's University Press, 1993.

Bourgon, Lyndsie. "Why women are coming to Canada just to give birth." *Maclean's,* 8 August 2017. https://www.macleans.ca/society/health/why-women-are-coming -to-canada-just-to-give-birth.

Bramham, Daphne. "Citizenship battle ends, but tangled web of rules remain." *Vancouver Sun,* 13 September 2010.

– "Loss of citizenship a mystery for son of war bride: Nobody can say why the man is no longer a citizen of Canada." *Vancouver Sun,* 2 June 2006.

– "War bride, 87, denied new passport; bureaucrats prevent Canadian resident of 67 years from seeing her great-grandchildren." *Vancouver Sun,* 4 September 2010.

Brodie, Janine. "From Social Security to Public Safety: Security Discourses and Canadian Citizenship." *University of Toronto Quarterly* 78, no. 2 (2009): 687–708.

Bronskill, Jim. "'Not consistent and uniform': Birthplace doesn't necessarily guarantee citizenship, feds tell Supreme Court." *National Post,* 8 September 2018.

Burns, Ian. "Ottawa changes law to allow non-biological Canadian parents to pass citizenship to their children." *Lawyer's Daily,* 10 July 2020.

Campbell, Alan. "Richmond MP presents anti-birth tourism petition to Parliament." *Richmond News,* 5 October 2018.

Campbell, Angela. "Law's Suppositions about Surrogacy against the Backdrop of Social Science" *Ottawa Law Review* 43, no. 1 (2012): 29–57. Updated in 2020.

Canada, Department of the Secretary of State. *Citizenship '87: Proud to be Canadian.* Ottawa: Supply and Services Canada, 1987.

Canada, Royal Commission on the Status of Women. Ottawa, 1970.

Canadian Press. "Feds studying birth tourism after new data shows it is more common than previously reported." *Global News,* 22 November 2018.

Carens, Joseph. *The Ethics of Immigration.* New York: Oxford University Press, 2013.

– *Immigrants and the Right to Stay.* Cambridge, MA: MIT Press, 2010.

Carlaw, John. "Authoritarian Populism and Canada's Conservative Decade (2006–2015) in Citizenship and Immigration: The Politics and Practices of Kennyism and Neoconservative Multiculturalism" *Journal of Canadian Studies* 51, no. 3 (2017): 782–816.

Castañeda, Heide. "Paternity for Sale: Anxieties over "Demographic Theft" and Undocumented Migrant Reproduction in Germany." *Medical Anthropology Quarterly* 22, no. 4 (2008): 340–59.

CBC News. "Second-generation Canadians get into the act" (March 2007), https://www.cbc.ca/news2/background/lostcanadians/born-abroad-babies.html.

CBC Radio. "Committee report urges citizenship for 'lost Canadians.'" 5 December 2007. http://www.cbc.ca/canada/story/2007/12/05/lost-canadians.html.

– "John McCallum on rolling back controversial Citizenship Act." *The House,* 27 February 2016.

Chapman, Don. *The Lost Canadians*. Vancouver: Pugwash Press, 2015.

Chesterton, G.K. *The Defendant: Essays*. Open Road Media, 2015. *ProQuest Ebook Central*, https://ebookcentral.proquest.com/lib/ualberta/detail .action?docID=4749313.

Citizenship and Immigration Canada. "Frequently Asked Questions: New Citizenship Rules, Question #4. 'Why is Government Doing This?'" (2009).

– "Operational Bulletin 381 – Assessing who is a parent for citizenship purposes where assisted human reproduction (AHR) and/or surrogacy arrangements are involved" (2012). https://www.canada.ca/en/immigration-refugees-citizenship /corporate/publications-manuals/operational-bulletins-manuals/bulletins -2012/381-march-8-2012.html.

"Club Native." Directed by Tracey Deer. 2008. https://www.nfb.ca/film/club_native.

Cohen, Elizabeth. *The Political Value of Time: Citizenship, Duration, and Democratic Justice*. Cambridge: Cambridge University Press, 2018.

– "Reconsidering US Immigration Reform: The Temporal Principle of Citizenship." *Political Perspectives* 9, no. 3 (2011): 575–83.

Conservative Party of Canada. *National Policy Committee Convention Package*. 2018. https://cpcassets.conservative.ca/wp-content/uploads/2019/04/03155332/DUCw9 _byfAlGSAE.pdf.

Cornes, Paul. *No More Damned Secrets: An Anglo-Canadian War Child's Quest for Roots and Identity*. Sussex: Book Guild, 2013.

Costello, John. *Love, Sex, and War 1939–1945*. London: Pan Books, 1985.

Coulthard, Glenn. *Red Skin White Masks: Rejecting the Colonial Politics of Recognition*. Minneapolis: University of Minnesota Press, 2014.

Cowen, Deborah, and Emily Gilbert. "Citizenship in the 'Homeland': Families at War." In *War, Citizenship, and Territory*, edited by Deborah Cowen and Emily Gilbert, 261–79. New York: Routledge, 2008.

CTVNews.ca. "Is 'birth tourism' a problem in Canada? Doctors on frontline of debate." *CTV News*, 10 August 2016.

Day, Richard. *Multiculturalism and the History of Canadian Diversity*. Toronto: University of Toronto Press, 2000.

Dhamoon, Rita. *Identity/Difference: How Difference Is Produced and Why It Matters*. Vancouver: UBC Press, 2009.

Dhamoon, Rita, and Yasmeen Abu-Laban. "Dangerous (Internal) Foreigners and Nation-Building: The Case of Canada." *International Political Science Review* 30, no. 2 (2009): 163–83.

Dhamoon, Rita et al., eds. *Unmooring the Komagata Maru: Charting Colonial Trajectories*. Vancouver: UBC Press, 2019.

Dickson, Janice. "Scheer defends birthright policy, says ending 'birth tourism' is objective." *The Star* (Toronto), 27 August 2018.

Dolin, Benjamin, and Margaret Young. *Legislative Summary: Bill C-18: The Citizenship of Canada Act*. Library of Parliament Research Publications, 2 November 2002.

Dua, Enakshi. "Exclusion through Inclusion: Female Asian Migration in the Making of Canada." *Gender, Place and Culture* 14, no. 4 (2007): 445–66.

Duffy, Andrew. "Baby born in midair granted citizenship." *Edmonton Journal,* 8 January 2009, A5.

Dumbrava, Costica and Bauböck, Rainer, eds. "Bloodlines and Belonging: Time to Abandon *jus sanguinis*." European University Institute Working Papers, 2015. http://cadmus.eui.eu/bitstream/handle/1814/37578/RSCAS_2015_80 .pdf?sequence=1&isAllowed=y.

Durbach, Nadja. "Private Lives, Public Records: Illegitimacy and the Birth Certificate in Twentieth-Century Britain." *Twentieth Century British History* 25, no. 2 (2014): 305–26.

Email from Douglas Chute to Lois Harder (21 August 2015).

Favaro, Avis, and Ryan Flanagan, 2019. "'Birth tourism' rising fast in Canada; up 13 per cent in one year." *CTV News,* 16 September 2018.

Ferguson, Kennan. *All in the Family: On Community and Incommensurability.* Durham: Duke University Press, 2012.

Foot, Richard. "Bill to restore citizenship for 'lost Canadians.'" *Ottawa Citizen,* 11 December 2007.

– "'Lost' citizen regains status." *Calgary Herald,* 6 December 2007.

Forcese, Craig. "A Tale of Two Citizenships," W-Five. "Citizens of Canada." *CTV TV.* 8 November 2008.

– "A Tale of Two Citizenships: Citizenship Revocation for Traitors and Terrorists." *Queen's Law Journal* 39 (2014): 551–85.

Forcier, Mathieu, and Frederick Guillaume Dufour. "Immigration, Neoconservatism, and Neoliberalism: The New Canadian Citizenship Regime in the Light of European Trajectories." *Cogent Sciences* 2, no 1 (2016): 1–18.

Freeman, Tabitha, and Martin Richards. "DNA Testing and Kinship: Paternity, Genealogy, and the Search for the 'Truth' of Our Genetic Origins." In *Kinship Matters,* edited by Fatemeh Ebtehaj, Bridget Lindley, and Martin Richards. Oxford and Portland: Hart, 2006.

Friscolanti, Michael. "Still-present dangers: Very little movement has been made on arrange of promises – from better equipping spies to jet purchases." *Maclean's,* 24 October 2016.

Gallant, Mavis. "Introduction." In *The War Brides,* edited by Joyce Hibbert, xi–xix. Toronto: PMA Books, 1978.

Gardels, Nathan. "Two Concepts of Nationalism: An Interview with Isaiah Berlin." *New York Review of Books,* 21 November 1991.

Gaucher, Megan, and Lindsay Larios. "Birth Tourism and the Demonizing of Pregnant Migrant Women." *Policy Options,* 17 January 2020.

Gaudry, Adam, and Darryl Leroux. "White Settler Revisionism and Making Métis Everywhere: The Evocation of Métissage in Quebec and Nova Scotia." *Critical Ethnic Studies* 3, no. 1 (2017): 116–42.

Gazze, Mary. "60 years later, European war kids still seek Canadian dads." *Canadian Press,* 10 November 2010.

Girard, Philip. "'If two ride a horse, one must ride in front': Married Women's Nationality and the Law in Canada 1880–1950." *Canadian Historical Review* 94, no. 1 (2013): 28–54.

Gold, Kerry. "'Growth coalition' kept foreign money flowing into B.C. real estate, professor says." *Globe and Mail,* 5 June 2018.

Goodin, Robert E. "Enfranchising All Affected Interests, and Its Alternatives." *Philosophy and Public Affairs* 35, no. 1 (2007): 40–68.

Granfield, Linda, ed. *Brass Buttons and Silver Horseshoes: Stories from Canada's British War Brides.* Toronto: McClelland and Stewart, 2002.

Griffith, Andrew. "What the previous government learned about birth tourism." *Policy Options,* 28 August 2018. https://policyoptions.irpp.org/magazines/august-2018 /previous-government-learned-birth-tourism.

"Guitarist Clapton finds lost family here." *Toronto Star,* 20 March 1998.

Hammerton, James. "The Quest for Family and the Mobility of Modernity in Narratives of Postwar British Emigration." *Global Networks* 4, no. 3 (2004): 271–84.

Hansen, Lene. "A Case for Seduction?: Evaluating the Poststructuralist Conceptualization of Security." *Cooperation and Conflict* 32 (1997): 369–97.

Harder, Lois. "'In Canada of All Places': National Belonging and the Lost Canadians." *Citizenship Studies* 14, no. 2 (2010): 203–20.

– "Does Sperm Have a Flag? On Biological Relationship and National Membership." *Canadian Journal of Law and Society* 30, no. 1 (2015): 109–25.

– "'Maternity Tourism,' Civic Integration, and *Jus Soli* Citizenship in Canada." *Revue Européenne des Migrations Internationales* (REMI) vol. 36, no. 4 (2020): 35–54.

Harder, Lois, and Lyubov Zhyznomirska. "Claims of Belonging: Recent Tales of Trouble in Canadian Citizenship." *Ethnicities* 12, no. 3 (2012): 293–316.

Helfend, Neil. "Asian Organized Crime and Terrorist Activity in Canada, 1999–2002." Washington: Library of Congress, Field Research Division. July 2003.

Henderson, James (Sa'ke'j) Youngblood. "*Sui generis* and Treaty Citizenship." *Citizenship Studies* 6, no. 4 (2002): 415–40.

Hibbert, Joyce., ed. *The War Brides.* Toronto: PMA Books, 1978.

Hobsbawm, Eric. *Nations and Nationalism since 1780.* Cambridge: Cambridge University Press, 1990.

Hoerder, Dirk. "'Of Habits Subversive' or 'Capable and Compassionate': Perceptions of Transpacific Migrants, 1850s–1940s." *Canadian Ethnic Studies* 38, no. 1 (2006): 1.

Honig, Bonnie. *Democracy and the Foreigner.* Princeton: Princeton University Press, 2001.

Horn-Miller, Kahente. "How Did Adoption Become a Dirty Word? Indigenous Citizenship Orders as Irreconcilable Spaces of Aboriginality." *AlterNative* 14, no. 4 (2018): 354–64.

Houdt, Friso van, Semin Suvarierol, and Willem Schinkel. "Neoliberal Communitarian Citizenship: Current Trends towards 'Earned Citizenship' in the United Kingdom, France, and the Netherlands." *International Sociology* 26, no. 3 (May 2011): 408–32.

Humphrey, Matt. "Tory motion to end birthright citizenship is 'just not workable,' says immigration lawyer." *CBC News,* 27 August 2018.

Isbister, John. "A Liberal Argument for Border Controls: Reply to Carens." *International Migration Review* 34, no. 2 (2000): 629–35.

Jarratt, Melynda. *War Brides: The Stories of the Women Who Left Everything behind to Follow the Men They Loved*. Stroud: Tempus, 2007.

Johnson, Darlene. "First Nations and Canadian Citizenship." In *Belonging: The Meaning and Future of Canadian Citizenship*, edited by William Kaplan, 349–58. Montreal and Kingston: McGill-Queen's University Press, 1993.

Jonaitis, Aldona, and Aaron Glass. *The Totem Pole: An Intercultural History*. Vancouver: Douglas and McIntyre, 2010.

Junn, Jane. "Citizenship in an Unequal World: A Discussion of *The Birthright Lottery: Citizenship and Global Inequality*." *Political Perspectives* 9, no. 3 (2011): 633–7.

Kaplan, Amy. "Homeland Insecurities: Reflections on Language and Space." *Radical History Review* 85 (Winter 2003): 82–93.

Keshen, Jeffrey. *Saints, Sinners, and Soldiers: Canada's Second World War*. Vancouver: UBC Press, 2004.

Knowles, Valerie. *Forging Our Legacy: Canadian Citizenship and Immigration, 1900–1977*. Ottawa: Department of Citizenship and Immigration, 2000.

Kolopenuk, Jessica. *Canada's Indians [sic]: (Re)racializing Canadian Sovereign Contours through Juridical Constructions of Indianness in McIvor v. Canada*. MA thesis, University of Alberta, 2012.

Kymlicka, Will. *Finding Our Way: Rethinking Ethnocultural Relations in Canada*. Toronto: Oxford University Press, 1998.

Lau, Rachel. "'Bring back Don Cherry' petition by conservative Alberta magazine amasses more than 200,000 signatures," *CTV News*, 13 November 2019.

Lawrence, Bonita. "Regulating Native Identity by Gender." In *Daily Struggles: The Deepening Racialization and Feminization of Poverty in Canada*, Edited by Siu-ming Kwok and Maria Wallis, 59–79. Toronto: Canadian Scholars Press, 2008.

Letter from William Janzen to Jason Kenney (20 September 2010) on file with author.

Ley, David. "Global China and the Making of Vancouver's Residential Property Market." *International Journal of Housing Policy* 17, no. 1 (2017): 15–34.

– *Millionaire Migrants: Trans-Pacific Life Line*. Chichester: John Wiley and Sons, 2010.

Li, Peter. "Reconciling with History: The Chinese-Canadian Head Tax Redress." *Journal of Chinese Overseas* 4, no. 1 (2008): 127–40.

Llana, Sara Miller. "When does birthright citizenship become citizenship for sale?" *Christian Science Monitor*, 8 May 2019.

Loewen, Royden. *Village among Nations: "Canadian" Mennonites in a Transnational World, 1916–2006*. Toronto: University of Toronto Press, 2013.

MacInnis, Laura. "Having children abroad? Your country may not want them." *Reuters*, 25 November 2010.

Macklin, Audrey. "Citizenship Revocation, the Privilege to Have Rights, and the Production of the Alien." *Queen's Law Journal* 40, no. 1 (2014): 1–54.

Manitoba Law Commission. 2014. *Assisted Reproduction: Legal Parentage and Birth Registration*. Winnipeg.

Martin Sr, Paul. "Citizenship and the People's World." In *Belonging: The Meaning and Future of Canadian Citizenship*, edited by William Kaplan, 64–78. Montreal and Kingston: McGill-Queen's University Press, 1993.

Matrix, Sidney Eve. "Mediated Citizenship and Contested Belongings: Canadian War Brides and the Fictions of Naturalization." *Topia* 17 (2011): 67–86.

McLaren, Angus. "Stemming the Flood of Defective Aliens." in *The History of Immigration and Racism in Canada: Essential Readings*, edited by Barrington Walker, 189–204. Toronto: Canadian Scholars Press, 2008.

Meloni, Francesca, Cécile Rousseau, Catherine Montgomery, and Toby Measham. "Children of Exception: Redefining Categories of Illegality and Citizenship in Canada." *Children and Society* 28, no. 4 (2014): 305–15.

Mouritsen, Per, K. Kriegbaum Jensen, and Stephen J. Larin. "Introduction: Theorizing the Civic Turn in European Integration Policies." *Ethnicities* 19, no. 4 (August 2019): 595–613.

Mulgrew, Ian. "Canadians who aren't; Don Chapman 52, was born in Vancouver. His father fought for Canada in the Second World War. Yet he and many others were stripped of their status by a defunct citizenship law." *Vancouver Sun*, 15 September 2007.

Mykitiuk, Roxanne. "Beyond Conception: Legal Determinations of Filiation in the Context of Assisted Reproductive Technologies." *Osgoode Hall Law Journal* 39, 4 (2001): 771–815.

Napoleon, Val. "Aboriginal Self Determination: Individual Self and Collective Selves." *Atlantis* 29 no. 2 (Spring–Summer 2005): 31–47.

– "Thinking About Indigenous Legal Orders." In *Dialogues on Human Rights and Legal Pluralism*, edited by Colleen Shepard and Kirsten Anker, 229–45. New York: Springer, 2013.

Nath, Nisha. *Far from Belonging: Race, Security Dissent, and the Canadian Citizenship Story after 9/11* PhD diss., University of Alberta, 2016.

Ngai, Mae. "Birthright Citizenship and the Alien Citizen." *Fordham Law Review* 75 (2007): 2521–30.

Nichols, Robert. *Theft Is Property! Dispossession and Critical Theory*. Durham: Duke University Press, 2020.

Nyers, Peter. "Alien Equality." *Issues in Legal Scholarship* 9, no. 1 (2011). https://doi-org.ezproxy.library.uvic.ca/10.2202/1539-8323.1131.

Off, Carol. "Dream merchants." *CBC News*, 27 October 2003.

O'Neill, Juliet. "Arcane law strips Canadians of their citizenship." *Calgary Herald*, 25 January 2007.

O'Regan, Seamus. "Child of WWII couple finally wins citizenship." *Canada AM* (CTV Television). Interview with Joe Taylor, 25 January 2008.

Palmater, Pamela. *Beyond Blood: Rethinking Indigenous Identity*. Saskatoon: Purich, 2011.

Pammett, Jon H., and Lawrence LeDuc. *Explaining the Turnout Decline in Canadian Federal Elections: A New Survey of Non-Voters*. Ottawa: Elections Canada, 2003.

Peterson, V. Spike. "Political Identities/Nationalism as Heterosexism." *International Feminist Journal of Politics* 1, no. 1 (1999): 34–65.

Pillay, Sukana. "Pillay: It was Canada's sloppy counter-terrorism that led to $31M payout." *Ottawa Citizen*, 3 November 2017.

Quebec. Comité consultative sur le droit de la famille. 2015. *Pour un droit de la famille adapté aux nouvelles réalités conjugales et familiales*. Quebec City.

Rains, Olga, Lloyd Rains, and Melynda Jarratt. *Voices of the Left Behind: Project Roots and the Canadian War Children of World War Two*. Fredericton: Project Roots, 2005.

Raj, Althia, and Ryan Maloney, "Federal Tory delegates vote that being born in Canada shouldn't guarantee citizenship," *Huffpost*, 25 August 2018.

Razack, Sherene. *Race, Space, and the Law: Unmapping a White Settler Society*. Toronto: Between the Lines, 2002.

– "'Simple Logic': Race, the Identity Documents Rules, and the Story of a Nation Besieged and Betrayed." *Journal of Law and Social Policy* 15 (2000): 181–209.

Regehr, T.D. *Mennonites in Canada 1939–1970: A People Transformed*. Toronto: University of Toronto Press, 1996.

Satzewich, Vic. "Racism and Canadian Immigration Policy: The Government's View of Caribbean migration 1962–1966." *Canadian Ethnic Studies* 21, no. 1 (1989): 77–98.

Schuck, Peter. "Birthright of a Nation." *New York Times*, 13 August 2010.

– *Citizens, Strangers, and In-Betweens: Essays on Immigration and Citizenship*. Boulder: Westview Press, 1998.

Schuck, Peter, and Rogers Smith. *Citizenship without Consent: Illegal Aliens in the American Polity*. New Haven: Yale University Press, 1985.

– "Citizenship without Consent." *The Social Contract* (Fall 1996): 19–25.

– "The Question of Birthright Citizenship." *National Affairs*, 1 June 2018, 50–67.

Shachar, Ayelet. *The Birthright Lottery: Citizenship and Global Inequality*. Cambridge, MA: Harvard University Press, 2009.

Sharma, Nandita. *Home Economics: Nationalism and the Making of "Migrant Workers" in Canada*. Toronto: University of Toronto Press, 2006.

Simpson, Audra. "Consent's Revenge." *Cultural Anthropology* 31, no. 3 (2016): 326–33.

– *Mohawk Interruptus: Political Life across the Borders of Settler States*. Durham: Duke University Press, 2014.

Smith, Anthony. *The Antiquity of Nations*. London: Polity, 2004.

Smith, Rogers M. "Birthright Citizenship and the Fourteenth Amendment in 1868 and 2008." *Journal of Constitutional Law* 11, no. 5 (2008): 1329–35.

– *Civic Ideals: Conflicting Visions of Citizenship in US History*. New Haven: Yale University Press, 1997.

– "'Living in a Promiseland?' Mexican Immigration and American Obligations." *Political Perspectives* (2011): 545–57.

– *Stories of Peoplehood: The Politics and Morals of Political Membership*. New York: Cambridge University Press, 2003.

Somerville, Siobhan. "Notes toward a Queer History of Naturalization." *American Quarterly* 57, no. 3 (2005): 659–75.

Stacey, C.P. and Barbara M. Wilson, *The Half-Million: The Canadians in Britain, 1939–1945*. Toronto: Toronto University Press, 1987.

Stasiulus, Daiva. "The Political Economy of Race, Ethnicity, and Migration." In *Understanding Canada: Building on the New Canadian Political Economy*, 141–71. Montreal and Kingston: McGill-Queen's University Press, 1997).

Stasiulus, Daiva, and Darryl Ross. "Security, Flexible Sovereignty, and the Perils of Multiple Citizenship." *Citizenship Studies* 10, no. 3 (2006): 329–48.

Stevens, Jacqueline. *Reproducing the State*. Princeton: Princeton University Press, 1999.

– *States without Nations: Citizenship for Mortals*. New York: Columbia University Press, 2010.

Strathern, Marilyn. *Kinship, Law, and the Unexpected: Relatives Are Always a Surprise*. Cambridge: Cambridge University Press, 2006.

"Survey shows Canadian war brides contented: NB taken as example." *New Brunswick Telegraph Journal*, 22 May 1947.

Tasker, John Paul. "'It's fraudulent': Former immigration official says action needed on 'passport babies'." *CBC News*, 28 August 2018.

Thobani, Sunera. *Exalted Subjects: Studies in the Making of Race and Nation in Canada* Toronto: University of Toronto Press, 2007.

Tuck , Eve, and K. Wayne Yang, 2012. "Decolonization Is Not a Metaphor." *Decolonization: Indigeneity, Education, and Society* 1, no. 1: 1–40.

UN General Assembly. *Convention on the Reduction of Statelessness*. Treaty Series, vol. 989, 30 August 1961.

Wang, Sean. "'Fetal citizens'? Birthright Citizenship, Reproductive Futurism, and the 'Panic' over Chinese Birth Tourism in Southern California." *Environment and Planning D: Society and Space* 35, no. 2 (2017): 269–70.

Weil, Patrick. *How to Be French: Nationality in the Making since 1789*. Durham: Duke University Press, 2008.

Whitaker, Reg. *Canadian Immigration Policy since Confederation*. Ottawa: Canadian Historical Association, 1991.

Windsor Star. "A war story; the fight for citizenship." *Editorial*, 4 November 2007.

Wolgin, Philip E., and Irene Bloemraad. "'Our gratitude to our soldiers': Military Spouses, Family Re-Unification, and Postwar Immigration Reform." *Journal of Interdisciplinary History* 41, no. 1 (2010): 27–60.

Wong, Jan. "Canada's birthright citizenship policy makes us a nation of suckers." *Toronto Life*, 20 May 2014.

Wood, Graeme. "Birth tourism rates smash earlier records in Richmond." *Richmond News*, 13 January 2015.

Yeates, Neal. "Government of Canada briefing on birthright citizenship." Prepared for Jason Kenney. Ottawa: Citizenship and Immigration Canada, 2012–13: 1. https: //multiculturalmeanderings.files.wordpress.com/2013/06/citizenship-reform -proposal-19-birth-on-soil.pdf.

Yelaja, Prithi. "Birth tourism" may change citizenship rules, *CBC News,* 5 March 2012.

Yuval-Davis, Nira. *The Politics of Belonging: Intersectional Contestations.* London: Sage, 2011.

Index

www.ingramcontent.com/pod-product-compliance
Lightning Source LLC
Chambersburg PA
CBHW020253030426
42336CB00010B/748